WITNESS OF THE BODY

THE EERDMANS EKKLESIA SERIES

Editors

Michael L. Budde
Stephen E. Fowl

The Eerdmans Ekklesia Series explores matters of Christianity and discipleship across a wide expanse of disciplines, church traditions, and issues of current and historical concern.

The Series is published in cooperation with the Ekklesia Project, a network of persons for whom "being a Christian" is seen to be the primary identity and allegiance for believers — superseding and ordering the claims on offer by the modern state, market, racial and ethnic groups, and other social forces. The Ekklesia Project emphasizes the importance of the church as a distinctive community in the world, called to carry into contemporary society the priorities and practices of Jesus Christ as conveyed in the Gospels.

The Ekklesia Series will draw from the broad spectrum of the Christian world — Protestantism of many traditions, Roman Catholicism, Anabaptism, Orthodoxy — in exploring critical issues in theology, history, social and political theory, biblical studies, and world affairs. The Series editors are Stephen E. Fowl, Professor of Theology at Loyola College in Baltimore; and Michael L. Budde, Professor of Political Science and Catholic Studies at DePaul University in Chicago.

Additional information about the Ekklesia Project, including submission guidelines for the Eerdmans Ekklesia book series, may be found at www.ekklesiaproject.org.

WITNESS OF THE BODY

The Past, Present, and Future of Christian Martyrdom

Edited by

Michael L. Budde and Karen Scott

William B. Eerdmans Publishing Company
Grand Rapids, Michigan / Cambridge, U.K.

Published 2011 by
Wm. B. Eerdmans Publishing Co.
2140 Oak Industrial Drive N.E., Grand Rapids, Michigan 49505 /
P.O. Box 163, Cambridge CB3 9PU U.K.

Printed in the United States of America

17 16 15 14 13 12 11 7 6 5 4 3 2 1

Library of Congress Cataloging-in-Publication Data

Witness of the body: the past, present, and future of Christian martyrdom /
edited by Michael L. Budde and Karen Scott.
p. cm. — (The Eerdmans Ekklesia series)
ISBN 978-0-8028-6258-7 (pbk.: alk. paper)
1. Martyrdom — Christianity. 2. Martyrdom — Christianity — History.
I. Budde, Michael L. II. Scott, Karen, 1954-

BR1601.3.W58 2011
272 — dc22

2010045308

www.eerdmans.com

Contents

Part III: Martyrdom Destroys the Church

Part IV: Martyrdom and the Future Church

Introduction

Michael L. Budde

Martyrdom sits uneasily among the settled notions of our time. Like a piece of furniture that clashes with a carefully choreographed décor, or brown shoes paired with a tuxedo, martyrdom seems both out of place and a source of unease.

For some people, martyrdom conjures unbelievable stories of miraculous and heroic figures from the past, or perhaps a near-pathological glorification of torture and pain. For others, the willingness to endure and impose martyrdom represents an outdated certainty about truth that legitimates intolerance toward other value systems. More recently, martyrdom has been smeared by blood shed by political actors who kill others and themselves in hopes of becoming "martyrs" who are then showered with blessings in the afterlife.

The purpose of this book is simultaneously modest and ambitious. It aims to suggest why some notions of martyrdom (like that of a suicide bomber) are incompatible with Christian martyrdom rightly understood — a modest goal by any measure. Doing so, however, necessarily involves returning martyrdom to a more central place in the self-understanding of the church, a move with profound and perhaps audacious implications.

This book focuses on Christian martyrdom, not martyrdom as a generic category, nor martyrdom in other religious or ideological traditions. In its attempt to explore martyrdom in ways helpful to contemporary readers — scholars and interested persons in churches and elsewhere — this volume ranges widely across historical eras, scholarly disciplines, ecclesial traditions, and geographic areas. Far from being the final word on the many issues and debates attendant to martyrdom and the Christian tradition, the chapters that follow might be seen as invitations to deeper and more sustained exploration of the many topics related to martyrdom as lived and understood by Christians.

The title, *Witness of the Body,* suggests two terms that are central in the Christian encounter with martyrdom. The term "martyr" initially meant "witness" in the Greek-speaking world of New Testament times; of course, discerning the multiple and sometimes conflicting understandings of "witness" is no easy or straightforward matter. Similarly, while martyrdom represents witness written on or by the bodies of persons killed for their faith, the Christian tradition has never considered martyrdom an individualistic or private matter. As many of the contributors to this book assert and demonstrate in diverse ways, the "body" giving witness is the church, the new people formed by God as disciples of Christ, whose murdered and resurrected body is the paradigmatic witness to God's love of and hope for the world.

In many ways, this book aims to reduce the freak-show element attached to martyrdom in some precincts of modern culture, as well as the assumption that it represents an act of heroic exceptionality (the "heroic" virtues of antiquity being something distinct from the Christian virtues of faith, hope, and love). Rather than seeing it as an object of fascination or dread, most of the contributors to this volume resituate martyrdom within the everyday practices of the church. As the place where people take on a new identity in baptism, learn to reconcile with and love their enemies, and become part of Christ's body via the sharing of bread and wine, the church will sometimes encounter hostility aimed at these practices and the people they produce. And while the church rightly resists the temptation to instrumentalize martyrdom — that is, seeing it as a tactic or weapon wielded against the unbelieving or oppositional (much of the rhetoric of "persecuted Christians in secular America" fits here) — it also resists the exploitation of "Christian martyrs" by groups outside the church pursuing their own agendas (e.g., states whipping up political support by selectively opposing rivals who persecute Christians and others).

Another reason to consider anew the role of martyrdom in Christian life and history is to address some of the pathologies and wrong turns that have found their way into the church. Not every Christian understanding of martyrdom has contributed to the health of the body of Christ, and not every Christian practice, in matters of prayer, piety, or politics, has been faithful to the call of discipleship as exemplified by Jesus. When one adds the scandal of Christians as killers — making martyrs of others, even other Christians — the need for reappraisal and repentance becomes even more apparent. For the body of Christ to speak a healing word to a world in which lethal force is still thought to be determinative, it must heal the wounds it has inflicted on others.

In drawing scholars from across the confessional divides of Christianity, this volume both reflects and contributes to a process of ecumenical reconciliation and practice built around a resituated understanding of martyrdom. Pope John Paul II demonstrated something of this by recognizing the Protestant martyrs of the twentieth century as part of the Catholic Jubilee commemoration in 2000, as well as in asking forgiveness for the killing of Protestants by Catholics. Being able to embrace one another's martyrs — and all that that entails — is no small matter, and it is one that opens hopeful avenues for the churches witnessing more faithfully as one in a divided and divisive world.

About This Book

This book arranges its chapters under four general, broadly chronological categories: Martyrdom as the Church's Witness (part I); Martyrdom Builds the Church (part II); Martyrdom Destroys the Church (part III); and Martyrdom and the Future Church (part IV). This is a loose-fitting chronological structure, however, and several contributors tend toward a thematic disposition that ranges more widely across eras.

As will become apparent, some contributors hope to model the enduring importance of martyrdom in Christian practice, either in a particular era or in relationship to other foundational Christian practices. Several demonstrate the interpretive and formative power of witness in its many expressions, including that of the martyr and his or her communities of memory. While the performance of martyrdom is not the only authentic expression of a Christian life well lived, many contributors suggest that it is one that should not be expunged or edited from the repertoire of the Christian way. At the same time, some contributors ask whether too much emphasis on martyrdom has damaged the capacity of the church to witness to the good news of Christ, or whether the sheer power of martyrdom in contemporary culture makes its invocation especially hazardous or incendiary.

Some of these chapters were presented as part of a lecture series at

DePaul University during the 2006-7 academic year. The remaining chapters were solicited for this volume, and they complement and extend the inquiry represented by the invited lecturers.

Many people and offices within DePaul University brought this project to life. The Vincentian Endowment Fund, directed by the Reverend Edward Udovic, CM, provided generous financial support, as did the College of Liberal Arts and Sciences under the leadership of Dean Chuck Suchar via its Religion and Society lecture series. Speakers in the "Witness of the Body" lecture series received generous and effective cosponsorship from a variety of academic units and programs, including the departments of history, religious studies, political science, women and gender studies, international studies, the Religion and Society lecture series, and the LA&S "Confronting Empire" series.

Staff members in the program in Catholic Studies and the department of political science provided essential and effective work in all phases, from logistics to promotion and more. In particular, we wish to express our appreciation to Brenda Washington in Catholic Studies and Wilma Kwit in political science. We also thank Mark Laboe and his staff in University Ministry for their encouragement and assistance.

PART I

Martyrdom as the Church's Witness

CHAPTER 1

Christian Martyrdom: A Theological Perspective

Lawrence Cunningham

> *We offer thanks to God for their victories and by renewing their memory we encourage ourselves to emulate their crowns and victories. . . .*
>
> Saint Augustine, *The City of God,* VIII.27

Introduction

Edward Gibbon's *Decline and Fall of the Roman Empire* is not much read anymore except by those interested in matters of historiography or lovers of eighteenth-century prose (and sonorously wonderful prose it is). This neglect is understandable because Gibbon is not a read for the faint of heart. After he published volume 1 in 1776, six more volumes would appear, until he finished the project in 1788 with the seventh one, provoking the Duke of Gloucester to exclaim: "Another damned, thick, square book! Always scribble, scribble, scribble! Eh! Mister Gibbon?" Despite the fact that in my long-distant school days Gibbon was out of bounds for me — since my church had put his works on the Index — I enjoy dipping into Gibbon not so much for history but for the sheer pleasure of his rounded Ciceronian prose and his pugnaciously expressed judgments, of which I will provide an example soon.

Gibbon, in chapters 15 and 16 of volume 1, derides the pride of place that the Christian church had given to its earlier martyrs. Gibbon's negative brief can be economically summarized: there were not as many martyrs as the church proclaimed; some who did die were clearly fanatics; and subsequently, Christians themselves were, in their various wars, responsible for more deaths than were the Romans. Gibbon's judgment, of course, was colored by the extravagant claims of hagiography with which he would have been familiar (the *Legenda Aurea* was still read in pious circles in his day), as well as the sixteenth-century exploration of the Roman catacombs, in which, it was thought — erroneously — all of those buried there were martyrs. Bones of deceased Romans were sent all over the world as putative relics of martyrs. Of course, beyond these testable facts there was the seeming hypocrisy of a church trumpeting martyrdom while ignoring its own bloody hands in the Wars of Religion.

Gibbon, of course, did not deny that the Christians were persecuted. What he did deny was that the number of martyrs was great; second, he asserted that the phenomenon of death under persecution ought not to be overemphasized from a historical point of view or overly praised from within the Christian tradition. Gibbon thought that too much of early Christian history in general, and martyrdom in particular, was seen through the rose-colored lens of piety. At the end of the first volume of his great work, he has a concluding paragraph that is both beautiful in its sonority and economical in stating his thesis:

> We shall conclude this chapter by a melancholy truth which obtrudes itself on the educated mind that, even admitting, without hesitation or inquiry, all that history has recorded or devotion has feigned, on the subject of martyrdom, it must still be acknowledged that the Christians, in the course of their intestine dissensions, have inflicted far greater severity on each other than they had experienced at the hands of the infidels.

At the other end of the doubting spectrum, asserted rather than argued historically, would be Frederick Nietzsche's claim, in various of his works, that the Christian martyr died out of *ressentiment* and a will to power. Nietzsche saw the martyr as an example of self-exaltation who embraced death in order to possess power after death. Famously, he turned a line from Jesus into a summary of his own take on martyrdom: "Everyone who humbles himself, *wills* to be exalted."[1]

1. Quoted in J. Warren Smith's illuminating article "Martyrdom: Self-Denial or Self-Exaltation; Motives for Self-Sacrifice From Homer to Polycarp; A Theological Reflection," *Modern Theology* 22, no. 2 (April 2006): 169-96, quoting 170.

Some of Gibbon's or Nietzsche's jibes echo similar ones made by those in Roman antiquity who were antagonistic to the claims of the early Christians. As Robert Wilken demonstrated two decades ago, the Christians were not followers of what the pagans considered a religion, but fell under the Roman rubric of the superstitious.[2] Wilken makes it clear that, from the perspective of the Romans, it was unthinkable to consider the followers of Jesus Christ religious; they were merely the victims of some fanatical ideas that put them outside the realm of *religio*. Book Fifteen of the *Annales* by Tacitus, one of the classical non-Christian sources for the study of Christian martyrdom, actually uses the word *superstitio* in describing the growth of Christianity from Palestine into Rome, with the subsequent persecution that happened under the reign of Nero.[3]

The Latin word *superstitio*, to quote that gold standard dictionary for Latin, Lewis and Short's *A Latin Dictionary*, is "excessive fear of the gods, unreasonable religious belief . . . different from *religio*, a proper reasonable awe of the gods." It is clear from the sources that that famous dictionary provides that the word *superstitio* was a very pejorative term; thus Seneca's declaration (Epistle 123): *superstitio error insanus est.*[4]

Now, it was bad enough to be considered superstitious from the Roman perspective, but what was worse from that perspective was the fact that this superstition made the Christians resistant to many claims of Roman religion. Central to these claims was that *pietas* was the essential glue ("religion" derives from the Latin verb *religare:* "to bind together") that held together the family, the state, and the gods, which in turn created, when all was in harmony, the *pax deorum*. From the perspective of the Romans, Christians were a kind of fifth column undermining the essential structure of Roman society.[5] While the very charge of bearing the *nomen* of a Christian could hail one before the Roman tribunal, it was the concomitant refusal to sacrifice to the genius of the emperor and the gods and the refusal to swear oaths before the gods that sealed the deal. That the Christians were seen as disloyal or as traitors is

2. Robert L. Wilken, *The Christians as the Romans Saw Them* (New Haven: Yale University Press, 1984).

3. *Exitabilis superstitio rursum erumpebat non modo per Judaeam . . . sed per urbem etiam. . . .*"

4. I cite from the 1993 impression of Lewis and Short's *A Latin Dictionary* (Oxford: Clarendon Press, 1993).

5. On this point, see Everett Ferguson. "Early Christian Martyrdom and Civil Disobedience," *Journal of Early Christian Studies* 1, no. 1 (1992): 73-83.

clear from the extant *Acta* that have come down to us from the times of the persecutions.[6]

The Christian Martyrs Considered

Christians were persecuted in the Roman Empire, as the testimony of both pagan and Christian sources clearly attest. This assertion has very few nay-sayers. For generations scholars have investigated a whole series of questions, ranging from the reason(s) for the persecutions, their geographical extent, their intensity, and — more controversially — the number of Christians who actually suffered.[7]

It is beyond the scope of this chapter to give any detailed answers to those questions, but, following what most scholars agree to, I will here stipulate that in the early period, persecutions were localized, of varying intensity, and of undetermined length. It is also agreed that it was not until the middle of the third century, with the legislation of Decius in AD 250, that an empire-wide persecution of Christians occurred.

The issue of how many Christians were subject to persecution is very hard to determine for a number of reasons that go beyond the simple fact that we do not possess anything in the way of reliable statistics. Further, it is difficult to extrapolate from the historical records that we do have, because of the equally simple fact stated above: the periods of persecution were episodic and almost always somewhat localized. The persecution under the emperor Decius in 250 was, for the first time, empire wide, as was that of Diocletian on the cusp of the fourth century. However, prior to that time, it is not absolutely certain from the writings that reflect Christians dying in Rome or Lyons in Roman Gaul or in North Africa whether those deaths were or were not peculiar to those places or whether they were emblematic of larger persecutions. Estimates mentioned in the literature ranging from a few thousand to many thousands are just empirically too suspect to trust.

6. The extant *Acta* are collected in *Acts of the Christian Martyrs,* ed. Herbert Musurillo, SJ (Oxford: Clarendon, 1972). Hereafter, references to this work appear in parentheses in the text.

7. Among other works, see W. H. C. Frend, *Martyrdom and Persecution in the Early Church* (Oxford: Blackwell, 1965); Herbert Workman, *Persecution in the Early Church* (New York and London: Oxford University Press, 1990); G. W. Bowersock, *Martyrdom and Rome* (New York and Cambridge: Cambridge University Press, 1995); Elisabeth Castelli, *Martyrdom and Memory* (New York: Columbia University Press, 2004).

On the issue about the "why" of the persecutions, especially since the Romans were notoriously indifferent to what people actually believed except when their belief threatened the power of the state: one is on safe ground saying that the disapproval of the Christian movement by the Roman state is best understood as politically and not religiously inspired. If we look at both the pagan and Christian accounts of the persecutions from the earliest period, it seems that the very name *(nomen)* "Christian" was sufficient to trigger the punitive arm of Roman justice. Looking at the earliest redaction of the *Acta,* involving Justin and his companions from about AD 165, it is clear that the crucial point was the question, repeated to them, "Are you a Christian?" and the reply, "I am a Christian . . ." (Musurillo, 45ff.). Other *Acta* pretty much show the same pattern. Even those *Acta* that have been heavily redacted by Christian hands to highlight the polarity of Roman cruelty and Christian forbearance (as, for example, in the *Passion of Perpetua and Felicity*) still reflect that simple exchange between the Roman authority's question and the Christian confession: "I am a Christian."

Of course, there had to be a deeper meaning and motive behind the mere utterance of the name — of being a Christian — that brought such dire consequences to the one who bore the name "Christian." The legal basis on which Romans relied has been the subject of much research, but those who argue that no sure conclusion can be deduced in the early period, that is, before the Christian noncompliance with Decius's decree demanding that all Roman citizens sacrifice throughout the empire, seem cogent to me. Neither the classic description of Tacitus nor the famous letter of Pliny to the emperor explains why the name "Christian" should bring with it such a ferocious reaction. What we can guess is that the distaste for a *superstitio* — especially connected to the seemingly noxious deconstruction of Roman *pietas* — is the most plausible reason for the Roman persecution of the Christians.

Whatever the legal reason for the persecution(s) of Christians might have been, martyrdom, from the Christian side, if not welcomed, was at least seen as a logical price to pay for one's faith. Untangling the motives of Christians who were willing to face death during the periods of the Roman persecution is not an easy task. From the Roman point of view, they seemed to be fanatics; from the Christian side, judging from the considerable martyrdom literature that has come down to us, the motives seem inextricably entangled with the way they understood their faith in general and their Founder's story in particular.

The primary motive, of course, rested in the fact that at the center of their faith was a person who himself died in defense of his faith. Not only had Jesus died, but he died by crucifixion following a Roman prosecution. In the Roman view, this form of execution was a quite horrific and loathsome punishment that was typically preserved for the worst malefactors: rebellious slaves or non-Roman felons. We have so domesticated the religious language of the Bible that it is almost impossible for a contemporary audience to understand the shocking rhetoric of Paul's outcry to the Corinthians: "For Jews demand signs and Greeks desire wisdom, but we proclaim Christ crucified, a stumbling block *(skandalon)* to Jews and foolishness to Gentiles, but to those who are called, both Jews and Greeks, the power of God and the wisdom of God" (1 Cor. 1:22-24). Later in that same letter, reflecting a core tradition *(paradosis)* of the nascent Christian faith, Paul hands over to the Corinthians one of the earliest formulas of faith in Christianity: "Christ died for our sins according to the scriptures and that he was buried and that he was raised on the third day according to the scriptures . . ." (1 Cor. 15:3-14).[8]

Furthermore — and this point is often overlooked — the essential core of the Christian faith is not the doctrines of Jesus or his teaching, but Jesus himself. Christianity is not a religion of the book, *pace* the fundamentalists, but a faith directed to a person. Jesus does not say, "Come, follow my teachings," but "Come, follow me." Paul conceptualizes baptism not as washing in water but in a symbolic death and rising up in Christ. It would take too long and would take us too far from our topic to further elucidate this primary fact about the Christian faith, but it needs to be noted for a simple reason. If a follower of Jesus finds him- or herself in a hostile situation in which faith is set over against possible punishment or death, there is a certain logic that, from the believer's perspective, urges one to accept death precisely because there is a paradigm for such behavior, namely, that the fundamental object of faith himself accepted death at the hands of the hostile.

It is patent in the early Christian martyrdom literature that the trials of the Christian martyrs were seen in the light of the experience of Christ. as the author of the *Martyrdom of Polycarp* clearly declares:

> We would never abandon Christ, for it was he who suffered for the redemption of those who are saved in the entire world, the innocent one

8. On the connection of martyrdom and the imitation of Christ, see Larry Hurtado, *Lord Jesus Christ: Devotion to Jesus in Earliest Christianity* (Grand Rapids: Eerdmans, 2003), 619-25.

dying on behalf of sinners. Nor could we worship anyone else. For him we reverence as the Son of God, whereas [we] love the martyrs as the disciples and imitators of the Lord and rightly so because of their unsurpassed loyalty towards their king and master. May we too share with them as fellow disciples. (Musurillo, 15-17)

A similar paean may be observed at the conclusion of the *Passion of Perpetua and Felicitas* (by Tertullian?): "Ah, most valiant and blessed martyrs! Truly are you called and chosen for the glory of Christ Jesus our Lord! And any man who exalts, honors, and worships his glory should read for the consolation of the church these new deeds of heroism . . ." (Musurillo, 131).

It would be otiose to cite other such texts. Anyone who has read through the martyrdom literature can cull similar sentiments. In fact, Tertullian, who lived through a period of persecution in North Africa in the late second century, aimed several of his writings at the subject of martyrdom (e.g., *Scorpiace, De Fuga, Ad Martyres,* etc.), and anyone who looks at those treatises will soon see that not only does Tertullian link martyrdom to the death of Jesus, but he reads the life of Christ typologically as shedding light on the plight of the martyrs as well as on the witness of every Christian.[9] So did the author of the *Martydom of Polycarp* nearly a century earlier. In fact, that earlier text, with any number of explicit allusions, retells the story of Polycarp in terms of the life of Jesus.

We must keep the biblical tropes in mind when we read the bemused, impatient, and hostile responses of the Roman prefects and the pagan onlookers who have the accused Christians standing before them. At times they seem genuinely puzzled at the obstructive resistance of the accused. The *Martyrdom of Perpetua and Felicitas* is especially poignant in that regard. Perpetua's father is desperate in the face of her seeming obstinacy. He pleads: "Have pity on my grey head — have pity on your father. . . . Do not abandon me to be the reproach of men. Think of your brothers, think of your mother and your aunt, think of your child. . . ." When Perpetua arrives before the tribunal, he urges her: "Perform the sacrifice — have pity on your baby!" The father's pleading in the court was so vehement that the officiating officer ordered the father to be thrown down to the ground and to be beaten with a rod (Musurillo, 113-15).[10]

9. Thus, Eric Osborn says of Tertullian's own teaching: "Every Christian lives the life of a martyr, through testimony to Jesus in every part of his life" (Osborn, *Tertullian: First Theologian of the West* [Cambridge: Cambridge University Press, 1997], 233).

10. The highly complex literary and rhetorical character of this text has recently been

At times, of course, the substance of the Roman charge against the Christians seems to have a more substantive claim. From the time of Nero it was the mere *nomen* of being a Christian that seems to have been sufficient reason to bring down the iron arm of Roman justice. There may have been an echo of the charge of the *nomen* in 1 Peter: "Beloved, do not be surprised at the fiery ordeal that is taking place among you to test you, as though something strange were happening to you. But rejoice in so far as you are sharing Christ's suffering, so that you may be glad and shout for joy when his glory is revealed. If you are so reviled *for the name of Christ*, you are blessed because of the spirit of glory which is the Spirit of God resting upon you" (1 Pet. 4:12-14).

More expanded reasons for Roman persecution orbit around the Christian refusal to participate in Roman *religio*. And there were other reasons flowing from that refusal. Thus, by the end of the third century, a certain Maximilian was brought before a Roman tribunal in Roman North Africa on the charge that, in the name of Christianity, he had refused induction into the Roman military. The proconsul demanded: "Serve. If you despise you will perish miserably." To which Maximilian responded: "I shall not perish and if I depart from this world, my soul lives with Christ my Lord" (Musurillo, 249). A variation of the same charge was brought against a Roman centurion, Marcellus, who, during the time of Diocletian, abandoned his military duties in a public act on the feast day of the emperor. He was executed on the charge that he profaned his solemn oath and was thus liable under military law. His passion is recorded in two recensions (Musurillo, 250-59), which are very interesting to read because they reveal much about military custom and allegiance.[11]

In the case of those who would not abandon the *nomen* of Christian and would not offer sacrifice, and in the cases of those who sought relief from military service, it is clear that the disjunction between what the Christians felt was the logic of their faith commitment and what the Romans saw as a threat to the well-being of the state led the two parties on an inevitable collision course.

It is also clear that the issue of martyrdom cannot be read as simply a theological subject; it was also an issue that had a deep social and political

explored in Erin Ronsse, "Rhetoric of Martyrs: Listening to Saints Perpetua and Felicitas," *Journal of Early Christian Studies* 14, no. 3 (2006): 283-328.

11. The classic study of the military saints is Hippolyte Delehaye, *Les legendes grecques des saints militaires* (Paris: Picard, 1909).

component, a component that is not all that alien to contemporary discourse when, to cite one instance, legitimate courts have to make adjudications about persons who, for deep reasons of conscience, act contrary to the law. From the perspective of the court, selective obedience and disobedience could easily be a precedent that erodes the whole fabric of law; from the perspective of the individual, there is that ultimate arbiter that must be named, namely, the sovereign voice of conscience. As Joseph Ratzinger (Pope Benedict XVI) has wisely noted in commenting on the legitimacy of the state to demand obedience:

> The faith of the New Testament acknowledges not the revolutionary but the martyr, who recognizes both the authority of the state and its limits. His resistance consists in doing everything that serves to promote law and an ordered life in society, even when this means obeying authorities who are indifferent or hostile to his faith; but he will not obey when he is commanded to do what is evil, to oppose the will of God. His is not the resistance of active force, but the resistance of one who is willing to suffer for the will of God.[12]

It may be worth noting in passing that it is this fact that, when fully explored, sheds light on the moral question of conscientious objection and other such moral questions.

The Making of the Martyr Tradition

Of course, already in the second century, the Christian church had absorbed the witness of the martyr into the liturgical practice of the church by commemorating the death of the martyr by formal rites and, where possible, by the sacralizing of their tomb memorials. These practices would be a signal mark of Christian practice by the fourth century within the community, and it was recognized as such in the non-Christian communities of the time. Here is a suggestive sermon preached by Saint Augustine of Hippo on the martyred Saint Cyprian of Carthage:

> Today we celebrate the birthday of the most glorious martyr, Cyprian. This expression *natales* [birthdays] is regularly employed by the

12. Joseph Cardinal Ratzinger, *Values in a Time of Upheaval* (New York: Crossroad/Ignatius, 2006), 21.

> Church in this way so that it calls the precious deaths of the martyrs their birthdays. This expression, I repeat, is regularly employed by the Church to the extent that even those who don't belong to her join her in using it. Is there anyone to be found, I ask you, and I don't mean just in this city of ours, but throughout the whole of Africa and the regions overseas, and not only any Christian, but any pagan or Jew or even heretic who doesn't call today the birthday of the martyr Cyprian.
>
> Why is this, brothers and sisters? What date he was born on, we don't know; and because he suffered today, it's today that we celebrate his birthday. We wouldn't celebrate that other day, even if we knew when it was. On that day we contracted original sin, while on this day we overcame all sin. On that he came forth from the wearisome confines of his mother's womb into the light, which is so alluring to our eyes of flesh; but on this day he went away from the deep darkness of nature's womb to that light, which sheds such blessing and good fortunes upon the mind.[13]

What is reflected in this excerpt from Augustine represents the maturation of impulses in the development of early Christianity that includes the exaltation of the *imitatio Christi* motif that is detectable in the second century, as well as the slow evolution of a calendar marking the "birthdays" of the martyrs, the honoring of their burial places, the perceived power of their relics, the growth of liturgical practices, and the other elements that are at the root of the Catholic veneration of the saints. What is happening here is, as a recent author has nicely put it, the slow making of a culture as the memory of the martyrs is institutionalized in various modalities within the Christian community.[14] It is not possible here to do more than mention these practices, because a consideration of their evolution would take us too far afield.[15] Nor is it possible to trace out the attitudes of the pagan contemporaries during the time of their development, except to mention in passing that the pagans were at a minimum bemused by such a fascination with the dead, which seemed to them polluting and unclean. That repugnance may also explain, as has often been noted, why Gnostic Christians had neither a penchant for martyrdom nor an appreciation of it,

13. *Sermo* 310.1.

14. Elizabeth A. Castelli, *Martyrdom and Memory: Early Christian Culture Making* (New York: Columbia University Press, 2003).

15. Lawrence S. Cunningham, *A Brief History of the Saints* (Oxford: Blackwell, 2005), where I have considered these issues in the opening chapters.

since, almost to a person, Gnostics were docetists with little evidence that they valued the material in general and the body in particular. That reaction in itself says something about the distance between pagans and Christians with respect to the meaning of the body.[16]

Some Reflections on Martyrdom

When writing or thinking about martyrs from within the Catholic household, which is my natural home since I write as a Catholic theologian, it is very difficult for me to bracket the nearly two-thousand-year history of the memory of the Roman martyrs as it has been received, elaborated on in everything from the plastic arts to the highly theologized accounts in the liturgy, and used as a template to understand subsequent periods in which there were other occasions for martyrdom. The memory of the martyrs is simply part of the fabric of the Catholic experience. I can walk into any church anywhere and, without a guide, look at the stained-glass window and pick out Catherine with her wheel, Laurence with his gridiron, and the arrow-specked figure of Sebastian. In that sense, at least, the Roman martyr is frozen in time and veneration by iconography, veneration, nomenclature, and interpretation.

The martyr stories, further, have themselves gone through a long period of development so that between the relatively chaste *Acta*, remembered from the actual Roman judicial processes, to the elaborated legends (*legendum*: "that which is read out loud") we move from austere question-and-answer to highly stereotypical fictions that use the martyrdom story to become a launching pad for the human imagination. The Roman court officer now takes on the character of a demon, while the accused, whether male or female, is virginal, resolute, and often possessed of grace-aided miraculous powers. Furthermore, the punishments are no longer merely the stake or the sword but elaborately woven punishments that, more than occasionally, have just a tinge of the pornographic about them.

Such elaborations, of course, are nothing new. They are, in fact, part and parcel of all folk history in which a nugget of possible historical truth becomes enveloped in a cocoon of mythic exaggeration. There may well have been a third-century martyr who was given the name "Christ-bearer"

16. On this topic, see Judith Perkins, *The Suffering Self: Pain and Narrative Representations in Early Christianity* (London: Routledge, 1995).

(Christopher) posthumously, but his career as a ferryman and the story of his bearing the Christ child over the river is a late elaboration that found its way into the *Golden Legend* and from there became one of the "Fourteen Holy Helpers." Erasmus of Rotterdam bitterly assailed this cult in the *Praise of Folly* and, with some plausibility, saw his story as being shaped by the Hercules legend, just as he thought that the brothers Cosmas and Damien were retellings of the Castor and Pollux of mythic fame.

The very elaboration of these hagiographical legends makes it necessary to posit a question that is not easily or tidily answered: Just what is a saint in general and a martyred saint in particular? In the Roman period, the answer with respect to the martyr is simple enough: a martyr is anyone who confesses his or her faith openly and dies as a direct result of that confession. That confession and subsequent penalty provides the baseline for the title of martyr, despite whatever exaggeration, elaboration, or fiction might have accrued over the course of time. In the more technical language of the church, the martyr is one who dies *in odium fidei.*

In the subsequent history of the church, that criterion becomes a bit muddled. There are those who are honored as martyrs in the church who did not die directly because of *odium fidei.* Saint Thomas Aquinas defended the appellation of martyr for the Holy Innocents and for John the Baptist despite the fact that neither died strictly after a confession of faith: the Holy Innocents were too young to make such a confession; John the Baptist lived before the redemptive work of Christ was finished (this is a fortiori true of the Old Testament Maccabee sons, who were honored as martyrs).

In our own day, a furious debate raged in the papers when Pope John Paul II canonized Edith Stein (Sister Benedicta of Holy Cross) as a martyr when — in the minds of many — she died, not *in odium fidei,* but because she was a Jew.[17] Similarly, while Maximilian Kolbe was without a doubt a heroic figure in offering to replace a married man in a concentration camp starvation bunker, it was not strictly the case that he died *in odium fidei,* but as a gesture of heroic self-sacrifice. It is for that reason that some have called for a new reflection on martyrdom to more easily accommodate those who demonstrate heroic virtue even unto death. As one theologian has put it,

17. I have explored in depth all of these issues in my essay "On the Contemporary Martyrs," in *More than a Memory: The Discourse of Martyrdom and the Construction of Christian Identity in the History of Christianity,* ed. Johan Leemans (Leuven: Peeters, 2005), 451-64.

such persons, especially those in the contemporary period, have died not *in odium fidei* but *in odium caritatis* ("out of hatred for love"). This is especially true where the persecutors come from countries where, nominally at least, the antagonists themselves were at least culturally Catholic.[18]

The whole issue of the intentions behind the willingness of the martyr to die for what he or she believes has become a burning subject in contemporary life because of the almost weekly accounts we have in the press about Islamic suicide bombers, who immolate themselves as part of the jihad against the perceived enemies of Islam. At the offset it is important for me to stipulate that my reflections on this topic derive from no special expertise on Islamic matters. Indeed, my reflections come only from my attention to the media and whatever wisdom I have gleaned from essays in journals of opinion. With that caveat in mind, let me make the following observations.

First, there is an honorable tradition of venerating the *shahid* (martyr) in Islam, with a warrant that goes back to the Qur'an. In fact, the Shia branch of Islam is only understandable against the concept of martyrdom. Islamic countries often possess a shrine *(mashhad)* commemorating the place where a martyr died and where he or she is buried. My remarks do not concern themselves with this strain of martyrdom theology in Islam. My focus is on the appellation "martyr" for those who kill themselves as an Islamic duty to further holy war (jihad) against infidels.

From a purely phenomenological perspective, the suicide bombers from Palestine who venture into Israel to kill themselves seem to have a family resemblance to martyrdom as it is understood in the Christian West. Those young people (and they are, in the vast majority of cases, young men and women) seem to be motivated out of a deep faith that what they are doing is within the dictates of Islamic faith and, further, that they will be rewarded in the next life for submitting to the will of Allah. Next, they are honored by the community who remember them by wall posters, mosque sermons praising their sacrifice, and families who are proud to have offered a child in this enterprise. In short, they enjoy in the community a form of anamnesis: they are remembered with honor and praise, though I am not aware that this form of anamnesis has any form of liturgical significance.

18. Lawrence S. Cunningham, "*Non Poena sed Causa:* A Contemporary Understanding of Martyrdom," in *Martyr and Prophet for the New Millennium,* ed. Robert Pelton (Scranton: University of Scranton Press, 2006), 59-72.

Second, from the perspective of Christian theology, the most notable difference between the Muslim martyr and the Christian one revolves around two issues: the legitimacy of suicide and the problem of the taking of human life as a result of the martyr's action.[19] On the issue of suicide, one must say that there are some instances where early Christian martyrs did put themselves in harm's way in order to die for the faith; but those instances are very marginal ones and their legitimacy is debated.[20] Typically, Catholic moral theology would judge such activities (e.g., Origen desiring to run after his arrested father to die with him as a Christian martyr)[21] as cases of indirect suicide, while direct suicide has always been regarded, following the common opinion of Thomas Aquinas, as intrinsically immoral.[22]

Aquinas, of course, was drawing his arguments from Augustine's celebrated discussion in *The City of God* (book 1, chaps. 17-27), where he argues that despite the praise among the pagans for suicides like Cato's and even the cases of some few Christian martyrs who, like Saint Pelagia, threw themselves to an almost certain death to avoid rape, suicide was always to be condemned. If a Christian acted like Saint Pelagia, it must have been under the force of divine command (Augustine thinks that to be the case for Samson in the Old Testament); but, he adds, "let him take care that there is no uncertainty about the divine command."

Saint Augustine is an apt figure to recall since his interest in suicide and its relationship to martyrdom was partially fed by his knowledge of the so-called "Circumcellions," who were an extreme wing of the schismatic Donatist Church. They acted as marauding warriors who fought in the name of religion, had a fixation on the cult of the martyrs, and at times committed suicide in the name of their faith. There was an outbreak of such suicides among the Circumcellions near the middle of the fourth century and again in the early fifth century. Even the Donatists expressed distaste for their fanaticism. Augustine did not accept the Donatist mar-

19. For one negative reaction to suicide bombers from an Islamic perspective, see Munawar A. Anees, "Salvation and Suicide: What Does Islamic Theology Say?" *Dialog: A Journal of Theology* 45, no. 3 (2006): 275-79.

20. Augustine, *The City of God*, trans. Henry Bettenson (Harmondsworth, UK: Penguin, 1984), 37.

21. For a discussion of this story told by Origen's biographer, Eusebius of Caesarea, see Henri Crouzel, *Origen* (New York: Harper, 1989), 5-7.

22. *ST* II II ae 64.5. For a traditional casuistic discussion, see "Suicide," in *New Catholic Encyclopedia* (Washington, DC: Catholic University of America Press, 1967), 13:781-83.

tyrs as martyrs as such, and he had nothing but contempt (mixed with horror) for the activities of the Circumcellions.[23]

One can be more apodictic about the case of someone who commits self-immolation in order to kill others in that very act. Since those instances always or almost always involve the direct killing of innocent persons, Catholic moral theology would regard such acts as intrinsically immoral. By that fact alone, they would never be considered martyrs from the Catholic point of view. While Pope Benedict XVI did not refer directly to suicide bombers in his now-infamous address of September 12, 2006, at the University of Regensburg on the relationship of faith and reason, his stern warning about never justifying violence in the name of faith (with some reference to Islam) must be seen as part of the background of that speech. From the perspective of Catholic moral theology, such actions are simply immoral. Furthermore, to apply the word "martyr" to such persons is to evacuate the meaning of the term in any Christian way of understanding.

Some Conclusions

As I have indicated earlier in this chapter, there is some conceptual haziness about who qualifies as a martyr in the Catholic tradition. While the Catholic Church had a pretty clear concept of what it meant by naming someone a martyr in the pre-Constantinian era, it is also clear that the title was used somewhat loosely in the medieval period and even in contemporary times, for example, the canonization of Edith Stein as a martyr (where it became an interreligious dispute) during the papacy of the late Pope John Paul II. Even before that time, theologians suggested that the entire concept of martyrdom be studied in more detail — not only in the light of history, but in terms of contemporary experience.[24]

In a letter to the Congregation for the Causes of the Saints (April 24, 2006), Pope Benedict XVI asked the Congregation to apply the classical understanding of martyrdom when considering causes brought before them.[25]

23. See "Circumcellions," in *Augustine Through the Ages: An Encyclopedia*, ed. Allan D. Fitzgerald, OSA (Grand Rapids: Eerdmans, 1999), 193-94 (with a good bibliography).

24. See the 1983 issue of *Concilium*, under the title "Martyrdom Today," edited by J. B. Metz; see also the 2003 issue of the same journal, under the title "Rethinking Martyrdom," edited by Teresa Okure.

25. See my remarks on that letter and its implications in Lawrence S. Cunningham, "Martyrs Named and Nameless," *America* (October 2, 2006): 10-13.

It is not clear what motivated the pope to express himself on the topic, but it may well be that he thought that the title had been used too elastically in common parlance and, further, that he did not want the title, which has an honorable history behind it in the Catholic tradition, to become too attenuated. After all, the word "martyr" has become bandied about in the popular press somewhat promiscuously, with the result that the concept itself is not only frequently used flabbily, but the precise meaning of the word becomes blurred.

Any definition of the term "martyr" from within the Catholic tradition must take into consideration a number of pertinent factors. I will limit myself to three of these factors.

(1) A distinction must be made between using the term generously for anyone who died as a member of the Catholic community as a result of political or social outrage (e.g., religious believers who were sent to Gulags because they were considered class enemies of the state) and those who died *ex professo,* that is, because they openly professed their faith before a hostile regime.

(2) We must take care when we use the term "martyr" if the canonization mechanism is to be put in play, since the canonization process inevitably involves the liturgy, which is, by its nature, traditional, conservative, and implicated in the way our common faith is expressed. In this regard, it is useful to recall that "orthodoxy" means both "right belief" and "right praise." It is significant that official documents of the Catholic Church see in the person of the martyrs witnesses of the truth of Christ's death and resurrection; witnesses to the truth of the faith and doctrine of the church; and a living lesson in Christian fortitude.[26]

(3) A thicker analysis needs to be made so that the traditional criterion of "hatred of the faith" *(odium fidei)* be understood not only in its plain sense of the term but in ways in which that *odium* might be expressed. We are yet to have a full theology of martyrdom written within the context of contemporary realities. It is clear that the official church is keenly aware of the critical importance of martyrdom. It has been a theme running through the encyclicals of the late John Paul II (see *Veritatis Splendor* and *Ut Unum Sint,* for two examples) and was a highlighted feature of the millennial celebrations. Pope Benedict XVI, in the second part of his first encyclical, *Deus Caritas Est,* singles out *marturia* as one of the

26. I am paraphrasing the formulation of paragraph #2473 of the *Catechism of the Catholic Church.*

three essential elements of the church. The pope saw *maturia* (witness) in its broad sense, but it seems to me that it is precisely in that sweeping theological category that we should understand martyrdom as it is more restrictively understood.

Finally, we need a new synthetic theological understanding of martyrdom because, as of now, no such account adequately plumbs the "thickness" of the term as it has come down to us in the tradition. In the end, any comprehensive theological account of Christian martyrdom will have to take into account not only the broad history of hagiography and the tradition of commenting on that history, but also the role of the martyr in the liturgical life of the church (and hence a look at the canonization process), and also, as a standard trope in contemporary theology, the historical situation in which our understanding has shaped and been shaped by human experience, not in the abstract but in the messiness of history. At the core of any such account, of course, is the icon of the primordial witness — Jesus crucified. When he wrote *Nachfolge* in 1937, Dietrich Bonhoeffer, who himself would be executed by the Nazis less than a decade later, got to the heart of the matter, and his words on the martyr make a fitting end to this essay: "No other Christian is so closely identified with the form of Christ crucified. When Christians are exposed to public insult, when they suffer and die for his sake, Christ takes on the visible form in his church. Here we see the divine image created anew through the power of Christ crucified."[27]

27. Dietrich Bonhoeffer, *The Cost of Discipleship* (New York: Macmillan, 1966), 342.

CHAPTER 2

Early Church Martyrdom: Witnessing For or Against the Empire?

Tripp York

In the year 295, a twenty-one-year-old man, Maximilian of Tebessa, was beheaded for his refusal to serve in the Roman military. Maximilian, whose father was a soldier in the Roman army, refused his obligation to join the military because of his commitment to the path of Jesus. When this was brought to the attention of the proconsul of Africa, Dion, Maximilian was asked for his name. "Why should you want to know my name? I cannot serve in the army, I am a Christian." The young Christian was not even interested in providing his name, for how could he even be tempted to carry a sword and make a pledge to a worldly leader when those indications of loyalty are bound to Christ?

This response did not interest the proconsul, who went ahead and measured the young man so that he could wear the badge symbolizing his place in the Roman military. Maximilian repeatedly protested this action, explaining to the proconsul that he was incapable of serving in this capacity because he was not a "soldier of this world"; rather, he was a soldier of God. Dion refused to accept this early case of conscientious objection, and the two engaged in a heated conversation over whether or not he would wear the insignia of the empire. Finally, Dion ordered that the badge be placed around Maximilian's neck, to which Maximilian responded:

> I will not take the badge of worldly warfare . . . . If you put it on me, I shall tear it off. It is of no use. I am a Christian. It is unlawful for me to wear this bit of lead around my neck after receiving the sign of my Lord Jesus Christ. . . . My service is for my own Lord.

Dion explained to him that, if he refused service, he would surely perish. Maximilian disagreed. He claimed that it was impossible for a Christian to die, because they live in Christ. After being told that his refusal to oblige their oath demanded his beheading, Maximilian responded: "Thanks be to God."[1]

Eight years later, the emperor Diocletian issued his first edict against Christianity, and that would be considered the beginning of the last great persecution of the Christians under Roman rule. In his imperial decree, Diocletian demanded that all houses of assembly for Christians, along with their scriptures, be burned. Any Christian leaders maintaining their practice of religion were to be imprisoned and tortured until they sacrificed to the Roman gods.[2] Within a year (AD 304), Diocletian had issued three more edicts against the Christians, with the fourth edict rendering the persecution of Christianity in more sweeping terms. That last edict said that any Christians found within the domain of the empire — regardless of their position in the church or as a Roman citizen — who did not sacrifice to the gods were to be put to death. Imprisonment was no longer an option. The practice of Christianity carried with it a death sentence.[3]

This was not the first time Christians were executed for their confession of Christ. Ignatius and Polycarp, along with other martyrs such as Stephen, Perpetua, and Felicitas, are all representative of celebrated martyrs prior to the rule of Diocletian. However, I begin with Diocletian because he represents the last emperor of the Roman Empire, save for the brief reign of Julian (361-363), to represent a physical threat against the church. For its almost 300-year history, Christianity, on its better days, had to merely deal with the indifference of pagan Rome toward its rather innovative and unusual practices and beliefs; on its not so fortunate days, the church had to face torture, suffering, imprisonment, and death at the hands of the Romans. Though there were a few exceptions to the rule, for the most part, beginning with the death of Jesus and lasting until 311,

1. Mark Water, *The New Encyclopedia of Christian Martyrs* (Grand Rapids: Baker, 2001), 351-52.

2. See Book 8 of Eusebius's *The History of the Church from Christ to Constantine*, trans. G. A. Williamson (New York: Penguin Books, 1989), 256-81.

3. For a detailed account of the four edicts issued by Diocletian, see chaps. 1 and 2 of G. E. M. de Ste. Croix, *Christian Persecution, Martyrdom, and Orthodoxy*, ed. Michael Whitby and Joseph Streeter (Oxford: Oxford University Press, 2006), and chap. 15 of W. H. C. Frend, *Martyrdom and Persecution in the Early Church* (New York: Doubleday, 1967).

Christians rarely exercised positions of great authority in the empire: there was not a single bishop during this time who approved of Christian participation in warfare (that is, the church was, by and large, a body politic that espoused and practiced nonviolence during this golden age of martyrdom); and Christians understood that their social place in worldly order was never a secure one. Though Christian persecution was often sporadic in the early church, Christians lived with the knowledge that at any given moment they might have to pay the price for their baptisms. This was so true that early Christians had to develop a theology of two baptisms: the first by water, the second by blood. Baptism, in the early church, was concretely connected to death.

Yet, within less than eighty years, all of this would change. Only a few years after Diocletian's last decree against the Christians, Galerius would decriminalize Christianity in 311, demanding that Roman citizens tolerate all religious creeds. In 313, following a vision and a military victory that they both attributed to the God of the Christians, Constantine and Licinius issued the Edict of Milan (though it was neither an edict nor from Milan), which not only furthered toleration toward all religious faiths but opened the doors to a closer relationship between the church and the empire. Constantine ordered that any confiscated material previously taken away from the Christian church be returned to the church. Not only were the goods of the church returned to her, but, following the controversial "conversion" of Constantine, the church began to enjoy the political and social privileges that were based on an emperor's favor. Some groups within the church even found an ally in the emperor on certain doctrinal issues that threatened to rend the church asunder. The most important of these was about Nicene Christianity. Constantine called the Council of Nicea in 325 in order to settle the relationship between the Father and the Son — so that there would be unity both within the church and the empire. Heretics were named, opposition was silenced, and orthodoxy was solidified via imperial might.[4]

4. I am not suggesting that the Nicene Creed was merely established due to the whims of an emperor, or that it should be discredited because it did find imperial favor. The battles that were waged over correct doctrine that would eventually lead to the grammar that we now call Christian faith were being hammered out long before emperors joined the fray (with basic creedal formulations arising as early as the first century). The Nicene Creed was not an invention of Constantine. With regard to the creation of those creeds that became imperial mandate, the major facet of concern should, I think, reside with the ability of those in the church to call on the strong-arming of the state to enforce its orthodoxy so that dis-

Before the fourth century had concluded, the emperor Theodosius made Christianity the official state religion. Eventually, under the reign of Theodosius, all citizens of the Roman Empire were required to be baptized at the time of their births. By 416, only Christians could serve in the military. With this new establishment in place, Christians were no longer persecuted by Rome; instead, Christians often became the persecutors for Rome. Christian discipleship was no longer optional, and along with what many consider to be the triumph of Christianity came, arguably, the domestication of Christian witness.[5]

There has been more than enough ink spilled about whether or not what has been coined the "Constantinian shift" signifies the "fall" of the church. My goal is not to add to this discussion, much less attempt to resolve this problem. Rather, I intend to provide a brief examination of the development of martyrdom within Rome prior to Rome's conversion to Christianity, and what can be considered the loss of martyrdom after that "conversion." Whether or not one period speaks more or less in terms of faithfulness to Jesus is beyond the scope of this chapter. This chapter merely wishes to briefly examine the creation and development of martyrdom as the archetypal act of Christian witness that affords the empire the ability to see that it is something that the church is not. Through the church's development of blood-witness as an act stemming from one person's confession of Christ and another's *odium fidei*, this form of witnessing became a public sacrament for the world to see.

Accordingly, martyrdom is missiological. Maximilian's refusal to serve in the military was his way of showing the world — in his case the Roman Empire — that it was not an end in itself and that it was worshiping false gods. Though the empire killed him for his refusal to worship their gods, his act, as any act of martyrdom, was not against the empire — as if Christian witness is merely reactionary or defined by what it is

---

senting positions can be quelled. Any criticism of this arrangement, therefore, has little to do with the content of the creeds, only the manner in which they were established. For a sound defense of classical orthodoxy that not only argues against current trends that would disregard creedal Christianity but also finds within the creeds the resources to resist being coopted by the state, see A. James Reimer, *Mennonites and Classical Theology: Dogmatic Foundations for Christian Ethics* (Kitchener, ON: Pandora Press, 2001), 247-71.

5. The work of Oliver O'Donovan (specifically his *The Desire of the Nations*) and John Howard Yoder (specifically his *For the Nations*) is a good place to start in terms of attempting to adjudicate contrasting accounts of what it means, in terms of discipleship, for the empire to "convert" to Christianity.

against. Rather, his martyrdom and early Christian martyrdom in general was *for* the empire. Any act of witness is always a testimony to the good news that is the resurrected Christ, which gives those watching the ability to see the world as it really is: redeemed. Martyrdom is not an end in itself. It is a public bodily confession that hopes to transform all that is not of Christ into the mystical body of Christ. It is an act that seeks the good of the city, though not as the city might imagine.

Confessors and Martyrs

> *Martyrdom contends with idolatry, not from some malice that they share, but from its own kindness; for it delivers from idolatry.*
>
> TERTULLIAN

In his book *Martyrdom and Rome,* G. W. Bowersock convincingly argues that, whatever martyrdom is, it is an invention of second-century Christianity.[6] In the first century, the term "martyr" simply signified one who was a witness to an event. A martyr was a person who had firsthand information of something and could share that information. More often than not, this generally implied that one could testify to something in a court of law. By the time of the recording of certain books in the New Testament, the term began to shift. In the book of Acts (possibly recorded in the 60s) it comes to signify those people, specifically the apostles, who will be witnesses to Jesus: "You will be my witnesses in Jerusalem, and in all Judea and Samaria, and to the ends of the earth" (Acts 1:8). According to Acts 1:22, one of the essential qualifications for the replacement of Judas Iscariot was that the eligible person be a witness to the resurrection of Jesus.[7] In both of these cases the word "martyr" *(martus)* is being used, but not in any way that indicates the death of the witness.

By the time John records his revelation (mid-90s), the language begins to shift even more: "Yet you are holding fast to my name and you did not deny your faith in me even in the days of Antipas my witness, my faith-

6. G. W. Bowersock, *Martyrdom and Rome* (Cambridge: Cambridge University Press, 2002), 1-21.

7. Later in Acts, Stephen is referred to as a witness to God whose blood was shed because of his testimony (Acts 20:22). Nevertheless, *martus* is still being used here in the technical sense of being a witness. His witness resulted in the shedding of his blood, but at this point it did not necessitate it.

ful one, who was killed among you, where Satan lives" (Rev. 2:13). And in Revelation 6:9: "When he opened the fifth seal, I saw under the altar the souls of those who had been slaughtered for the word of God and for the testimony they had given. . . ." In both of these passages, especially the latter, confession of God is becoming linked with the death of the confessor. Nevertheless, prior to the middle of the second century, there is no Christian literature that ever designates the term "martyr" as one who necessarily dies for his or her beliefs. The subject becomes even more convoluted when we see that many times Christians who ended up in prison because of their confession of Christ were labeled martyrs despite not being killed for their confession. Much of this has to do with the categorizing of certain Christians as confessors and the fluidity of language that permeated the early church's thinking.

Confessors were, simply, those Christians who had confessed their allegiance to Christ in light of hostile public authorities.[8] All Christians are called to be confessors, but much of a Christian's initial confession takes place in the security of a private, unthreatening setting. It is a very different story when the actual body of the confessor is at stake. Those Christians who publicly pronounced their confession of Christ, regardless of whether or not it landed them in prison or in the arena, were labeled "confessors." This group maintained a special status in the early years of Christianity, because at that time the temptation to lapse, given the persecution, was always a threat to the unity of the church. Confessors were praised for their ability to face prison, torture, and even death because of their commitment to Christ, because it also solidified, through their bodies, the validity of Christian claims.

Therefore, the development of martyrdom is better understood in its relationship with those known as "confessors." In the work of the second- and third-century theologian Tertullian we find that, though he generally speaks of "martyrs" as those people who died because of their confession of faith, he occasionally uses that word to refer to those — as I have mentioned above — who are not yet dead. A few examples can be found in his letter entitled *Ad Martyras* and *The Prescription Against Heretics.* In the former, Tertullian is addressing those Christians who are, presumably, going to die; yet he is already referring to them as martyrs (or martyrs desig-

8. Cyprian, *Treatise III, Epistles VI and X,* in *The Ante-Nicene Fathers,* vol. 5, ed. Alexander Roberts and James Donaldson (Peabody, MA: Hendrickson, 1999; hereafter referred to as *ANF*).

nate). In his treatise against heretics, Tertullian asks whether or not one who falls away from faith proves heresies to be true. Interestingly, he acknowledges the possibility of not only leaders in the church apostatizing but even martyrs:

> For to the Son of God Alone was it reserved to persevere to the last without sin. But what if a bishop, if a deacon, if a widow, if a virgin, if a doctor, if *even* a martyr, have fallen from the rule (of faith), will heresies on that account appear to possess the truth?[9]

Tertullian argues against such logic and contends that "no one is a Christian but he who perseveres to the end." At this point within Christianity, one can be considered a martyr and yet not have persevered to the end.[10]

It was Tertullian who coined the term "confessor," and he did so in view of the development of martyrdom meaning a blood-witness. He writes in *The Chaplet, or De Corona,* "I affirm that not one of the Faithful has ever a crown upon his head, except at a time of trial. That is the case with all, from catechumens to confessors and martyrs, or (as the case may be) deniers."[11] This passage suggests that Tertullian sees three distinct groups within Christianity: the catechumens, the confessors and the martyrs, and those that, under trial and persecution, deny Christ. Tertullian does not think of confessors and martyrs as two distinct groups within Christianity; rather, they are one group, as opposed to the catechumens or those that would deny Christ. This does not necessarily mean that Tertullian uses the words "confessor" and "martyr" as synonyms; it is just that, when he does use the term "confessor," according to Edelhard Hummel, he places the

> emphasis primarily on oral confession of faith before a pagan magistrate, and refers only secondarily to the martyr's death by which such a confession is confirmed; while, when he uses the word martyr, he wishes to place the emphasis rather on the torture and death suffered by such a Christian.[12]

9. Tertullian, *The Proscription Against Heretics,* III, *ANF,* 3:244.

10. Perhaps it is for this reason that the Christian tradition, over time, decided that a martyr can only be named a martyr after her death. The naming must occur by a community who recognizes an imitation of Christ in both her life and death.

11. Tertullian, *The Chaplet, or De Corona,* III, *ANF,* 3:94.

12. Edelhard L. Hummel, *The Concept of Martyrdom According to St. Cyprian of Carthage,* The Catholic University of America Studies in Christian Antiquity, ed. Johannes Quasten (Washington, DC: Catholic University of America Press, 1946), 5.

As we have seen, however, Tertullian is not always consistent in such usage. What we can gather from his use of the words "confessor" and "martyr" is that, when he does use such language, he generally assumes at least the possibility of death for such confession, if not immediate death. That it does or does not happen does not necessarily change his use of the language because, according to Tertullian, the fact that one was capable of confessing Christ, in light of a possible early death, was often enough to warrant the use of such language as confessor or martyr.

Saint Cyprian, the slightly later third-century theologian and bishop of Carthage, leans on the work of Tertullian but is a bit more precise in his choice of words. Cyprian never applies the term "confessor" to one who has already died because of his or her confession of faith; he thus avoids some of the confusion over the constitutive differences between a confessor and a martyr.[13] Nevertheless, Cyprian often addresses those Christians who are facing death as both martyrs and confessors and continues to place both of them in the same camp.[14] He even refers to Aurelius, the "illustrious youth, already approved by the Lord, and dear to God," who, because of his "twice confession," Cyprian has ordained as a reader for the priest, as a martyr.[15] Cyprian does refer to those who have given up their lives for Christ as martyrs, but he is also compelled to name those who are still living as martyrs. This makes sense inasmuch as both Tertullian and Cyprian are merely holding to the original meaning of the word *martus.*

Cyprian does, however, make strides in solidifying a more precise account of martyrdom by drawing distinctions between those whose struggle ended in death and those whom he categorizes as confessors. He begins this process by granting confessors the title of martyrs if physical torture and mistreatment were part of their imprisonment. Cyprian argues that "scripture speaks of the tortures which consecrate God's martyrs" and thus sanctifies "them in the very trial of suffering."[16] He quotes the Wisdom of Solomon from the Apocryphal literature as evidence of the tortured confessors' sanctification:

> And if they have suffered torments in the sight of men, yet is their hope full of immortality; and having been a little chastised, they shall be greatly rewarded: for God proved them, and found them worthy of

13. Hummel, *Concept of Martyrdom*, 5.
14. Cyprian, *Epistles VIII, X, LI, ANF*, 5:5.
15. Cyprian, *Epistle XXXII, ANF*, 5:312.
16. Cyprian, *Epistle LXXX, ANF*, 5:407.

> Himself. As gold in the furnace hath he tried them, and received them as a sacrifice of a burnt-offering, and in due time regard shall be had unto them. The righteous shall shine, and shall run to and fro like sparks among the stubble. They shall judge the nations, and have dominion over the people; and their Lord shall reign forever.[17]

As I have mentioned above, this was part of his reasoning for ordaining Aurelius, one who "vanquished torture" through his body, a reader in the church. Those who have endured torment for their confession will be those who will, with God, judge over the nations (Rev. 6:11). How much more should a person be recognized in the church as one of special status!

As this progression moved forward, ranging from the good of private confession to public confession, to public confession resulting in torture, it reached the point where it became necessary for language to describe the confessor who not only endured pain but died on account of his confession. There needed to be a way, in terms of language, to distinguish between those confessors who went to prison because of their confession, yet returned home, and those confessors who never came back. For the latter, those who either died in prison or were executed as punishment, Cyprian refers to as consummated martyrs.[18] For the bishop of Carthage, martyrdom is the consummation of the testimony of one's faith. Any "right," so to speak, to the title of "martyr" would eventually require that the confessor die because of his confession. Such is the glory of those who suffer as their Lord did:

> He who under the eyes of God has offered himself to tortures and death, has suffered whatever he was willing to suffer; for it was not that he was wanting the tortures, but that the tortures were wanting to him. "Whosoever shall confess me before men, him will I also confess before my Father which is in heaven" saith the Lord. They have confessed Him. . . . They have persevered in their faithfulness, and steadfastness, and invincibleness, even unto death. When to the willingness and the confession of the name in prison and in chains is added also the conclusion of dying, the glory of the martyr is consummated.[19]

17. Cyprian, *Epistle LXXX, ANF,* 5:407; Wisdom of Solomon 3:4-8.

18. For a more in-depth account of *martyres consummati,* see Hummel, *Concept of Martyrdom,* 7-14.

19. Cyprian, *Epistle XXXVI, ANF,* 5:315.

The ultimate consummation for one who witnesses to Jesus, this side of resurrection, is death. The martyr is no longer simply a witness; she is a blood-witness.

The Spectacle of a Second Baptism

> *Let us remember also the sins that we have committed, and that except by baptism it is not possible to obtain remission of sins. But according to the laws of the Gospel one cannot be baptized twice in water and the spirit for the remission of sins. We are given, however, the baptism of martyrdom.*
>
> ORIGEN

The confession that led to death took on liturgical significance in the early church. Martyrdom became a sacrament, a second baptism that was greater than the first:

> Let us only who, by the Lord's permission, have given the first baptism to believers, also prepare each one for the second; urging and teaching that this is a baptism greater in grace, more lofty in power, more precious in honor — a baptism wherein angels baptize — a baptism in which God and His Christ exult — a baptism after which no one sins any more — a baptism which completes the increase of our faith — a baptism which, as we withdraw from the world, immediately associates us with God. In the baptism of water is received the remission of sins, in the baptism of blood, the crown of virtues.[20]

Such a baptism, since it is a gift from God, should both be embraced and desired, as such an act renders possible full communion with God. To this end, Cyprian suggests that martyrdom is a kind of medicine, an antidote to both sin and death:

> Assuredly God, who cares for all, gave to life a certain medicine as it were in martyrdom, when to some He assigned it on account of their

20. Cyprian, *The Treatises of Cyprian,* 11, *ANF,* 5:497. For a more detailed account of the sacramental nature of martyrdom, as well as my following comments on martyrdom as a spectacle, see the first chapter of Tripp York, *The Purple Crown: The Politics of Martyrdom* (Scottdale: Herald Press, 2007), 27-48 (on which I lean heavily in the following).

> deserving, to others He gave it on account of his mercy. Martyrdom is medicinal because it leads to the death that leads to life.[21]

Not all deaths are the same, argues Cyprian. Yet, through the death that is martyrdom, "death finds the glory that was lost" and restores the communion that was lost with God.[22]

Cyprian is not the only theologian of the early church to refer to martyrdom as a second baptism. Tertullian, Cyril of Jerusalem, and Origen also claim the act of blood-witness as a second baptism, and as a baptism that fully eradicates sin in a way that the first cannot, as it eradicates the sinner. This second baptism makes it possible for sinners to be purged of their sins in order to be raised in the presence of the most Holy God. Much of this theology of martyrdom arises from Jesus' question to his disciples: "Are you able to drink the cup that I drink, or to be baptized with the baptism with which I am baptized?"[23] To drink of this cup is to fully embody the first baptism. The second baptism fulfills the commitment made to follow the path of Jesus in the first baptism. This is why Tertullian argues that Christians have a "second font" inseparable from the first.[24] Just as Jesus underwent two baptisms, the first of water, the second of blood, so too should his followers expect the possibility of a second baptism. Jesus did, after all, promise that if the world hated and persecuted him, then the world would hate and persecute those who followed him. His "servants are not greater than their Master" (John 15:18-20).

21. Cyprian, *On the Glory of Martyrdom, ANF,* 5:585.

22. Cyprian, *On the Glory of Martyrdom, ANF,* 5:585. It is not that martyrdom is the only means by which communion with God is restored, as that would suggest that redemption comes through human action. This is an idea deemed heretical within Christian orthodoxy. Creation is restored to God through the atonement of Jesus and nothing else. However, the early church did argue that, because Christians are still fallen creatures, full communion with the triune God is something that is only made possible after the resurrection and subsequent judgment of the dead. The special place this reserves for martyrs is the consideration, entertained by the church, that martyrs were given immediate entrance into heaven following their death (Cyprian, *Exhortation to Martyrdom, Addressed to Fortunatus;* Tertullian, *On the Resurrection of the Flesh;* and Eusebius, *History of the Church,* bk. 6). Such an argument finds scriptural grounds in Rev. 6:11, where God instructs the slain witnesses to wait a little while longer for their deaths to be avenged on those who dwell on the earth. The argument being made in these texts is that the martyrs have already been judged by God in this life, hence the gift of martyrdom, and that they are resurrected before the rest of the world so that they can judge with God.

23. Mark 10:38; see also Jesus' words on the baptism he had yet to receive in Luke 12:50.

24. Tertullian, *On Baptism,* 16, *ANF,* 3:677.

That the early church would take this so seriously should not be surprising, because their context lent itself to a literal interpretation. Due to the rather large number of martyrdoms that occurred in the early church, many Christians simply assumed that what it meant to follow Jesus required a death like his. A teleological necessity was attached to persecution for the sake of the gospel. Just as Jesus suffered, so too would his followers. Tertullian reminds his readers that just as Jesus came by means of blood and water (1 John 5:6), his disciples would, likewise, be called by water and "chosen by blood."[25] Tertullian tells the story of the martyr Saturus in order to reinforce his theology of martyrdom. Saturus, who predicted that he would be consumed with only one bite of a leopard, was fed to this creature and after being bitten "he was bathed with such a quantity of blood, that the people shouted out to him as he was returning, the testimony of his second baptism, 'Saved and washed, saved and washed.'"[26] Despite the mocking nature of the crowds, Tertullian concludes that, given his faithful performance of discipleship, Saturus was indeed "assuredly saved."[27]

Counter to the early practice of the sacraments of the Eucharist and baptism as being private events in the church, martyrdom, the second baptism, was primarily intelligible in light of its public display.[28] Though this baptism of blood was dependent on the private practices of the Eucharist and baptism, the second baptism was a public event on which everyone could focus their gaze.[29] Many of the martyrdoms during the first three hundred years of Christianity occurred within the Roman arena, and they often coincided with Roman feasts celebrating the gods or certain nobility. When these "battles" between the bodies of Christians and the body politic of Roman power occurred, careful attention was given to what kind of victory Roman power would be gaining, and in whose name such victory

25. Tertullian, *On Baptism*, 16, *ANF*, 3:677.

26. Tertullian, *The Passion of Perpetua and Felicitas*, 6.4, *ANF*, 3:705.

27. York, *Purple Crown*, 44-45.

28. In referring to private practices, I am not suggesting or attempting to keep in line with our contemporary culture's account of keeping our religious convictions to ourselves. The early Christians, especially in the case of the martyrs, refused to accept this dichotomy between the private and the public. By private I am merely referring to the practice that the early Christians had of performing these sacraments in their homes and out of view of those who were not Christian. The Eucharist was even practiced out of view of many catechumens. However, these private practices necessitated a public response of the Christian when it came to embodying Christianity.

29. Cyprian argues that an indispensable means of preparing for martyrdom occurs through the "daily" partaking of the Eucharist (*Epistle LV*, *ANF*, 5:347).

would be won. For instance, the martyrdoms of Perpetua and Felicitas occurred on the birthday of Geta, the son of Septimius Severus. The martyrdom of Ignatius of Antioch was properly delayed until the occurrence of an appropriate feast day of the Romans (which one remains unclear).[30] The reason for this is that the games themselves revolved around a liturgical cycle designed to praise and honor the Roman gods.[31] That many Christians were executed on birthdays of royalty, feast days, and other "holy" days was not a coincidence; rather, it was a carefully laid-out process designed to pay tribute to the forces sustaining Roman power. Hence, Rome's execution of its enemies, as in the case of the martyrs, was a practice of Roman doxology.

Much of the reasoning for the careful planning of such a spectacle was the understanding that the arena, the Roman coliseum, was a holy space where the fate of the empire was thought to reside.[32] Though the Roman arena had many functions, its primary reason for existence revolved around what Joyce Salisbury calls the "ritual ordering and controlling the world." This intimate connection between what took place in the arena and the well-being of the Roman Empire is expressed in the proverbial saying:

> As long as the Colosseum stands, Rome shall stand;
> When the Colosseum falls, Rome will fall;
> When Rome falls, the world will fall.[33]

Assuming the seriousness with which this proverb was taken, it would be difficult to overstate the importance attached to the arena in terms of Roman politics. Indeed, Thomas Wiedemann suggests that the arena cannot be separated from politics because it is precisely within the arena where the ever-extending perimeters of Roman civilization are created. For instance, it is within the arena where the battle between nature and civilization is decided through the bodies of humans and nonhuman animals. It is also

> where social justice confronted wrongdoing, in the shape of criminals who were executed there, and where the Roman empire confronted its

30. York, *Purple Crown*, 28-29.

31. Robin Darling Young, *In Procession Before the Word: Martyrdom as Public Liturgy in Early Christianity* (Milwaukee: Marquette University Press, 2001).

32. For a more detailed account of the following comments on the sacred space that was the Roman amphitheater, see York, *Purple Crown*, 32-36.

33. Joyce Salisbury, *Perpetua's Passion: The Death and Memory of a Young Roman Woman* (New York: Routledge, 1997), 120.

> enemies, in the persons of the captured prisoners of war who were killed or forced to kill one another in the arena.[34]

Through the doxological ordering of the events that transpired within the arena, whether they were the games of the gladiators or the consumption of Christians by various animals, the Romans assured themselves that they were very much in control of the world, because such control was both symbolically and literally being created and perpetuated in the holy space of the Roman arena.

If such was the place where the gods were thought to either look favorably or unfavorably on the Romans, it also mattered how well the Christians performed in such an arena. The results of any contests, especially between Roman law and usurpers of Roman law, were of crucial importance to both body politics. What occurred in the arena was not just a statement about earthly battles, but about the battles that rage in the heavens. This was not just an event in which one human refused to acquiesce to the desires of another (i.e., Caesar demanding that Christians consume sacrificial meat or burn incense); instead, something cosmic was at stake. A battle raging in the heavens is taking place in the very bodies of those who are Christian and those who are hostile to Christianity.

Just as the Romans imagined their gods rendering judgments based on the performances that transpired in the arena, Christians also imagined that their God was making judgments based on the events that took place. The real battle, argued the Christians, was not between a sole Christian and a beast or a gladiator; rather it was between Christ and those forces antagonistic toward Christ. Christ was again assuming flesh in each believer as martyrs perished under the weight of the mighty empire — the same one that earlier killed their master. But this was the resurrected Christ living in each Christian. As such, the Christian could not lose her life because she had already gained resurrection. This led to the rather odd practice of Christians dying happy. Christians were led into the arena and forced to participate in games they abhorred; yet their ability to perform well, that is, to die well, turned the games against the Romans. Criminals were not supposed to have good deaths. Instead, precisely because they were criminals — and therefore at odds with the good that the Romans imagined the gods would reward — these Christians/criminals were supposed to die in fear, pain, and agony. This was not simply hoped for or expected, but de-

34. Wiedemann, *Emperors and Gladiators,* 46.

manded by the political worldview of the Romans. However, Christian martyrdom undermined this worldview.

> During these executions, Rome demonstrated its control over those who threatened the social order, and Christians fit this category. . . . Romans expected gladiators to show how to die bravely, and they equally expected Rome's criminals to die badly. . . . When Christian martyrs bravely and indeed cheerfully met their deaths during the midday executions, Romans were shocked because their understanding of human behavior had been violated. . . . The public executions of Christian martyrs caused Romans to reconsider their realities.[35]

The reality of the Romans, so carefully crafted and sustained by the events occurring within the arena, was being called into question by the very way the martyrs died. So much so that some Romans abandoned their reality altogether and converted to the path of Christianity. Indeed, the purpose of Christian confession, of baptism, of showing how to both live and die, is so that the world may know that there is an alternative to it. Martyrdom, like all other forms of Christian witness, is not merely an end in itself, since it has a particular reason for being: the conversion of all that is not Christian.

Better to Die Than to Live?

> *Therefore, sublime and illustrious as martyrdom is, it is the more needful now, when the world itself is turned upside down, and while the globe is partially shattered, failing nature is giving evidence of the tokens of its final destruction.*
>
> CYPRIAN

In his *Apology*, after proclaiming that he owed a greater obedience to God than to his audience, Socrates told the Athenian assembly: "I assure you that if I am who I claim to be, and you put me to death, you will harm yourselves more than me. . . . I do not believe that the law of God permits a better man to be harmed by a worse."[36] Socrates claimed that he was at-

35. Salisbury, *Blood of Martyrs*, 19.

36. Plato, *Socrates' Defense (Apology)*, 30cd, in *The Collected Dialogues: Including the Letters*, ed. Edith Hamilton and Huntington Cairns (New York: Pantheon Books, 1966), 16.

tempting to save his fellow Athenians from misusing a gift God had given them in the presence of himself, since his concern was, ultimately, for the good of the city.

A similar sentiment is echoed in both the voices of Ignatius of Antioch (ca. 35-107) and Polycarp of Smyrna (ca. 69-155). These two Christian bishops represented two of the most famous martyrdoms in Christian history, and their own understanding of their deaths, as expressed in their response to the powers that would put them to death, is quite informative. When the emperor Trajan called Ignatius a "wicked wretch" who teaches others to transgress the commands of Roman law, Ignatius simply responded that no one should call him wicked as "all evil spirits have departed from the servants of God. But if, because I am an enemy to these [spirits], you call me wicked in respect to them, I quite agree with you, as I have Christ the King of Heaven [within me]." Trajan then asked who Theophorus (i.e., Ignatius) was, to which Ignatius responded: "'He who has Christ in his breast.' Trajan said, 'Do we not then seem to you to have the gods in our mind, whose assistance we enjoy in fighting against our enemies?' Ignatius answered, 'Thou art in error when thou callest the demons of the nations gods.'"[37] Ignatius was eventually led away in order to be devoured by the beasts in the amphitheater, that sacred site of contests between the Roman gods and those who did not worship them.

Polycarp faced a similar fate. After being arrested, the eighty-six-year-old bishop had the opportunity to either recant or convince the bloodthirsty crowd in the stadium of the good of Christianity. Polycarp passed on both, though he did tell the proconsul that he would give the latter a hearing of the gospel at a later time. The Roman official also declined and told him to "swear by Caesar's fortune; change your attitude; say, 'Away with the godless!'" But Polycarp, with his face set, looked at all the crowd in the stadium and waved his hand toward them, sighed, looked up to heaven, and cried: "Away with the godless!"[38]

Of course, Polycarp knew that no words were going to convince this hostile crowd about the truth of Christianity, and given that recantation was not an option, he took the only faithful option left: martyrdom. His executed body would have to suffice as an argument for the crowd. Following his retort, the crowd grew even more indignant and immediately demanded his death. The politics of the arena could only demand one re-

37. Ignatius, *The Martyrdom of Ignatius, ANF,* 1:129.

38. Eusebius, *The History of the Church,* 120.

sponse to such disrespect: death. Polycarp was executed, and the harmony of the city was restored.

Just as Socrates understood himself as a gift from God for the well-being of the ancient polis, so did the early Christians imagine that their presence on earth was for the good of the temporal cities. The church is a body politic, as extended through Israel, whose purpose is to reveal to the world who God is and what it means to worship this God well. Polycarp's attitude toward the hostile crowd that wanted him dead should not be viewed as arrogant any more than Socrates' genuine thoughts of himself as a divine aid for the good of the social order should be seen as presumptuous. Socrates argued that "no greater good has ever befallen you in this city than my service to my God."[39] Socrates' entire life had been consumed with the desire to convince "both young and old" that the most important concern one should have is not for bodily pleasure or material goods but for the welfare of their souls. Likewise, both Ignatius and Polycarp understood that the presence of the church, as a very particular formation of people in the world, was about the prophetic calling away from idolatry that the world, inasmuch as it is the world, practices.

The key difference between Socrates and the latter two Christian martyrs, other than the explicit confession of Christ that makes the deaths of Ignatius and Polycarp martyrdoms, is that, whereas Socrates might imagine that he would do more good for the polis by being alive, Ignatius and Polycarp understood that they might do more good in death. That is, in their deaths both Ignatius and Polycarp continued to serve both the church and the world. It is for this reason that Ignatius was so adamantly opposed to those who would attempt to rescue him from his impending death: "For it is not my desire that ye should please men, but God, even as also ye do please Him. . . . Pray, then, do not seek to confer any greater favor upon me than that I be sacrificed to God, while the altar is still prepared." Ignatius asked not only that his friends not attempt to save him from death because he thought it would be difficult to otherwise "attain God"; he feared that if he did not seal his confession with the death of his body, then he would become but a mere voice — as opposed to a word. Ignatius understood that one's voice was not always enough; rather, for the good of his own community and the watching world, he thought it best to seal his testimony with his life.[40]

39. Plato, *Socrates' Defense,* 30ab, 16.
40. Ignatius, *Letter to the Romans,* II, *ANF,* 1:74.

The actions taken against both Ignatius and Polycarp were, according to Roman wisdom and authority, a morally legitimate response. Allowing them to live would have resulted in the possible destruction of the social harmony enjoyed by the Roman citizenry. Just as Socrates was viewed as a threat to the order of his own city, Athens, Christians posed a similar threat, because their understanding of what constitutes the good conflicted with that of the Roman Empire. Their continued existence, like that of Socrates, had to be denied.

The above comments about Socrates, Ignatius, and Polycarp run the risk of suggesting that the early pagan and Christian attitudes toward martyrdom and/or noble death (as in the case of Socrates) are really about the profession of one's principles — honor and virtue (Socrates) or faith (Ignatius and Polycarp), including the foundational belief that the greater, in terms of morality, cannot be harmed by the lesser — even through death. Martyrdom, the ultimate act of *imitatio Christi,* is a far more complex act of the Christian than a simple dying for one's principles (though that is no small feat). As we have seen, the early church understood martyrdom in general, and the body of the martyr in particular, as the arena for the cosmic battle between God and the powers of evil, which begins with public confession and culminates in the Christian's "second baptism." This is a baptism that is not just for the believer, but for the sake of the world. It is a liturgical rite at odds with the formative liturgy of the empire. It is an oath not to Caesar but to what is above Caesar *for* Caesar.

The early Christians, as "resident aliens," occupied a distinctive place in and under the empire, as their territory was that of the divine: the city of God. Given that the city of God is not a place on earth, and thus is not a territory capable of being defended, one of the most basic ways a Christian bore witness to the heavenly city on earth was by being slain by the earthly cities. Archbishop of Canterbury Rowan Williams argues that the "simplest" possible demonstration of what it meant to be the church under the empire in the first three hundred years of Christianity was through martyrdom. He says that martyrdom is a "demonstration of Christian 'legitimacy,' of the foundational charter of that community which is called the *ekklesia:* this is what the rule and law of God means, and why the legitimacy of the empire cannot be the last word."[41] The martyrs laid down their lives in order to be faithful to the church, whose faithfulness to Jesus

41. Rowan Williams, *Why Study the Past? The Quest for the Historical Church* (Grand Rapids: Eerdmans, 2005), 34.

demands that it provide a witness to all that is not the church. This is why the early church had no desire to rebel against the empire. They were not "subversive for subversiveness' sake." Indeed, the early Christians paid their taxes and prayed for their emperors. Tertullian, in an attempt to reiterate why it was the case that Christians were good for Rome, declares:

> A Christian is an enemy to none, least of all to the Emperor of Rome, whom he knows to be appointed by his God, and so cannot but love and honor; and whose well-being moreover, he must needs desire, with that of the empire over which he reigns so long as the world shall stand — for so long as that shall Rome continue.[42]

Many in the early church claimed that the emperor belonged more to them than to the pagan Romans, as Christians were the only ones capable of recognizing the true God who ordained the power of the emperor. God ordained all powers, yet these powers are often rebellious and require the presence of the church to let them know when they are transgressing the will of God. The bodies of the martyrs were themselves the physical evidence that God's will was being transgressed. Rowan Williams comments further on this reality, and on Polycarp's witness in particular, when he argues that the

> expulsion of the Christian from the would-be sacred order of the Roman city or the Roman empire is the very moment in which the holiness of the Christian is perfected: holiness, in the sense not of exceptional goodness but of the active presence of a holy and terrifying power, is indeed identical with marginality in the terms of the empire. The holy place is the suffering body expelled from the body politic, Polycarp uttering his great thanksgiving as the flames are lit.

As Polycarp offers his prayer, the divine presence of God is made tangible and "vindicates the claim to another citizenship." Within the body of the martyrs all power is subordinate to what the martyr worships and the "definition of the vocabulary of being an *ekklesia* of aliens, the citizens' assembly of the non-citizens, a people whose political legitimacy and loyalty lay outside the imperial system."[43] It is for this reason that the witness of Ignatius, Polycarp, and Maximilian transgresses, to this day, all national

42. Tertullian, *Ad Scapula, ANF,* 3:105.
43. Williams, *Why Study the Past?* 36.

borders. Their witness endures through time as does the church and only seeks to show the vision that is the peaceable kingdom that is the hope for all nations.

Swords and Deserts

That the early Christians found themselves on the receiving end of a blade, a beast, or a stake was neither odd nor unexpected. Taking up the cross of Jesus promised such occurrences, and the early church was well aware of what they were getting into when they pledged themselves under the baptismal waters. The world had crucified their savior and if they were to follow him, they too might be crucified. Yet within less than a century of Maximilian's death, Christians would be in power. The threat of torture, exile, and executions were over — for some. However, the power that Christians would seize would return the favor, not just on pagans, but on other Christians as well. As early as 314, with the Synod of Arles, the Christians would condemn Donatists as heretics; as a result, many Donatists had their goods confiscated, were sent into exile, or were killed by angry Christian mobs. This was also true with the Circumcellions, Luciferians, and the first officially ordained killing of one Christian by another: the beheading of Bishop Priscillian of Avila in 383.[44] I have little doubt that, if the Donatists or the Luciferians had been in power, they would have not also committed the same acts against those they deemed heretical. In fact, Donatism was a rather large movement prone to acts of violence that proved dangerous to many non-Donatists.[45] The question of interest resides not so much in which "side" was correct, but how it was possible for either side to come to imagine that violence and persecution (or prosecution, for that matter), the very same tactics that were used against Christians by the pagan Roman Empire, would become the tools used by the Christian Roman Empire.[46]

44. For more on Priscllian of Avila, see Henry Chadwick, *Priscillian of Avila: The Occult and the Charismatic in the Early Church* (Oxford: Oxford University Press, 1976).

45. For an in-depth analysis of the Donatist movement, see David Benedict, *History of the Donatists* (Paris, AR: The Baptist Standard Bearer, 2001); see also Maureen Tilley, *Donatist Martyr Stories: The Church in Conflict in Roman North Africa* (Liverpool: Liverpool University Press, 1996).

46. In his stellar account of martyrdom in the sixteenth century, Brad Gregory draws important distinctions between persecution and prosecution, suggesting that these two

The enthronement of Christianity ended the golden age of martyrdom. There could no longer be any persecution of Christians under the Roman Empire because the empire had become Christian. In order to produce Christian martyrs, the church would have to seek out new lands to evangelize: their taking of the gospel into non-Christian regions would provide the possibility of martyrdom. This would demand a different account of martyrdom, one that would include flights to the desert as well as the possibility of military martyrs.

Though desert asceticism became a strong replacement for the early church martyrs, it is the development of the military martyr that clearly reveals the reversal of early church thinking. In the desert the Christian would flee the comforts of city living and battle those demons that attempted to overcome the Christian's flesh. Mortification of the flesh and severe forms of asceticism in general became more common forms of practice for Christians attempting to suffer with Christ as well as having their bodies/desires disciplined for Christ. Asceticism — that is, bodily disciplining — was nothing new to fifth-century Christians; it was necessary for the training of the pre-Constantinian martyrs. The flight to the desert may very well be the logical response to the loss of martyrdom, though it is doubtful that is a necessary one.[47]

The development of the military martyr, on the other hand, is an attempt to maintain continuity with the early church while accepting the newly ordained role of being in charge. The first historian of the church, Eusebius, was privy to the "before and after" of the Constantinian development, and he had little problem praising both those Christians who once refused allegiance to Caesar and those Christians who now serve and have

terms should not be conflated, since they point to different realities and processes that, at least in terms of the latter, belong to the state and are not ecclesiastical in nature. See Gregory, *Salvation at Stake: Christian Martyrdom in Early Modern Europe* (Cambridge, MA: Harvard University Press, 1999), 74-96. No doubt this is an important distinction, but I cannot help wondering how and at what cost it became an intelligible practice for Christians to think it was their duty to prosecute religious deviants in the first place. I also question making much of this distinction, considering that Jesus understood himself as being persecuted, yet he was "prosecuted" in full accordance with the law. This set the stage for how the early church understood itself as being persecuted, not simply prosecuted, while use of the latter term became justification for the post-third-century Christian underwriting of capital punishment against its enemies.

47. For an account of why it is true that desert asceticism should not be read as a replacement for early church martyrdom, see Teresa M. Shaw, *The Burden of the Flesh: Fasting and Sexuality in Early Christianity* (Minneapolis: Augsburg Fortress, 1998).

become Caesar. Christians of both eras, for Eusebius, were simply serving God — and thus the city — in the most appropriate manner as dictated by their particular circumstances. For Eusebius, the persecution of the early church was necessary in order to pave the way for the overcoming of paganism, so that Christ could rightly rule over the nations first through his martyrs and, second, through his emperors.

> But once again the Angel of great counsel, God's great Commander-in-Chief, after the thoroughgoing training of which the greatest soldiers in His kingdom gave proof by their patience and endurance in all trials, appeared suddenly and thereby swept all that was hostile and inimical into oblivion and nothingness, so that its very existence was forgotten.[48]

The age of the martyrdom was over; it had served its purpose well. A new era, the "recovery of the church," as Eusebius calls it, had begun.

This new epoch would call for a different kind of martyr, or at least the possibility of a different kind of martyr, one predicated on serving the empire in a new way: not simply by praying for it, as early church theologians such as Tertullian, Hippolytus, and Cyprian demanded, but, if need be, by killing for it. The church has never been fond of the idea of losing martyrdom altogether as a possible form of witness, as the early church's insistence on this practice — especially during times of relative peace — makes clear. But this new era would demand a different kind of martyr. The good of the city now rested on the Christian citizens of the empire defending it, and hence this martyr, this witness to the way of Christ, might now take up the sword for God as a service to the city. The social harmony of the city may require that the Christian defend it in order to preserve the good that the city intends for her citizens. These martyrs, of whom there is rarely a short supply, may find it necessary to defend the city in order to preserve the good that the city intends for her citizens. It is this continuity located within the desire of the Christian to seek the peace of the city that makes it intelligible for the church to honor both Maximilian, the conscientious objector, and, many centuries later, Santiago Matamoros, or even Saint James, the son of Zebedee, referred to in Spain as the "Moor-slayer."[49]

48. Eusebius, *History of the Church,* 309.

49. The apostle James, one of the first martyrs of Christianity, was slain by the sword of King Herod, as reported in Acts 12:1-2. Though he died in the first century, legends during the sixth and seventh centuries suggested that, prior to his death, James spent some time

Though one of the basic long-standing requirements of Christian martyrdom has been that an act of violence can never precede one's death (and thus why calling crusaders who died on the battlefield martyrs has generally not happened, despite their being promised automatic absolution of their sins and the immediate inheritance of the kingdom of God), the transition of the early church's posture from being a suffering body politic to a conquering body politic forever altered the way she understood her witnesses.

With respect to the conversion of Rome to Christianity, one must ask if this was indeed a victory for Christianity, since martyrdom, the ultimate act of witnessing to Christ, was no longer necessary — at least not within the empire. Once the witness of those like Polycarp, Ignatius, and Maximilian are no longer necessary, we must ask what form Christian witness must take in order for it to not simply be against the empire, but for the empire. This same question must be addressed in our contemporary context. How do North American Christians today, especially in terms of how they remember the witness of the early church martyrs, best serve the empire they find themselves under today? The current position is an even more precarious one, as Christians are no longer officially the empire, yet the remnants of Constantinianism remain in practice. How does the church, living in a post-Christian culture, remain faithful to her own body politic in such a way as to be truly for the empire?

---

performing missionary work in Spain. Though there are no written texts to prove whether or not James made it to Spain, the idea that he did became an important part of Spanish Catholicism, especially with respect to the late seventh-century spread of Islam. With the spread of Islam, many Christians saw another opportunity for a battle between the forces of good and evil, and many "believed new martyrs were being created as Christians fell in battle fighting Islam," which required, so argues Joyce Salisbury, "supernatural help," hence the warrior martyr Saint James of the Starry Field (*Blood of the Martyrs,* 68-69).

CHAPTER 3

The Primacy of the Witness of the Body to Martyrdom in Paul

Stephen Fowl

Let me begin by noting two truisms:

First, anyone familiar with Paul's letters, our earliest insights into the lives of the first Christian communities, will recognize how different these texts are from those stories we have of early Christian martyrs of the second and third centuries.[1] This is not simply because Paul's letters rarely, if ever, directly address the issue of martyrdom.

Second, in recent works on early Christian martyrdom it has become a truism to note that one of the constitutive elements of martyrdom — if not the primary one — is the narration of the martyr's death.[2] Without a particular story of the death of a specific believer, it becomes difficult to call that death martyrdom. This is true in a number of different respects. First, in the absence of an alternative account, the authorities, in this case Rome, will always narrate the death of believers as the justified execution of stubborn and potentially dangerous criminals. To narrate the death any other way would raise questions about Roman justice. Therefore, martyrdom requires an alternative account that narrates a believer's death as an act of steadfast and even joyous fidelity to the Lord in the face of hostile powers.

In another respect, narration — either oral or written — is essential

1. See H. Musurillo, *The Acts of the Christian Martyrs* (Oxford: Clarendon, 1977).

2. Several recent works that make this point in various ways are D. Boyarin, *Dying for God: Martyrdom and the Making of Christianity and Judaism* (Stanford: Stanford University Press, 1999); G. Bowersock, *Martyrdom and Rome* (Cambridge: Cambridge University Press, 1995); P. Middleton, *Radical Martyrdom and Cosmic Conflict in Early Christianity* (Edinburgh: T. & T. Clark, 2006).

for martyrdom to fulfill any formative purpose in the lives of those believers who remain alive. That is, the stories of the martyrs not only offer an alternative account of these believers' deaths at the hands of the authorities; they also serve to make the martyrs' lives imitable. Attention to the accounts of the martyrs' deaths can help to form subsequent believers into people capable of offering their lives back to God in like manner. Without such accounts, the formative capacity of martyrdom ceases when there are no longer eyewitnesses. These are simply two respects that indicate the centrality of narration to martyrdom.

In addition, those who study Paul's Epistles have also come to see the relationships between Paul's claims, directives, and admonitions and a larger, sometimes unexpressed narrative web that holds those claims, directives, and assertions together.[3] Indeed, one way to think about the social and moral directives in Paul's Epistles is to see Paul as helping believers fit their lives into a new narrative world.

In this chapter I wish to press on with these truisms about narrative relative to Paul and martyrdom a bit further to argue that martyrdom is but one species of a larger narrative genre that comprehends the death of believers at the hands of hostile authorities within a wide range of other faithful practices that I will call the witness of the body to God's drama of salvation. While this distinction may prove useful to historians of early Christianity or to literary critics interested in this period, this distinction is primarily of theological importance. It is theologically important to fit the lives and deaths of martyrs into the larger category of witness of the body because martyrdom is such a contingent activity. That is, martyrdom is always contingent on the authorities. Believers can and should always participate in the witness of the body. Whether or not the authorities will kill them for this is largely out of their hands. Moreover, I will point out that one finds in Paul's Epistles some of the most important reflection on both the witness of the body and the importance of believers fitting their lives in word and deed into an account of bodily witness.

In addition, comprehending martyrdom as one species of the witness of the body may have two additional benefits. First, for American Christians such as those I teach and those with whom I worship, martyrdom can often appear to be the act of such fanatical extremity that it can

3. See Richard Hays, *The Faith of Jesus Christ* (Chico, CA: Scholars Press, 1983); Stephen Fowl, *The Story of Christ in the Ethics of Paul* (Sheffield: Sheffield Academic Press, 1990).

only be a reflection of mental illness. Hence, for those who seek to live faithfully before the triune God in the early part of the twenty-first century, coming to grips with the more primary category of the witness of the body may help make them better able to contemplate both the lives of the martyrs of previous times and other places and the possibility that they, too, may find themselves in the contingent circumstances of having to offer their lives back to God in the face of hostile authorities. Furthermore, fitting martyrdom within the larger category of witness of the body can help establish far stronger lines of continuity between the New Testament and those narratives of martyrs from later centuries.

Given the constraints of a single chapter, I will find it useful to sharpen my focus on the witness of the body by limiting my discussion to a few key texts in Paul's Letters. Perhaps the most familiar text where we might begin reflection on the witness of the body is Romans 12:1-2. By the end of Romans 11, Paul has reached the rhetorical climax of that Epistle. When confronted with the issue of Israel's unbelief and the questions this raises about God's fidelity to the covenant, Paul begins by sharing his anguish over the unbelief of his fellow Jews. He is convinced that this unbelief plays a significant role in God's drama of salvation, contributing to the inclusion of the Gentiles. He also reminds the Gentiles not to become arrogant in the face of God's extravagant mercy. He then concludes this reflection by reasserting God's faithfulness to Israel, boldly asserting that "all Israel will be saved" (Rom. 11:26). This is one of the merciful gifts of God; it may be imponderable, but it is not revocable. Romans 11 concludes by praising the gifts of God's mercy to both Jews and Gentiles.

In the light of God's gifts of mercy,[4] Paul calls on both Jewish and Gentile believers to "present your bodies as a living sacrifice, holy and acceptable to God" (Rom. 12:1).[5] The great praise of God's gifts that concludes Romans 11 makes it clear that the kind of sacrifice Paul speaks of at the beginning of Romans 12 has nothing to do with expiating sins. Rather, it is the offering to God of the first fruits of the harvest, a sacrifice of thanks (cf. Lev. 2:14-15; 23:9-14; cf. also Ps. 50:14).

Of course, offering one's life back to God in a world that is hostile to God may result in martyrdom. However, the crucial point in Romans 12:1

4. J. D. G. Dunn, *The Theology of Paul the Apostle* (Grand Rapids: Eerdmans, 1998), 543-44, is one of the few to see the close connection between the end of Romans 11 and the beginning of Romans 12.

5. There has been an ongoing discussion of Paul's "body" language since the time of Bultmann. I discuss this more thoroughly below with regard to Phil. 1:19-20.

is that believers offer their bodies back to God as a living sacrifice. The offering of living bodies may result in martyrdom, but the primary dispositions and activities that follow from offering oneself to God as a living sacrifice are directed at how believers are to conduct themselves in the world: they are directed to the witness of the body to God's drama of salvation.

Indeed, having offered their lives to God as a sacrifice, believers are enjoined to be transformed by the renewing of their minds (rather than conformed to the world) so that they may be able to discern what the will of God is, what is "good and acceptable and perfect" (12:2). These living sacrificial bodies are called into a process of formation whereby they learn to discern and love what is truly good, perfect, and acceptable. This may involve discerning the good from the bad, but it is much more likely that the discernment Paul wants for the Roman Christians is the capacity to recognize and pursue what is truly good from alternatives that might claim to be good, but are really idolatrous.[6]

One occasionally reads accounts of martyrdom where the authorities will urge Christian prisoners to recognize a set of "goods" that they should be attending to, but will not be able to attend to when they have died. A martyr's unwillingness to recognize these culturally approved goods helps to sustain the authorities' judgments that martyrs are stubborn and foolish. For women, this is often cast in terms of a call to think of their children and what will become of them.[7] In such cases, these women end up not only offering themselves to God as martyrs but, in effect, offering their children as living sacrifices to God in faithful expectation that God will sustain and maintain those children. The most obvious people to take on this task would be fellow brothers and sisters in Christ.[8] One might even suggest that such faithful expectation as these women display in their bodily witness can only be sustained in the presence of others who are also offering bodily witness to Christ.[9]

6. This renewed mind can be contrasted with the "darkened mind" of Gentiles, which is typified by idolatry in Rom. 1:18-23.

7. See, for example, *Perpetua's Passion,* 6.2-4, and the letter of Elizabeth, an Anabaptist martyr, to her daughter. The latter can be found in Hans Hillerbrand, ed., *The Protestant Reformation* (New York: Harper Torchbooks, 1968), 146-52.

8. This is what happened with Perpetua's son (*Perpetua's Passion,* 6.7-8).

9. In Shusako Endo's fictional account of the persecution of Christians in seventeenth-century Japan, it is precisely this kind of absence that leads Fr. Rodrigues to apostatize. See Stephen Fowl, "Paul's Riposte to Fr. Rodrigues," in *Post-Modern Interpretations of the Bible: A Reader,* ed. A. K. M. Adam (St. Louis: Chalice Press, 2001), 243-52.

The overwhelming majority of believers, however, are those who, despite offering themselves back to God as a living sacrifice, are not called to bear bodily witness to Christ through martyrdom. It is much more common for believers to be faced with a whole set of culturally approved goods that appear genuinely good, acceptable, and perfect. But the pursuit of such goods will gradually, over time, divert the attention of believers from the God to whom they have ostensibly offered up their lives. Failure of attention tends ineluctably toward idolatry.

It would appear that one of the central practices of the bodily witness to which God calls all believers manifests itself in a particular form of attention to God and God's will for them. Martyrdom may result from such attentiveness, but Paul is primarily concerned with the transformation of believers' perceptual skills — that is, with the renewing of their minds. With these skills in good working order, believers will both avoid being conformed to this world and will be able to participate in the Spirit's transformation of their lives. This will result in ever sharper and wiser perception, so that believers can better discern what is good, acceptable, and perfect. These living sacrifices will thus witness bodily to God's will.

This pattern appears in a much more developed form in Philippians. In this light, it is interesting to note that it was Ernst Lohmeyer who interpreted Philippians as a manual of martyrdom.[10] Most subsequent scholars reacted negatively to Lohmeyer's attempt to find references to martyrdom at every turn in that Epistle. Moreover, in comparison to second- and third-century martyrological texts, Philippians appears to be very different. Nevertheless, Paul pays persistent attention in that Epistle to his own disposition toward his imprisonment, trial, and possible death (Phil. 1:12-26; 2:17). He is concerned that the Philippians manifest a common life worthy of the gospel in the face of opposition (1:27-28). He notes that he and the Philippians have been granted the opportunity not only of believing in Christ, but also of suffering for his sake (1:28-30). He informs the Philippians of his desire to know "the power of [Christ's] resurrection, the fellowship of his sufferings and to be conformed to his death" (3:10). Hence, rather than offering a manual of martyrdom, Paul aims to display and to help form in the Philippians habits of perception, attention, and action necessary for a faithful bodily witness in a world hostile to Christianity. One of the places where he makes this most clear is Philippians 1:18-20.

10. E. Lohmeyer, *Die Briefe an die Philipper, und die Kolosser und an Philemon* (Göttingen: Vandenhoeck und Rupprecht, 1930).

After greeting the Philippians and assuring them of God's continued work in their midst and of his own continued prayers for them, Paul begins to bring the Philippians up to date on his own circumstances. The imprisoned Paul is convinced that, despite the limitations prison has set on his own life, the gospel of which he is a minister has continued to advance. He discusses briefly a conflict between those who preach the gospel out of love and those who preach from selfish motives (1:12-18). Paul is convinced that the God who advances the gospel through Paul's imprisonment is certainly capable of securing and advancing the gospel despite the motives of some preachers. This conviction leads Paul to rejoice.

Indeed, Paul commits himself both to rejoicing now and to rejoicing into the future. As Philippians 1:19 begins, Paul gives two reasons for his continued commitment to rejoicing. This commitment is based on knowledge about the future that Paul has. The subsequent clauses give two reasons for Paul's knowledge that will lead to his continued rejoicing. Paul articulates the first reason by quoting from Job 13:16: "This will result in my salvation." That is, Paul will rejoice in his circumstances because, like Job, he will be vindicated before God. There is much to be said about various allusions and echoes in Paul's use of Job, which one might explore. For the purposes of this chapter, I will leave those to one side.[11] Instead, it is the second part of Paul's knowledge about the future that is most important. He lays this out in 1:20: Paul will continue to rejoice, he says, "[b]ecause it is my eager expectation and hope that I will in no way be disgraced. Rather with all boldness, as I have always done, Christ will be magnified in my body whether I live or die."

Paul's language here about being "disgraced" is quite common in the Septuagint (cf. Isa. 50:7). In the LXX, "disgrace" does not so much reflect an inner feeling of shame as a failure of faith in word or deed, which brings with it a certain disgrace (see, esp., Ps. 24:3; 68:7; 116; 118:80; Jer. 12:13).

Rather than being disgraced, Paul plans — with all boldness and as he has always done heretofore — to magnify Christ in his body. The notion of "magnifying the Lord" has strong links to the Psalms.[12] Furthermore, Luke uses the same word in the *Magnificat,* which ascribes glory to God. What is striking here in Philippians is that the passive voice of the

11. For further comment on Phil. 1:19 and Job 13:16, see Stephen Fowl, *Philippians* (Grand Rapids: Eerdmans, 2005), 43-45.

12. See LXX Pss. 33:3; 34:27; 39:16; 56:10. In this light, the usage here conforms more to Paul's use of similar vocabulary in 2 Cor. 10:8 rather than Rom. 1:16.

verb allows Paul to make a significant distinction. While it is Paul who might be disgraced, it is Christ who will be magnified in Paul's body, whether the apostle lives or dies. Paul's body is a witness to Christ's glory or to his own disgrace.

Because the quotation from Job in Philippians 1:19 speaks of a heavenly vindication, there is a tendency among commentators to think that Paul is also talking here about a confidence directed toward the eschaton.[13] Such an eschatological view, however, seems to miss some important points. First, Paul's discussion of Christ being magnified in his body notes not only that such magnification will happen in the future, but that Christ is regularly magnified in Paul's body. This has the force of "as I have always done."[14] Paul's confidence is not primarily about the eschaton, but about his ability to continue, with the Spirit's help and in circumstances of extreme adversity, a practice he has carried on for some time.

A second interpretive issue here concerns Paul's use of the term "body" (σῶμα). Under Bultmann's influence, it became common to weigh down Paul's use of σῶμα with quite a bit of anthropological baggage.[15] In explicit reaction to Bultmann, Robert Gundry has argued that Paul's use of σῶμα simply cannot bear such a heavy anthropological load.[16] In general, Gundry would seem to have the weight of exegetical evidence on his side. However, he misses something when he limits Paul's use of σῶμα to his physical body.[17] That is, Gundry is correct in saying that we should not invest Paul's use of σῶμα with a great deal of anthropological weight; but we have to recognize that Paul's claims imply that whether he dies or lives, there is, in each instance, an opportunity for magnifying Christ or

13. A good example of this can be found in Peter O'Brien, *Commentary on Philippians* (Grand Rapids: Eerdmans, 1991), 113: "In other words, what is eagerly expected is the consummation of God's purposes. Here at Phil. 1:20, Paul's confident expectation and hope have to do with that consummation, and his future vindication by God will be in accordance (κατά) with it."

14. Gordon Fee, *Paul's Letter to the Philippians* (Grand Rapids: Eerdmans, 1995), is correct to pick this up (137). However, he incorrectly limits the practice of "magnifying Christ in my body" to the practice of the "praise of Christ."

15. See Rudolf Bultmann, *New Testament Theology,* trans. K. Grobel (London: SCM, 1952), 1:194-95; see also E. Schweizer, *TDNT,* 7:1065-66.

16. See Robert H. Gundry, *Soma in Biblical Theology with an Emphasis on Pauline Anthropology* (Cambridge: Cambridge University Press, 1976).

17. See Gundry, *Soma in Biblical Theology,* 37: "*Soma* therefore, does not signify the whole 'I' of Paul, but only that part of him more immediately affected by the outcome of his trial and through which he bears witness to the visible world around him."

disgracing himself. In dying, Paul could either be disgraced or magnify Christ; in living, he faces the same option. Magnifying Christ in life, however, will require a different set of practices than magnifying Christ in death. Aquinas recognizes this in his commentary when he observes: "Christ is honored in our body in two ways: in one way, inasmuch as we dedicate our body to his service by employing our bodies in his ministry . . . in another way by risking our body for Christ. . . . The first is accomplished by life, the second by death."[18] Both of these represent instances of the witness of the body.

What Paul understands — and what both Bultmann and Gundry in their own ways miss — is that in this particular matter Paul's body will display the disposition of his character, whether he lives or dies. For example, in dying in a way that disgraces himself — by recanting under torture, say — Paul's body would display something crucial about his character.[19] Paul understands what virtually all ancient moral philosophers would have recognized: bodily actions and bodily responses to specific situations display elements of a person's character. It is not simply Paul's death that is being discussed here, but the manner of his death and his abilities to describe that death as something that might give glory to God or that might bring shame on himself. In this respect, Paul's claims are not particularly surprising. It is significant, however, that the alternatives here are not between life or death but between glorifying God or disgracing oneself. Glorifying God in and through one's body can be done equally whether one lives or dies. These comments support the idea that a martyr's death, as well as life lived in particular ways, are both instances of the larger category of the witness of the body.

Of course, in Paul's particular situation, a Roman prison would be the last place in which one would be expected to have any control over one's own body. In the context of imperial imprisonment, the prisoner's body becomes the text on which the empire's power is inscribed.[20] In a sit-

18. Thomas Aquinas, *Commentary on Saint Paul's First Letter to the Thessalonians and the Letter to the Philippians,* trans. F. Larcher (Albany, NY: Magi Books, 1969), 69.

19. Chrysostom comments on this passage this way: "For if fear of death had cut short my boldness, death would have been worthy of shame, but if death at its approach cast no terror on me, no shame is here; but whether it be through life I shall not be put to shame, for I still preach the Preaching, or whether it be through death I shall not be put to shame; fear does not hold me back, since I exhibit the same boldness" [Homily 3].

20. This general point about imprisonment and punishment was first made by Michel Foucault in *Discipline and Punish,* trans. A. Sheridan (New York: Vintage Books, 1979).

uation where the Roman empire would be expected to have complete control over Paul's body, Paul declares that Christ will be magnified by the way in which he comports himself. Whether he lives or dies, Paul (especially his body) will be, as he has always been: Christ's text rather than the empire's.

Having confidently stated that whether he lives or dies he intends to continue to glorify Christ in his body, Paul now turns (in vv. 21-26) to reflect at greater length on what is at stake in living and dying. Either prospect can fit into Paul's bodily witness, but he clearly has views about which he prefers. "For me to live is Christ, to die is gain." That is, to live entails that Paul will continue to magnify Christ, engaging in fruitful labor for Christ, such as founding and building up various congregations. To die is to enter into a deeper union with Christ than is possible in the flesh.[21]

What is particularly interesting here is Paul's claim in verse 22 that he does not know which of these two options for magnifying Christ in his body he will choose. The Greek here is somewhat obscure because of the verb γνωρίζω. The most straightforward way to render the clause καὶ τί αἱρήσομαι οὐ γνωρίζω would be something like this: "I don't know which [of these two options] I will choose."[22] The complication comes from the fact that this is not the normal way Paul uses this verb. He normally uses γνωρίζω to speak of disclosure, of making known, often with regard to God's mysteries (cf. Rom. 16:26; 1 Cor. 15:1; 2 Cor. 8:1; Gal. 1:11). Commentators have used a variety of ways to try to bring this sense of γνωρίζω to bear on this verse as well. The results of these attempts range from the unsatisfying[23] to the downright confusing.[24] Moreover, though Paul does not tend to use οὐ γνωρίζω with the sense of "I don't know," there are a

21. See A. Lincoln, *Paradise Now and Not Yet* (Cambridge: Cambridge University Press, 1981), 104: "[T]he state into which Paul will enter at death is far better, bringing with it a greater closeness of communion with Christ, and yet it is still a state of expectation, less than the fullness of redemption described in 3.20f." Presumably, if Paul lacked conviction about what lay behind the grave for him, then death would have held little appeal.

22. I take Paul's use of αἱρήσομαι in its conventional sense, i.e., indicating a choice not a preference. For the best arguments in favor of this, see C. Wansink, *Chained in Christ* (Sheffield: Sheffield Academic Press, 1997), 96-102.

23. For an example of this, see Fee, *Philippians,* 164, which denies that Paul had any real choice to make.

24. See Lohmeyer, *Philipper,* 60-61; see also O'Brien, *Philippians,* 127-28: O'Brien thinks that Paul cannot make his decision known because God's mind has not yet been revealed to Paul. This is confusing because, by v. 25, Paul has both made up his mind and does not attribute this to a direct message from God.

host of extrabiblical references to support such usage.[25] Given that this makes the best sense of the passage, we should read the verb in this way.

Paul here seems to be deeply torn between his desire to die, which is Paul's personal preference, and the needfulness of living. He speaks as one faced with two incompatible possibilities, each with a certain appeal. By verse 25, however, Paul has both made up his mind and given the reasons for his resolve. While his personal preference is to die and be with Christ, it is more beneficial for the Philippians that he remain in the flesh, engaging in fruitful labor for Christ. What Paul's reasoning displays here is the habit of seeking the benefit of others, a habit that plays a crucial role in the argument of the Epistle.

Indeed, as the Epistle moves into the next chapter, it becomes clear that Paul takes seeking the benefit of others to be one of the essential habits of a bodily witness worthy of the gospel of Christ, and a habit he both exemplifies here and desires the Philippians to cultivate among themselves. Moreover, as Philippians 2:6-11 makes clear, it is precisely this activity of seeking the benefit of others that God has decisively displayed to the world in the life, death, and resurrection of Jesus. Thus, when faced with the choice of life or death, Paul opts for life. This is not because life is obviously superior to death; for Paul, this is far from the case. Rather, his choice here analogously replicates the climactic movement in the divine economy of salvation revealed in Christ. By seeing his situation as part of that larger story, Paul is provided with a compelling exemplar of how he should comport himself in his imprisonment.[26]

In this respect Paul is engaged in a fruitfully circular activity. The precise form of Paul's bodily witness is shaped by his understanding of the movements of God's drama of salvation and his apprehension of his role within that divine drama. Therefore, by fitting the movements of his life appropriately into the movements of God's drama of salvation, Paul bears witness bodily to that very drama. He claims that he has decided to live and remain with all of the Philippians, engaging in fruitful labor for Christ, because it is more beneficial to the Philippians and will advance their "progress and joy in the faith." Here, in verses 25-26, Paul is making a transition from speaking (at least ostensibly) about his own affairs to a discussion of the Philippians' affairs, a discussion he will take up directly in

25. See Philo, *Jos.* 165; *Conf. Ling.* 183; Josephus *Ant.* 2.97; *Life* 420; see also *TDNT.*

26. In Phil. 2:19-30, Paul will point to Timothy and Epaphroditus as further exemplars of this disposition.

verses 27 and following. He does this by bringing his affairs and their affairs into the same story, the story of God's salvation of the world.

Several verbal links in verses 25-26 to themes Paul has already introduced support this interpretation. For example, the phrase τοῦτο πεποιθὼς οἶδα introduces a bold statement about how Paul's situation will work itself out to the Philippians' advantage: they will advance and have joy. It also recalls the equally bold statement in Philippians 1:6 (πεποιθὼς αὐτὸ τοῦτο) about God's continued work in the life of the Philippian congregation.

Furthermore, in 1:12, Paul had already introduced the discussion of his circumstances in prison by declaring that, contrary to expectation, his circumstances have worked to advance the gospel (εἰς προκοπὴν τοῦ εὐαγγελίου). In 1:18 he notes that, despite the motives of some, he rejoices in the advance of the gospel. Here, in verse 25, he asserts that his remaining with the Philippians will lead to their advancement (εἰς τὴν ὑμῶν προκοπήν) in joy and faith. These verbal connections remind us that, from the very first part of the Epistle, when Paul declares his conviction that God has worked and will continue to work in the lives of the Philippians, Paul has already been reading the Philippians into the narrative of God's economy of salvation in much the same way that he has read himself into that story. His claims in verse 25 simply resume that activity.

In reading the Philippians into his account of the divine economy from the beginning of the Epistle, Paul is already laying the groundwork for the claim he is going to make in 1:30 that he and the Philippians are engaged in the same struggle. This claim is essential for the larger aims of Paul's argument. If he can establish that he and the Philippians are in similar circumstances, then he can argue that the Philippians ought to act in a similar way. The bodily witness of Paul and the Philippians should, therefore, have a great deal in common. Moreover, having heard Paul offer an account of their situation in a way that both ties their situation to his and accounts for their circumstances in the light of the larger movements of the divine economy, Paul is implicitly encouraging them to learn how to see their situation in a similar way. In a sense, by the time the argument reaches the explicit claim in 3:17 that the Philippians should be "fellow imitators" of Paul, he has already laid so much conceptual and rhetorical groundwork that the claim comes as no surprise.

According to Philippians 1:26, the result of Paul's decision to remain in the flesh, engaging in fruitful labor for and with the Philippians so that their joy and faith may advance, is the "boasting" that will happen when Paul and the Philippians are reunited and can see each other face to face. In the Greco-Roman world, boasting is quite compatible with a cultural system based on honor and shame: it is a way of rightly locating honor.[27] Of course, boasting in Christ, one who suffered a slave's death, would have struck many in Paul's world as foolishness. Paul makes this quite clear in 1 Corinthians 1:18-31, a passage that concludes with a citation of Jeremiah 9:23-24: "Let the one who boasts, boast in the Lord." As the passage from Jeremiah indicates, this practice of boasting or giving glory is a practice that, if done in the right way and for the right reasons, is the paradigmatic activity of the believer. If done in the wrong way or for the wrong reasons, it is fundamentally destructive of a believer's relationship with God. This reinforces the importance of being formed to recognize what is "good, acceptable and perfect," according to God's standard. In Philippians 1:26 the grounds for boasting are in Christ Jesus, and, more precisely, what Christ Jesus has done through Paul.[28] Paul is not the object of his own or the Philippians' boasting. Rather, Christ is the object, and Paul's circumstances simply provide the occasion.

In this passage Paul has consistently displaced himself (offered himself as a sacrifice?) as the primary actor in a story that is ostensibly about himself. His account here thus makes it clear that his story is part of a larger story, the story of God's economy of salvation. In the light of Paul's persistent emphasis on the *koinonia* that he shares with the Philippians, he starts to draw them into this larger story as well. Paul makes this explicit in Philippians 1:5, where he claims that he and the Philippians are fellow sharers in the gospel; it is also explicit in 1:30, where he claims that he and the Philippians are part of the same struggle; it is also evident in Paul's expression of thanks in 4:10-20.

Within 1:12-26, Paul's reflections about his own life and death and how his views and plans are shaped not only by his commitment to continue magnifying Christ in his body, but also by what is most beneficial to the Philippians, implicitly indicate that he and the Philippians share a common situation. Further, he has indicated that his future joy and boasting in the Lord are intimately connected to the destiny of the Philippian community, a point he makes explicit in 2:12-18.

27. See B. Witherington's discussion of this issue in *Friendship and Finances in Philippi: The Letter of Paul to the Philippians* (Valley Forge, PA: Trinity Press International, 1994), 47-49.

28. As Witherington rightly suggests, "Paul is trying in part of this discourse to deenculturate his audience from such values by indicating that they are part of a different commonwealth, holding a different sort of citizenship" (*Friendship and Finances*, 47).

In short, Paul sees that he and the Philippians are engaged in a project greater than themselves. This project is nothing less than participation in the economy of God's saving purposes, to which they and all believers are to offer a bodily witness. Because they are fellow participants in the divine economy, Paul's sufferings and the Philippians' sufferings can be narrated within the scope of that common project. As a result, it will be neither Paul's beliefs that might require the Philippians to suffer, nor the Philippians' beliefs that might require Paul to suffer. Rather, their common convictions about God's work in the world, particularly as that work is revealed in and through the story of Christ narrated in 2:6-11, lead Paul to claim that the Philippians have been granted the opportunity not only to believe in Christ but to suffer for his sake (1:29). Their bodily witness is to these convictions about God's work in the world. Should that result in martyrdom, they will be able to narrate that death within the ongoing story of their bodily witness.

In the light of present or immanent suffering, it is crucial for Paul to help the Philippians develop the skills of being able so to interpret the movement of God's economy and so to situate themselves both within the movements of that story and in the light of that story's ultimate end, that they, as a community, can remain as a faithful witness to the gospel in the midst of a hostile world, whether or not that witness takes the form of martyrdom. This point is brought home explicitly in 1:27-28. Of course, the divine economy is not a self-interpreting text; its movements can at times be hard to decipher, particularly in the midst of material realities such as suffering and imprisonment. This further reinforces the importance of renewing the mind.

Sometimes paying proper attention to the divine economy requires an ironic perspective, and at times Paul displays such a perspective. When I speak of Paul's ironic point of view with regard to both his own circumstances and the movements of the divine economy, it is important that I qualify that judgment in several important respects. Paul's point of view is ironic in that he is able to see that, despite their present appearance and contrary to expectation, his circumstances are working and will work to advance the gospel. Despite the fact that he is in prison and utterly powerless, he will magnify Christ in his body. In spite of the obvious benefits of death, he will pursue a course that is more beneficial to the Philippians. The stable point that can sustain this ironic perspective is Paul's unwavering confidence that God will ultimately bring all things to their proper end. This is very different, then, from a perpetual irony that infinitely defers judgment and commitment, an irony that cannot but lapse into cynicism. Such irony could not sustain a bodily witness, much less martyrdom.

Instead, Paul's ironic perspective is christologically dense. It is a perspective that is shaped by a narrative of God's economy of salvation that reaches its climax in the life, death, and resurrection of Jesus, especially as that story gets told in Philippians 2:6-11. In those verses we read about a Christ who, contrary to expectation, does not use equality with God for his own advantage.[29] Instead, seeking the benefit of others, Christ willingly empties himself, takes on the form of a slave, and obediently submits to crucifixion. As 2:9-11 indicates, surprisingly, this is precisely the pattern of seeing and acting that God vindicates by exalting the crucified one. Having been shaped by this narrative, Paul can see the temporal contingency of present circumstances and current configurations of power. As a result, he can comport himself in the midst of adverse circumstances in the knowledge that these circumstances are ultimately ordered by God's providential will. Moreover, this ordering ultimately ensures that all things will be subject to Christ.

In Philippians these perceptual skills and habits are crucial components of maintaining a faithful bodily witness. By displaying these skills for the Philippians and by urging them to manifest these same skills and habits in their own context (e.g., 2:1-4), Paul is contributing to their formation as Christians who will bear truthful witness to Christ and, when called upon, have the resources to narrate their own deaths as willed offerings of themselves to God.

Speaking of Paul's body as Christ's text or the site of Christ's magnification reminds us, as Romans 12:1-2 did, that the witness of the body involves the formation of christologically acute perceptual skills and habits. These habits allow one to give an account of one's own circumstances — no matter how dire — that fit the narrative of one's own situation into the larger story of the divine economy of salvation. This habit makes it possible to distinguish between the empire's execution of a recalcitrant deviant and the offering of one's life back to God in martyrdom. More fundamentally, however, these perceptual skills and habits are necessary for believers' bodily witness to magnify Christ appropriately in life.

Through the examples from Romans and Philippians, I have tried to situate martyrdom within a larger set of practices that I have called the

29. In this respect, the term ἀλλά in Phil. 2:7 plays a role similar to that of μᾶλλον in Phil. 1:12. I owe this observation to Mike Gorman.

"witness of the body." The call to bear bodily witness to Christ is incumbent on all believers; martyrdom is simply a distinct form of this larger practice. The Letters to both the Romans and the Philippians indicate that faithful bodily witness depends on the cultivation of a set of perceptual skills and habits that enable believers to fit their lives into the larger narrative of God's drama of salvation. As believers become skilled in doing this, they will be ever more adept at discerning God's "good, acceptable, and perfect" will, especially in contexts hostile to the gospel. Should believers in those contexts be required to offer their lives back to God in martyrdom, both those believers and those left behind will be able properly to account for this death as something that magnifies Christ.

In the light of having explored the witness of the body from Romans 12:1-2 through Philippians, I want to examine one further aspect of the witness of the body as it relates to the church as the corporate body of Christ. Forming patterns of thinking, feeling, and acting appropriate to faithful bodily witness is best understood as an activity of believers within the community of the church. The passages from Romans and Philippians discussed above reflect that. The New Testament also reflects on the witness of the communal body of Christ as a whole. In this sense, the witness of the body refers to the common witness of the church to God's drama of salvation. This is, perhaps, most clearly seen in Ephesians.

In Ephesians 2, Paul provides a rich summary of the "mystery" of God's drama of salvation.[30] Through the life, death, and resurrection of Jesus, God's eternal plan of blessing all nations through Abraham and his heirs is brought to its climax. In Christ, Jews and Gentiles have been reconciled and brought together into one body through the cross. As Ephesians 3 begins, Paul reminds his readers that because of his role in proclaiming this mystery, he is now in prison, offering his own bodily witness. Of course, once this mystery has been made known in Christ, it is no longer hidden and must be witnessed to and proclaimed.

Having referred to his own practice of witness and proclamation, Paul goes on to claim that the church has a particular mission: "[S]o that now the principalities and powers in the heavenly realms might know the manifold wisdom of God through the church according to the eternal purpose accomplished in Christ Jesus our Lord" (Eph. 3:10-11). One of the purposes for which Paul has been given grace to evangelize the Gentiles is

30. Although there are serious debates about the Pauline authorship of Ephesians, I will refer here to Paul as, at least, the inscribed author of this text.

that the church established in the light of Paul's preaching may bear bodily witness to God's wisdom to the principalities and powers.

Paul first introduces the "principalities and powers" in Ephesians 1:21. He does not give a very full description of these things, and that has provided opportunity for a great deal of theological and exegetical speculation, much of which is not relevant for our purposes.[31] It is clear that the principalities and powers are created beings. Furthermore, they reside in the "heavenly realms."[32]

Both Jews and pagans would have recognized that, though these powers are immaterial, they may stand behind and oversee a host of earthly practices and institutions hostile to God.[33] Even the New Testament recognizes that spiritual forces manifest themselves in a variety of concrete structures and events (see both Rom. 13 and Rev. 13), and in pagan worship (1 Cor. 10:20). Moreover, scholars now generally agree that in Ephesians, as well as in the New Testament more generally, the powers are taken to be either hostile to or alienated from God and God's purposes in Christ. Christ's superiority to these powers must in part depend on the fact that these powers, unlike the Son, are created (Col. 1:15-16). As such, they must have initially been part of God's good creation. Whatever good pur-

31. One finds similar terminology in Col. 1:16, Rom. 8:38, and 1 Pet: 3:22. These contexts do not add much to our understanding of these terms.

32. Paul's language about the "heavenly realms" is notoriously vague. Strikingly, according to Eph. 1:3, believers must in some sense currently participate in the "heavenly realms," for it is where they have received God's blessing. Moreover, 1:20 indicates that God has seated the resurrected Christ in the "heavenly realms." Further, as 1:20-22 indicates, these principalities and powers are not yet under Christ's dominion, at which time Christ will be established as "head of all things," including "the church which is his body." It is clear from the five times the phrase "in the heavenly realms" occurs in Ephesians that this is a way of talking about a location (see 1:20; 2:6; 3:10; 6:12). The "heavenly realms" refers to both a place where Christ is seated at the right hand of God (1:20) and a place where hostile principalities and powers seek to exercise authority (3:10; 6:12). It is also a place where believers have been raised with Christ and seated with him. It would appear, then, that the heavenly realms is a place that has been decisively marked by Christ's redemptive work, a foreshadowing of the final end of believers (see Aquinas, *Commentary on St. Paul's Epistle to the Ephesians,* trans. M. Lamb [Albany, NY: Magi Books, 1966], 46), and yet also a place whose final transformation into a place fully under Christ's rule has yet to be accomplished (see A. Lincoln, *Ephesians* [Waco: Word, 1990], 21).

33. There is a great deal of literature on the "principalities and powers," much of it technical. One can find a good introduction to the issues in P. O'Brien, "Principalities and Powers: Opponents of the Church," in *Biblical Interpretation and the Church,* ed. D. A. Carson (Nashville: Thomas Nelson, 1984), 110-50.

poses these powers might have initially fulfilled, they are now hostile to God. They no longer participate in or enhance God's good ordering of creation. Indeed, they may well attempt to thwart God's plans. Along with the rest of creation, they will ultimately be restored to their proper place under Christ's lordship. Indeed, Ephesians 3:10 indicates that the church, Christ's body, is the means by which these powers might be restored to their proper relationship to God and the rest of creation.

There can be a variety of ways in which this might happen, but Christians may well find resources for understanding the implications of Paul's claims here by reflecting on passages such as Isaiah 2:1-4, Isaiah 60:1-7, and Ezekiel 37. In particular, one might see Paul's claims here in Ephesians as a further unpacking of Isaiah 2:1-4. Recall that, according to Isaiah, when the redemption of Israel happens, the nations will be so attracted to the renewed people of God and their relationship to God and each other that these Gentiles will be drawn to God. The result of this will be the peace characteristic of the garden in Genesis 1–2. The church, the body of Christ, is the place where the redemption of Israel is made manifest in word and deed, a place where Gentiles are welcomed and reconciled both to God and to the renewed people of God. It should come as no surprise, then, that the attractiveness that first drew Gentiles to God should be made even more attractive in the light of the reconciliation of Jew and Gentile into one body in Christ. Indeed, it may appear attractive enough to induce the powers to return to their proper place under Christ.

I am not claiming that Paul consciously reflected on Isaiah as he thought about his own commission. Rather, if Isaiah thinks of the reconciliation of the nations with redeemed Israel as having significant social consequences for the world, it is not unimaginable that Paul and subsequent Christians might expect that the reconciliation in Christ of Jew and Gentile to God and to each other would have social and even cosmic consequences. This would be the aim of the church's bodily witness to the powers related in Ephesians 3:10. Therefore, it is striking that, although these powers are located in the heavenly realms, their understanding of and reconciliation to the wisdom of God is dependent on the material presence of communities such as Paul seeks to form in Ephesus and elsewhere.

Paul says that the corporate bodily witness of the church plays a decisive role in the ultimate reconciliation of the powers. As the argument of Ephesians unfolds, one can perhaps see some of the practices Paul takes as crucial to this witness of the corporate body. These practices are summarized in Ephesians 4:1 with the call to the Ephesians to walk in a manner worthy of their calling (cf. Phil. 1:27). Most important, this involves "maintaining the unity of the Spirit in the bond of peace" (4:3). The actual embodied unity of believers — particularly of Jew and Gentile — in Christ is the crucial element in the church's witness to the powers. Ephesians 4–6 goes on to speak widely and variously about the practices believers need to observe in order to walk worthily. For the most part, however, these practices can all be understood as practices designed to maintain the unity of the Spirit in the bond of peace.

From this one might infer that, to the extent that the principalities and powers seek to thwart the unfolding of God's drama of redemption, they will seek to undermine the unity of the church. Although martyrdom may be narrated as part of the concerted attempt by the principalities and powers to undermine the corporate witness of the church, it would appear that Christian disunity and division does a far better job of this. It seems far more plausible to argue that Christian division, particularly in Western Europe and the United States, so enfeebles the church's witness that principalities and powers, whether working through nation-states or not, need not bother harassing the church. Further, one might plausibly speculate that, should Christians overcome their current divisions to the degree that they can offer an articulate witness to the gospel, the principalities and powers will work to create the sort of hostility to the faith that will make martyrdom a realistic scenario for believers.

This focus on the church's corporate bodily witness in Ephesians has been more speculative than the earlier discussions of Romans and Philippians. Nevertheless, it is grounded in a common view about the comprehensive category of the witness of the body. That is, one continues to see that the witness of the body is a witness to God's drama of salvation. Attention to the scope and movements of this drama will lead believers (with the Spirit's help) to form and transform their lives in the light of what is truly good, acceptable, and perfect. Thus transformed, believers will be ever more able to maintain the unity of the Spirit in the bond of peace. Such transformations will also enable believers to bear ever more truthful and beautiful forms of witness to this drama of salvation. This, in turn, will generate further transformations, and then ever deeper forms of witness, both individually and corporately. Within such a circle of witness and transformation, the offering of one's life back to God in martyrdom can be seen as one exemplary type of the witness of the body.

PART II

Martyrdom Builds the Church

CHAPTER 4

Witness, Women's Bodies, and the Body of Christ

Joyce E. Salisbury

The early centuries of the Christian age — from AD 64 through 313 — brought forward stunning examples of bravery, as women and men stepped forward to bear witness to their faith. Crowds of pagans watched as Christians went to their deaths cheerfully, singing psalms and glorying in an expected victory in the afterlife. The causes of the persecutions varied a bit over time and space, and, most important for this discussion of the impact of the persecutions on Christian attitudes toward the body, the nature of the tortures changed over time.[1] From the persecutions of Nero in 64 to the early third century, the persecutions involved Christians who had been condemned to death as criminals. Such public condemnations (for Christians or other criminals) usually meant a sentence of execution by beasts or flames in the public space of the local amphitheaters. These deaths were horrible, but they were familiar to the witnesses.

After the third century, things changed. In 212, Emperor Caracalla extended citizenship to all free residents of the empire, and from that time on, Roman authorities did not want to simply execute criminals; they wanted the citizens to demonstrate their loyalty by worshiping the state cults, especially that of the emperor. How does one persuade people to change their beliefs — or do anything, for that matter? Like so many of the powerful who have been frustrated by the intransigence of the powerless, Romans turned to torture. Now the brave witness of the Christian confessors seemed even

1. For a description of the progress of the early Christian persecutions, see Joyce E. Salisbury, *Blood of Martyrs* (New York: Routledge, 2004), 9-29.

more miraculous, and it was eminently clear that it was the *bodies* of Christians that were tested. It was the flesh that was tortured horribly, and muscles, bones, and organs had to bear witness to the faith in men's and women's hearts and minds. Eusebius, the fourth-century church historian, was only one of many who wrote in loving detail of those who died horribly for their faith: "Sometimes they were killed with the axe . . . sometimes their legs were broken. . . . Sometimes they were hung up by the feet head down over a slow fire . . . sometimes noses, ears, and hands were severed."[2]

One important consequence of the physical witness of the martyrs was the victory over Gnosticism, an early heresy that devalued the flesh. Gnostics such as Valentinus claimed that the flesh was no more than a "leather tunic" to be discarded as a suit of clothes, and that Jesus was not a fleshly human at all, but a spiritual being who had adapted himself so humans could see him.[3] For the Gnostics, Christ's physical death was less significant than his spiritual ascendance; therefore, martyrdom, with its physical imitation of Christ's suffering, was pointless. One Gnostic writer claimed that physical sacrifice turned God into a cannibal who desires human flesh.[4] Yet the martyrs' brave deaths seemed to make a lie of Gnostic devaluation of the body.

Thus, as we see, the acts of the martyrs shaped the theology of early Christianity. Ideas of justice made people believe that the flesh that suffered so horribly during martyrdom would be rewarded; resurrection would not simply be of the soul, as the Gnostics believed, but of the body itself. The third-century church father Tertullian wrote:

> Now we are not permitted to suppose that God is either unjust or idle. Unjust, however, He would be, were He to exclude from reward the flesh which is associated with good works. . . . [It would be] unworthy of God . . . that this flesh of ours should be torn by martyrdom, and another [body] wear the crown.[5]

As Tertullian and others developed the theology of the resurrection of the actually tortured flesh of the martyrs, they claimed that there would

2. Eusebius, *The History of the Church,* trans. G. A. Williamson (Harmondsworth, UK: Penguin, 1984), 341-42.

3. Elaine Pagels, *The Gnostic Gospels* (New York: Vintage Books, 1981), 87.

4. Pagels, *Gnostic Gospels,* 111.

5. Tertullian, "On the Resurrection of the Flesh" in *Ante-Nicene Fathers,* ed. A. Roberts and J. Donaldson (Peabody, MA: Hendrickson, 1995), 3:555.

be a place in an unchanging heaven for mouths, teeth, and even bowels, even though resurrected bodies would not need to eat.[6] This focus on physicality of resurrected bodies led to speculation about women's bodies. What about women who imitated Christ in death? What about their witness in martyrdom? In this chapter I will consider how the accounts of female martyrdom transformed the idea of women's bodies, the church, and images of the body of Christ himself.

In their devaluation of the flesh, the Gnostics also downplayed a distinction between genders, looking to a salvation when "the two shall be one, and the male with the female, and there is neither male nor female."[7] Orthodox Christians, however, thought more carefully about the nature of resurrected bodies — and specifically the bodies of women. The experience of the female martyrs, in which their gendered flesh was tortured, affirmed the idea that women would rise as women. This notion, which seems pretty self-evident today, was not always taken for granted. In fact, those who thought women might be resurrected into "perfected" male bodies took as evidence the experience of Perpetua, a third-century Carthaginian martyr.

Perpetua, who died in 203, left a diary in which she recorded her visions, which the faithful took as inspired. In these visions, for example, Perpetua articulated views of heaven as a beautiful garden. In the final vision she received, on the eve of her martyrdom in the arena, Perpetua had a preview of her battle with the forces of evil. She saw herself appearing in the amphitheater with two young men as her assistants. She then described what happened next: "My clothes were stripped off, and suddenly I was a man."[8] What were believers to make of this much-quoted vision? Did this mean that women martyrs would become male as they claimed their victorious resurrected bodies?

While many Christians speculated that women would be "perfected" into men at the resurrection, the influential bishop Augustine established the orthodox view: that the resurrected bodies of women would retain the appearance of women, including their genitalia, that is; women would not be resurrected as male.[9] Augustine explained that Perpetua's vision was

6. Salisbury, *Blood of Martyrs,* 42-49.

7. Anne McGuire, "Women, Gender, and Gnosis in Gnostic Texts and Traditions," in *Women and Christian Origins,* ed. Ross Shepard Kraemer and Mary Rose D'Angelo (New York: Oxford University Press, 1999), 265.

8. Joyce E. Salisbury, *Perpetua's Passion* (New York: Routledge, 1997), 107.

9. Augustine, *City of God,* trans. H. Bettenson (Harmondsworth, UK: Penguin, 1972), 1057-58.

not a preview of the world to come. Instead, the bishop claimed that her vision demonstrated an interior change, in which her feminine frailty was transformed into a masculine strength that could withstand torture. He said that in her dream her body did not "keep the shape of its vagina," since the experience of martyrdom needed masculine strength.[10]

Perpetua's dream of her transformation may have revealed that she had internalized the prevailing misogynist views that women could not battle in the arena and that their flesh did not have the strength to withstand the torture required by the witness of the faith. Augustine's analysis of her dream certainly shows that he perpetuated these views. Perpetua's influential dream and Augustine's analysis of it provide a stark devaluation of women and their bodies. However, the full range of the texts of female martyrs shows a more positive view of women and their flesh.

Women were surprisingly visible as martyrs. In most of the Mediterranean world — especially the Greek East — women were to be silent and stay indoors; even most of the texts that brought shape to the early Christian church reinforced this image. The church father Origen (ca. 250) can serve as a typical example: he argued that a woman should keep silent even when she was moved by the Holy Spirit. He used the letters of Paul as his proof:

> Even if . . . it is granted that a woman is a prophetess, she is still not permitted to speak out in an assembly. . . . "For it is not right for a woman to speak out in an assembly" (1 Cor. 14:35) and "I am not giving permission for a woman to teach," still less "to tell a man what to do" (1 Tim. 2:12).[11]

However, the defining moment of a martyrdom was to bear witness to belief, that is, to speak out in public. Perpetua announced: "I cannot be called anything other than what I am, a Christian."[12] When asked why she would not perform a sacrifice to the emperor, Agatha, another confessor, said simply, "Because I am a Christian." Her companion Eutychia echoed the simple statement: "I am a Christian, a servant of almighty God."[13] The

10. Salisbury, *Perpetua's Passion,* 175.

11. J. Kevin Coyle, "The Fathers on Women and Women's Ordination," in *Studies in Early Christianity,* ed. Everett Ferguson (New York: Garland, 1993), 139.

12. "Of Perpetua and Felicitas," in *The Acts of the Christian Martyrs,* trans. Herbert Musurillo (Oxford: Oxford University Press, 1972), 109.

13. "Of Agape, Irene, and Chione," in *Acts of the Christian Martyrs,* 285.

verbal formula was expressed throughout the Mediterranean basin; even martyrs killed by the Persians repeated it. The fourth-century martyr Martha told her Persian inquisitor, "I am a Christian, as my clothing shows."[14]

While both men and women stepped forward bravely to announce their faith, women stepped outside their traditional roles of silent witness when they did so. The exceptional nature of this public declaration by women led observers to see the female martyrs in a different light than they saw the males, and the texts that record the witness of the women spoke with wonder about their bodies. These influential texts that bore witness to female bodily resilience have shaped the way Christians think of both women and the church.

One way the texts of women's passion are different from those of men is that the accounts of their torture are more sexual.[15] For example, the fourth-century church historian Eusebius writes: "Women were tied by one foot and hoisted high in the air, head downwards, their bodies completely naked without a morsel of clothing, presenting thus the most shameful, brutal, and inhuman of all spectacles to everyone watching."[16] Eusebius seemed more concerned about the sexual humiliation than with physical pain, and this was typical of many who described women's torture.

According to the texts, torturers often particularly struck at women's breasts. The Roman consul ordered that Agatha's "breasts be roughly twisted, and then commanded that they be torn off." Another martyr, Faith, was "beaten by thirty-six soldiers; then her breasts were torn off. . . ."[17] Were these examples of sexual sadomasochism actually part of the torturers' repertoire, or were they later additions of the martyrologists who recorded the event to emphasize the gender of the martyr? We cannot know for sure, but we may probably assume both went on. In either case, the actions revealed a deep awareness of the female bodies that bore witness to their faith.

In addition to attacking female sexual organs, torturers also used sexual humiliation to try to persuade women to abandon their faith. Dulcitius, the prefect questioning the virgin Irene, said, "I do not wish you

14. Susan Ashbrook Harvey, *Holy Women of the Syrian Orient* (Berkeley: University of California Press, 1987), 68.

15. Francine Cardman, "Acts of the Women Martyrs," in *Studies in Early Christianity,* 102.

16. Eusebius, *History of the Church,* 337.

17. Jacobus de Voragine, *The Golden Legend,* trans. G. Ryan (New York: Arno, 1969), 159, 592.

to die immediately. . . . Instead I sentence you to be placed naked in the brothel. . . ."[18] Sabina, a woman who was arrested at the same time as the famous martyr Pionius, was also threatened with prostitution: "You are going to suffer something you do not like. Women who refuse to sacrifice are put into a brothel."[19] None of Sabina's male companions were threatened that way, and this contrast within the same account testifies to the degree that the martyrdom of women was significantly sexualized.

One might ask whether there was a traffic in male prostitutes that would make for corresponding humiliation, and indeed there was. Not only were slaves regularly used as homosexual prostitutes, but in these early Christian centuries there was a bustling trade in eunuchs, many of whom were used as male prostitutes. It is surprising that accounts of male martyrs did not include threats of castration or other sexually charged tortures. Eusebius describes in graphic detail the torture of men beaten, burnt, and dismembered. For example, he describe martyrs who were "hung up by the feet head down over a slow fire . . . sometimes noses, ears, and hands were severed, and the other parts and portions of the body cut up like meat. . . ."[20] But in only one instance of Eusebius's detailed catalogue of tortures does he hint at attacks on men's sexual organs: "[O]thers endured in their private parts and bowels sufferings shameful, merciless, and unmentionable. . . ."[21]

I suggest that this omission lay less with the torturers' scruples than with the desire of the authors of these accounts to show men as masculine and heroic, "athletes of Christ" who withstood torture with their masculinity intact. By the fourth century, the church banned self-castration and forbade eunuchs to become priests, and the accounts of the martyrs reflected this ideal of masculine integrity. Torturing might break bodies into bits, but male genitalia would be left intact.

Even though accounts of female torture were heavily sexualized, there was a parallel between the treatment of men's sexual organs and women's: women's breasts might be ripped off, their thighs and buttocks cut; yet, in spite of repeated threats of rape, martyrs were reputed to have maintained their virginity intact. In the memories of the faithful who recorded the passion of the martyrs, in spite of horrible bodily dismember-

18. "Of Agape, Irene, and Chione," in *Acts of the Christian Martyrs,* 291.

19. "Of Pionius," in *Acts of the Christian Martyrs,* 147.

20. Eusebius, *History of the Church,* 342.

21. Eusebius, *History of the Church,* 343.

ment, the martyrs' genitalia — and sexual identity — would remain intact: men would not become eunuchs, and women would remain virgins.

Martyrs' accounts tell of many virgins who were martyred during the persecutions — so many, in fact, that one wonders whether only virgins held firm in their faith. This preponderance of virgins among martyrs was highly unlikely. In the first place, the early Christian communities were heavily made up of families, and even if we acknowledge that some of these families might have included unmarried daughters, the more likely female spokesperson in the household would have been the mother, not the young daughter. Furthermore, the membership of the church included many widows, who likely were able to follow their consciences after their husbands' deaths. For example, the third-century church in Rome alone was supporting more than fifteen hundred widows and "other persons in distress."[22]

Some of the most famous female martyrs were mothers, beginning with the Jewish Maccabean mother who, in the first century AD, was brought before the authorities for refusing to eat sacrificial meat. She encouraged her seven sons to remain firm unto death as they were tortured for maintaining the Jewish purity laws.[23] Perpetua was a young mother with her infant at her breast when she was called to witness her faith in the arena, and her prison diary tells of her anxiety for her infant. Ultimately, she had to renounce her motherhood and leave her child behind when she claimed the crown of martyrdom.[24]

The accounts of the martyrs show that the Roman authorities had to confront the problem of what to do with women who had family ties when they were arrested. Roman law forbade executing pregnant women, so Perpetua's pregnant companion and slave, Felicity, feared she would not be able to join her fellow Christians in the arena. However, the night before they were to face their ordeal, Felicity gave birth in prison. The account of her passion claimed that she was "glad that she had safely given birth so that now she could fight the beasts, going from one blood bath to another, from the midwife to the gladiator, ready to wash after childbirth in a second baptism." Even the crowd was shocked to see a new mother "fresh from childbirth with the milk still dripping from her breasts" led into the

22. Salisbury, *Blood of Martyrs,* 73.

23. 4 Macc. 14–15. For the association between motherhood and martyrdom, see Salisbury, *Blood of Martyrs,* 116.

24. Salisbury, *Perpetua's Passion,* 89.

arena.[25] Another confessor, Eutychia, was a pregnant widow when she was arrested. The prefect used Roman law to decide her case quickly, saying, "Since Eutychia is pregnant, she shall be kept meanwhile in gaol."[26]

With these and other similar examples of mothers and widows who stepped forward to accept martyrdom, it seems a bit odd that the prevailing view of martyrs is that they were virgins. There are several explanations for the tendency of authors of martyrs' passions to praise women's bodies as virginal. One reason, as described above, was that virgins' "intactness" served as a marked contrast to the dismemberment involved in torture, and as such it was a marker of the miracle of martyrdom itself. For examples, the virgins who were threatened with brothels and sexual exploitation were all miraculously saved from such ignominy. Irene, the virgin sent to a brothel, escaped sexual taint, for as the account states, "by the grace of the Holy Spirit which preserved and guarded her pure and inviolate . . . no man dared to approach her, or so much as tried to insult her in speech."[27]

Whenever possible, then, the accounts claimed that the female martyrs were virgin and intact. This observation leads to the question: What was so religiously significant about virginal integrity? In addition to intact bodies, I suggest that the regular association between virgins and martyrs has to do with blood; unlike pregnant women, virgins continue to bleed. From time beyond memory, people have associated blood with sacrifice, and this idea continued into Christian thought. In the Christian tradition, the blood of Christ was to be the full and sufficient sacrifice. As Tertullian succinctly charged his pagan contemporaries who flocked to the arena and temples to see sacrificial blood spilled, "Do you have desire for blood? You have the blood of Christ."[28] In spite of Tertullian's and others' claims that Christ's sacrifice was sufficient, many continued to see martyrs' deaths as continuing sacrifices in imitation of Christ's. Polycarp, for example, called himself "a sacrifice, rich and acceptable," as he prepared to die in flames.[29]

Virginal blood, with its seeming inexhaustible supply as women bled monthly, was seen as particularly efficacious. The fourth-century poet Prudentius captured this idea of the value of virginal blood sacrifice in his

25. "Of Perpetua and Felicitas," in *Acts of the Christian Martyrs,* 127, 129.

26. "Of Agape, Irene, and Chione," in *Acts of the Christian Martyrs,* 285.

27. "Of Agape, Irene, and Chione," in *Acts of the Christian Martyrs,* 291.

28. Tertullian, "Spectacles," in *Disciplinary, Moral and Ascetical Works,* trans. R. Arbesmann (New York: Fathers of the Church, 1959), 104.

29. "The Martyrdom of Polycarp," in *Early Christian Writings: The Apostolic Fathers,* trans. Maxwell Staniforth (New York: Dorset Press, 1968), 160-61.

poem of praise to the martyr Eulalia. He wrote of Merida, which housed the martyr's bones: "A powerful city, wealthy people, but made more prosperous by the blood of the virginal tomb." When Prudentius wrote that the land was hallowed by the "virginal tomb" of the martyr, he surely intended his readers to think of the virgin's "womb" as well as "tomb," for the two were linked in folk tales and other poems.[30] As virgins sacrificed their own fertility by withdrawing from reproduction, they were thought to bring fertility to the community. Martyrs who brought blessings to the neighborhood were seen as virgins, those who had traditionally brought fecundity to the land. In popular consciousness, then, the bodies of female martyrs were often transformed into virginal bodies.

In addition to retaining sexual integrity, men's and women's bodies appeared to undergo other changes in the crucible of martyrdom. As they were willing to sacrifice themselves, their bodies became more beautiful in the eyes of the beholders (if not miraculously in actual fact). Pionius stripped himself naked before his ordeal, and "realizing the holiness and dignity of his own body, he was filled with great joy. . . ." After he had been burned, the witnesses claimed:

> Those of us who were present saw his body like that of an athlete in full array at the height of his power. His ears were not distorted; his hair lay in order on the surface of his head; and his beard was full as though with the first blossom of hair. His face shone once again . . . so that the Christians were all the more confirmed in the faith, and those who had lost the faith returned dismayed and with fearful consciences.[31]

The ordeal of martyrdom took place on the body, and thus all the accounts revealed that the body, the tortured flesh, was transformed and made more beautiful. This was equally true, if not emphasized more, in women's bodies, which were always held to ideals of beauty. In the Acts of Crispina, the Roman judge threatened first to attack her beauty in order to defile her body: "Let her be completely disfigured by having her hair cut and her head shaved with a razor till she is bald, that her beauty might first thus be brought to shame."[32] The judge did not make good on this threat, and Crispina was decapitated — with her beauty, if not her body, intact.

Eusebius also describes the physical beauty that accompanied the

30. Salisbury, *Blood of Martyrs*, 141.

31. "Of Pionius," in *Acts of the Christian Martyrs*, 163, 165.

32. "Of Crispina," in *Acts of the Christian Martyrs*, 307.

commitment to Christian witness in his description of the martyrs of Lyons who died in about 177. As the condemned marched into the arena,

> [t]he faithful stepped out with a happy smile, wondrous glory and grace blended on their faces, so that even their fetters hung like beautiful ornaments around them and they resembled a bride adorned with golden lace elaborately wrought; they were perfumed also with the sweet savor of Christ so that some people thought they had smeared themselves, with worldly cosmetics.[33]

This description shows that the ideal of the beauty of women's bodies became the metaphor for the physical sanctity that martyrs' bodies gained. Both men and women were as beautiful as "brides" covered with the perfumes and cosmetics appropriate to the female sex. Even a physically ugly woman (although martyrs were seldom described as homely) was transformed by the experience into an object of more beauty. For example, Eusebius describes Blandina, who was among the martyrs of Lyons, that men regarded her as "mean, unlovely, and contemptible," yet that she was deemed worthy and indeed made lovely by her strength.[34]

As observers recast martyrs' bodies into objects of sanctity and beauty, they created one of the most striking shifts in the perceptions of pagan Romans. Pagans had a fear of dead bodies. In the second century, Celsus wrote: "For what sort of human soul is it that has any use for a rotted corpse of a body? . . . [C]orpses should be disposed of like dung, for dung they are."[35] And yet Christian Romans venerated these holy remains, like the Carthaginian woman Lucilla, who had purchased a bone of a martyr and brought it to church with her and kissed it before she took the Eucharist. Another pious Carthaginian noblewoman, Megetia, beat herself against the grill that protected the relics of Saint Stephen so hard that she broke the barrier and was able to lie upon the bones themselves.[36] In fact, the medieval practice of enshrining dry bones with magnificently jeweled reliquaries is a physical expression of the accounts of the martyrs' passions: the dead were made beautiful by the transformation achieved by the suffering of their bodies.

33. Eusebius, *History of the Church,* 199.

34. Eusebius, *History of the Church,* 196.

35. Celsus, *On the True Doctrine,* trans. R. J. Hoffman (Oxford: Oxford University Press, 1987), 86.

36. Salisbury, *Blood of Martyrs,* 50-51.

In order to really see the vindication of women's bodies that is the subject of this chapter, we need to note one more transformation of the body that took place at the moment of martyrdom. Not only did the body become beautiful; it became like the body of Christ. The homely slave Blandina might serve as the best example of this final transformation. When she was tortured, she was hung on a post to serve as food for the beasts that were released into the arena. To the onlookers, she seemed to be "hanging in the form of a cross" and the witnesses "saw with their outward eyes in the person of their sister the One who was crucified for them. . . ."[37] At the moment of her witness, Blandina's body became like the body of Christ, so it could no longer be dismissed as shameful, ugly, or simply an imperfect woman. What effect did this have on perceptions of all women's bodies?

To explore the result of Christian martyrdom on people's views of women's bodies, unfortunately, I have to dismember them a bit — or at least look at the body parts associated with different identities of women. In the ancient world, women primarily filled two roles. They were sexual beings, represented by their genital organs, and they were mothers, represented most often by their nurturing breasts. The most problematic parts of women's bodies for men of the ancient world were their sexual organs. In the case of the martyrs, men (torturers and witnesses alike) believed that the greatest torture was to violate and rupture a woman's hymen. As we have seen, virtuous women — including martyrs — were virgins whose genital organs remained intact. One of the principal metaphorical patterns by which the church fathers understood virginity was through images of things closed, and these images — drawn from the times of the martyrs — shaped future understandings of women's bodies.

In the fourth century, Ambrose explicitly listed metaphors for virginity so that, as he said, his readers might more easily understand its nature. He called virginity a "closed door," a "closed garden," and a "sealed fountain" (an image drawn from the Song of Songs).[38] As the fourth-century fathers developed these images of enclosure that signaled — and indeed ensured — an intact virginal body, they articulated a way of life for virginal women that was marked by closure. Ambrose expressed this with sexual associations: "What is more excellent (especially in a maiden whose

37. Eusebius, *History of the Church,* 200.

38. Ambrose, "De Institutione Virginitate," *PL* 16:335; see also Joyce E. Salisbury, *Church Fathers, Independent Virgins* (London: Verso, 1991), 29-30.

private parts demand modesty) than . . . retirement?"[39] Virgins were to keep their metaphorical doors closed behind literal closed doors.

The belief in the power and holiness of virgins' genitals found an expression in the apocryphal acts of Thecla, a purported confessor who faced a lion in the arena. As told by Ambrose, Thecla was arrested and sent to be eaten by a lion that had been starved for many days. As the lion charged at her, Thecla, "avoiding the gaze of men[,] . . . offered her vital parts to the fierce lion." The lion was awed by the exposure of her genitals, and lay down and licked her feet. Ambrose explained that "it could not injure the sacred body of a virgin. . . . Virginity has in itself so much that is admirable, that even lions admire it."[40]

This story of the power of virgin flesh to tame lions summarizes the ideas about women's genital organs that were shaped in the early centuries of Christianity. Like the bodies of martyrs, virgins' bodies, too, were made holy. Like miraculous resurrected flesh — like Christ's resurrected flesh — bodies on earth could be transformed into holy vessels that were different from the bodies of the fallen. Ambrose further testified to the physical expression of the holy bodies: they smelled different. He urged virgins to test this proposal:

> [P]resent your hands to your nostrils and explore with unwearied and ever-watchful alacrity of mind the perfume of your deeds. The smell of your right hand will be musty to you, and your limbs will be redolent with the odor of the resurrection; your fingers will exude myrrh. . . .[41]

Furthermore, he said that Christ "prefers the fragrance of . . . [her] garments . . . to all other perfumes. . . ." Ambrose argued that those who existed in the realm of the flesh bore the "odor of death," while those existing in the spiritual realm bore the "odor of life."[42]

All these images reinforce the view that virgins' bodies — at least their closed, intact genitals — were sanctified. But what of opened bodies? Was there any possibility of redemption for women whose genitals were no

39. Ambrose, "Letter No. 32," in *Saint Ambrose: Letters*, trans. Sr. Mary Melchior Beyenke (New York: Fathers of the Church, 1954), 159.

40. Ambrose, "Concerning Virgins," in *Nicene and Post-Nicene Fathers*, ed. P. Schaff and H. Wace (Peabody, MA: Hendrickson, 1995), 10:376.

41. Ambrose, *On Virginity*, trans. Daniel Callam (Saskatoon, SK: Peregrina Publishing, 1980), 17.

42. Ambrose, *On Virginity*, 23, 17.

longer intact? (The same question was asked of eunuchs, men whose sexuality had also been fragmented, but that question is for another essay.) Once the witness of the martyrs paved the way for married bodies to be transformed, we can trace some texts that argue for redemption of even vaginas that had been opened.

The idea that women who have had sexual intercourse, even within marriage, might have bodies that were sanctified was never easily accepted. We have seen that the acts of many female martyrs emphasized their sexual integrity (virginity), whether or not they were virgins. Even when martyrs were obviously mothers, like Perpetua, their sexual roles were downplayed. In the case of Perpetua, for example, the thirteenth-century author of a revised account of her passion inserted a question about her husband: "He asked, 'Hast thou a husband?' She answered: 'I have, but I disdain him!'"[43] This rejection of her married state was a way of renouncing sexual intercourse. The young mother could not be converted into a virgin, but the story could be transformed to praise virginity.

Tertullian is representative of the early church fathers (i.e., before Augustine) in rejecting sexual intercourse — and specifically women's bodies — in his much-quoted designation of women as the "devil's gateway." In the same passage he claims that a woman (and therefore all future women) was the "unsealer of that forbidden tree."[44] In this passage Tertullian uses the metaphors that had become so popular among Christian audiences: the forbidden tree was sexual intercourse, which opened (unsealed) the closed bodies of virgins and made their vaginas (and thus women themselves) the gateway through which sin entered the world.

This view of women's sexual bodies would seem to make them completely unredeemable. Would it be that only virgins' bodies could be sanctified? This is the case in most of the texts through the Middle Ages. However, there were many medieval saints' lives that preserve an alternative view of sexuality, one that praised all the parts of a woman's body. These texts demonstrate that an alternative view of womanhood persisted. One example of this vindication of women's bodies may be found in the *Life of Melania,* a fourth-century Roman noblewoman who renounced her family after her two children died and took on the life of a holy woman, albeit one who traveled rather than remaining enclosed. In one of the miracles attrib-

43. Jacobus de Voragine, *The Golden Legend,* 735.

44. Tertullian, "On the Apparel of Women," in *Fathers of the Third Century, Ante-Nicene Fathers* (Peabody, MA: Hendrickson, 1995), 4:14.

uted to Melania, she was called to the bedside of a woman whose child had died in her womb. A surgeon was cutting out the stillborn child in an attempt to save the mother. Melania intervened and tied her belt around the tormented woman's waist. The stillborn infant was delivered and the woman was saved. Melania comments on the disgust that was generated in the audience at the grisly description of the surgeon's actions — and on the fear and revulsion stimulated by childbearing. She says that reproduction could not be filthy because God had created it. Furthermore, vaginas that God had created could not be filthy because through these passages were born the patriarchs, prophets, apostles, and other saints.[45] In this story of dismemberment as vivid as any martyr's tale, Melania praises and calls blessed the "unsealed" opening of a woman's body.

Melania's hagiographer describes two other miracles that she performed. In each case a woman was "gripped by an evil demon. Her mouth and lips were closed for many days, so that she could neither talk nor eat. She was in danger of starvation."[46] Melania cured both women and opened their mouths. In these miracles Melania was directly opposing patristic requirements for virgins, the perfect women, to keep their mouths closed to demonstrate and preserve their closed genitals. Melania was arguing that a woman's open body could be as holy as a closed one. This kind of text vindicated women's vaginas. What about their uteruses?

A woman's uterus was less often disparaged by patristic writers, in part because most texts focused on the rupturing of the hymen in intercourse as the significant marker of sexuality rather than any change in the uterus. Furthermore, one of the central mysteries of Christianity — the incarnation of Christ — took place within the Virgin's womb. Patristic writers claimed that virgins who dedicated their sexuality to God might also hope to bear spiritual fruits. Ambrose promised: "In your uterus you will receive the Holy Spirit and bring forth the spirit of God."[47] This comment was certainly a praise for this part of the female body.

Two little-known letters from an anonymous fourth-century Spanish virgin vividly demonstrate how some people embraced the idea of spiritual fruits generated from virgins' wombs. She wrote the first of these letters to a friend to express the benefits that would come from her virginal vow: the images she uses are those most frequently associated with fertility.

45. Salisbury, *Church Fathers, Independent Virgins,* 113.
46. Salisbury, *Church Fathers, Independent Virgins,* 114.
47. Ambrose, "De Institutione Virginitate," *PL* 16:345.

In this three-page letter, she uses some form of the word "fertility" eight times. The complex images she uses echo Ambrose's promise of spiritual fruits centered in a woman's uterus. She writes: "Fruit pours forth from your womb; that you may carry your child [wisdom] about and show it . . . to us survivors of a darkened generation."[48] For this woman, the renunciation of fecundity yielded spiritual fruits that could benefit the community. This sentiment exactly paralleled the ideas that had surrounded virgin martyrs such as Eulalia, whose blood Prudentius promised would help the faithful.

The second letter shares the same themes, but the Spanish virgin addressed it to a married friend. She urges her friend to withdraw from her family for a while to an isolated retreat, where she can fast and pray for three weeks, a time meant to be restorative in its imitation of the Virgin Mary's postpartum recuperation. During this time, as she writes, "with the box of your body in flood," you might receive a divine revelation.[49] This is a remarkable letter for several reasons. In the first place, she claims that even a married woman could obtain the spiritual fruits that Ambrose promised virgins. Furthermore, the revelation might come during menstruation, a time that most men considered to be unclean. Texts like these appeared even in the most misogynist years of the Middle Ages, sanctifying all parts of a woman's body.

Women's breasts, while considered sexual, were also symbols of nurturing and motherhood, and as such they became rich symbols through which women's bodies became linked to Christ's body in the arenas of martyrdom. Maternal imagery came naturally to those who wrote about the martyrs: Christian deaths seemed like a "birth" into eternal life. Eusebius, for example, quotes confessors who acknowledged Christ as a "martyr-witness and firstborn of the dead." Eusebius continued the birth metaphor when he described Christians who were threatened with death in Gaul. Of those arrested, some were too frightened to confess and accept martyrdom. Of these he said, "Some ten proved stillborn, causing us great distress."[50] At their moment of potential rebirth, these failed the test and died.

However, we readily mix metaphors as we link related ideas in our

48. G. Morin, "Deux lettres mystiques d'une ascete espagnola," *Revue Benedictine* 40 (1928): 294.

49. Morin, "Deux lettres mystiques," 301.

50. Eusebius, *History of the Church,* 204, 195.

minds, and martyrs were quickly transformed from children newly born in the blood of torture to mothers, whose blood can nurture a growing Christian community. Eusebius and others who witnessed the fortitude of Christians standing firm while being tortured believed that they had acquired special intercessory powers, even if they had not died into eternal life. Eusebius describes these confessors as "mothers" who could help those Christians who had been weak in their resistance. Eusebius says that they had the power to forgive the lapsed, allowing the church to receive "her stillborn children back alive." He develops this idea further, writing that the confessors "bestowed [prayers] with motherly affection on those who lacked them. Shedding many tears on their behalf in supplication to the Father, they asked for life and He gave it to them."[51] Thus did martyrs become mothers.

Maternal images also applied to the church itself, an association that would ultimately serve to enhance the images of maternal breasts. Tertullian, for example, makes this association explicit in a letter he wrote at the beginning of the third century to Christians in jail awaiting martyrdom. He refers to food sent to the confessors purchased through the resources of the Christian community: "The nourishment for the body which our Lady Mother the Church [furnished] from her breast."[52] Thus do we have metaphors that link martyrs, mothers, and the church itself — all alike in nurturing the Christian community that grew rapidly through the fourth century, even as the martyrs' blood spilled abundantly.

These images were distributed through the early martyr accounts (through the fourth century), but they really bore fruit in the revision of the passions written later — during the Middle Ages. The most popular of these revisions was Jacobus de Voragine's *The Golden Legend.* Jacobus departed from the original texts as he elaborated on the Acts of the Martyrs, and his transformations reveal the wonderful medieval tendency to emphasize a metaphorical "truth" that underlay the accounts, even at the expense of literal truth that we moderns prefer. In Jacobus's accounts, which certainly stretch the credulity of the modern audience, he makes explicit the link between martyrs, mothers, breasts, blood, and milk.

In one case, Jacobus recounts the martyrdom of Sophia and her three daughters, Faith, Hope, and Charity. The three girls (all virgins) were

51. Eusebius, *History of the Church,* 200, 204-5.

52. Tertullian, "To the Martyrs," in *Disciplinary, Moral, and Ascetical Works,* trans. R. Arbesmann (New York: Fathers of the Church, 1959), 17.

tortured: "Faith therefore first was beaten by thirty-six soldiers; then her breasts were torn off, and from her wounds milk gushed forth, but from her breasts flowed blood."[53]

By describing blood coming from the maiden's breasts, Jacobus explicitly rejects any notion that the martyr was a mother — insisting, instead, that she is a virgin. Yet, by having milk flow from the wounds of martyrdom, he expresses the belief that martyrs served as nurturing mothers to the young church. Here, late in the Middle Ages, we can see that female martyrs are associated less with Christ than with the Virgin Mary, the only woman who was both virgin and mother.

Jacobus expresses the same truths in his account of the martyrdom of Catherine of Alexandria. When she was beheaded, milk — not blood — flowed from her veins.[54] Like Faith, this virgin became a mother at her death to nourish future generations of believers. Mothers like Perpetua had to renounce their maternity to become martyrs, but they joined the ranks of martyrs that future generations would see as mothers to a growing Christian community. These metaphors of maternity that were applied to martyrs helped contribute to the veneration of the Virgin Mother throughout the Middle Ages. But it also helped bring dignity to women's bodies that served to feed the community. In the process, it expanded the metaphors by which we understand the body of Christ.

Carolyn Walker Bynum, in *Holy Feast and Holy Fast*, makes a significant contribution to our understanding of the religious significance of food and of women's bodies in the late Middle Ages. She demonstrates that, in late medieval theology, "food equals body."[55] The theologians repeatedly wrote about Christ's body that had become flesh in the Incarnation, then became food in the Eucharist. The central mystery of the Mass was that humans could become Christlike by eating Christ's body in the wine and bread that had been miraculously transformed on the altar. The seeds of this powerful food metaphor of salvation lay in the early witness of the martyrs, and I will trace these images in order to make the final connection between women's bodies and the body of Christ.

We have seen that many martyrs saw their sacrifice as an imitation of Christ's sacrifice. In their suffering, their bodies were transformed, indeed

53. Jacobus de Voragine, *The Golden Legend*, 592.

54. Jacobus de Voragine, *The Golden Legend*, 715.

55. Carolyn Walker Bynum, *Holy Food and Holy Fast* (Berkeley: University of California Press, 1987), 250-51.

sanctified, into an imitation of Christ's broken body. If this was the case, were their bodies transformed into food just as Christ's had been when he urged the faithful to "take, eat, this is my body which is given for you"? The body as food metaphor is highly ambivalent. On the one hand, people feared the dismemberment and dissolution of the body, which was death itself. The flesh of the martyrs that was consumed by beasts in the arena was but a visible example of everyone's flesh, which is digested into death. Tertullian describes the process that consumed bodies: "[T]he devouring fires, and the waters of the sea, and the maws of beasts, and the crops of birds and the stomach of fishes, and time's own great gullet itself."[56] Therefore, death is dissolution by digestion, and even many of the images of hell drawn throughout the Middle Ages portray hell as a great mouth that consumes the damned.

Salvation, on the other hand, is a victory of decay, but how does this victory take place? Bodies were transformed into "indigestible" saved bodies when they consumed Christ's body, which was broken on the cross and consumed on the altar. Early in the second century the martyr Ignatius demonstrated how his imitation of Christ's death proved a victory over dismemberment and digestion. He says: "Leave me to be a meal for the beasts, for it is they who can provide my way to God. I am His wheat, ground fine by the lions' teeth to be made purest bread for Christ."[57] In imitation of Christ, Ignatius's body would become food to be consumed — then saved — by Christ himself.

It is within this understanding of the saved body as food that we can understand the focus on female martyrs' breasts and the spilling of nurturing milk. What more vivid image could there be of the body as food than this? The bodies of women martyrs become food, and this image continues into the late Middle Ages, long after the age of early martyrdom ended. The cult of the Virgin Mary's milk was extremely popular in the late Middle Ages, and the allegorical figure of the church was also frequently shown as a nursing mother.[58] The art of the late-medieval age and the visions of late-medieval mystics were full of the idea of the nursing mother as a vehicle for salvation. These images even contributed to an enriching of the idea of Christ's body as well: sometimes Christ himself was portrayed as a nurturing female.

56. Tertullian, "On the Resurrection of the Flesh," 548.

57. Ignatius of Antioch, "Letter to the Romans," in *Early Christian Writings*, 104.

58. Bynum, *Holy Food and Holy Fast*, 270.

In a striking reversal of Perpetua's dream, in which she was transformed into a man, the Montanist prophet Priscilla dreamed that Christ was transformed into a woman: "Christ came to me in the form of a woman clothed with a long, gleaming, flowing robe, and placed wisdom in me. . . ."[59] But it was not only a female heretic who described the body of Christ in female terms. The venerated Eastern church father Clement of Alexandria also developed this image, speaking of the "milk of Christ" and further claiming that Christ said, "I have given you milk to drink."[60] In fact, throughout the late Middle Ages, artists portrayed the wound in Christ's side as a breast that fed the faithful, and as Bynum has noted, "women found it very easy to identify with a deity whose flesh, like theirs, was food."[61]

What has this tour through the medieval images of martyrs shown us about witness, women's bodies, and the body of Christ? Certainly, these multivalent images demonstrate that orthodox Christianity, with its embrace of the body, took an approach to gender that was very different from that of the early Gnostics. In a Gnostic text that intended to devalue the flesh and the genders that make up the body's identity, the author claims that the Lord says, "When you trample on the robe of shame [that is, the body], and when the two shall be one . . . there is neither male nor female."[62]

The Christian martyrdoms, on the other hand, served to vindicate — indeed sanctify — the flesh, and the faithful believe that the genders will be maintained in heaven. Saved bodies will be both male and female. Here on earth there is also redemption for female bodies. In spite of much misogynistic commentary, the experience of the female martyrs offered the possibility that women here on earth need not suffer any shame. Their bodies, too, were created in the image of the body of Christ, which, like a good mother, spilled blood — and even milk — to nurture the faithful.

59. F. C. Klawiter, "The Role of Martyrdom and Persecution in Developing the Priestly Authority of Women in Early Christianity: A Case Study of Montanism," in Ferguson, *Studies in Early Christianity,* 253.

60. Clement, "The Instructor," in *Ante-Nicene Fathers,* ed. A. Roberts and James Donaldson (Peabody, MA: Hendrickson, 1995), 2:218.

61. Bynum, *Holy Food and Holy Fast,* 275.

62. McGuire, "Women, Gender, and Gnosis," 265.

CHAPTER 5

The Judgment of the Eucharist at the Trial of Joan of Arc

Ann W. Astell

Take everything peacefully. Have no care for thy martyrdom.

Voices of Saint Joan

Early on May 30, 1431, the morning of her execution at the stake, Saint Joan of Arc received communion devoutly in her prison cell with the express permission of the bishop of Beauvais, Pierre Cauchon (1371-1442), who had presided at her trial. The fact that the body of Christ had been granted to her before her death as a condemned heretic was so extraordinary in itself — so contrary in its witness — that it later provided one of several rationales for the nullification in 1456 of the verdict against her. More than anything in her remarkable history, Joan's final communion, her fervent feasting on the quintessential "food of martyrs," has come to symbolize her sanctity, ironically overturning the calculated strategy of her prosecutors, who had used the Eucharist during Joan's prolonged confinement as a means to test and ultimately to condemn her.[1]

In the trial of Joan of Arc, the movement "from judgment to passion" (to use Rachel Fulton's memorable phrase) is so rapid that it brings together in a single history the two poles of eucharistic understanding that had anchored the early and the late Middle Ages, respectively. In her mag-

1. On the meaning of this ancient eucharistic title, see Caroline Walker Bynum, *The Resurrection of the Body in Western Christianity, 200-1336* (New York: Columbia University Press, 1995), 56, 80.

isterial book *From Judgment to Passion: Devotion to Christ and the Virgin Mary, 800-1200,* Fulton has shown that the earlier Middle Ages brought to the fore the apocalyptical dimension of eucharistic reception as an anticipation of, and preparation for, the Final Judgment, whereas the High Middle Ages emphasized instead a compassionate identification with the suffering Jesus, whose death and resurrection were re-presented at every Mass.[2] In *Eating Beauty: The Eucharist and the Spiritual Arts of the Middle Ages,* I have observed that the early modern period saw a pronounced return (albeit in another key) to the theme of eucharistic judgment.[3] In this essay I argue that the late-medieval trial of Joan of Arc brings these contrary but intrinsically related images of the Eucharist — as just judge and as a suffering prisoner unjustly condemned — into a strongly marked opposition that resolves itself, ultimately, in a synthesis of the two. What was intended as a juridical proof of Joan's heterodoxy becomes the vindication of her Christian faith. The Eucharist whom Joan finally receives — and with whom she identifies herself in her martyrdom — becomes at once her advocate and her judge, effectively nullifying the historical verdict of her jurors at Rouen.

From the beginning of her trial, Joan herself kept the jury anxiously aware that its own actions were being witnessed not only by report throughout Europe, but also by a higher, heavenly court. The record of the 1431 trial of Joan of Arc at Rouen is saturated with her performative utterances, perlocutionary "speech acts" that render others imaginatively present to her addressees.[4] Again and again, Joan concludes her responses to her interrogators with the words: "I submit myself to God." She indicates that she must seek the counsel of her voices before replying to some questions. She reports what her voices have told her, thus allowing them to speak through her. She remembers what she herself has said to others and what others have said to her, representing the past dramatically. She appeals to the Council of Basel (1431-39) and to the pope, the very mention of

2. Rachel Fulton, *From Judgment to Passion: Devotion to Christ and the Virgin Mary, 800-1200* (New York: Columbia University Press, 2002).

3. Ann W. Astell, *Eating Beauty: The Eucharist and the Spiritual Arts of the Middle Ages* (Ithaca: Cornell University Press, 2006). See, esp., chap. 6, "The Eucharist, the *Spiritual Exercises,* and the Art of Obedience: Saint Ignatius of Loyola and Michelangelo."

4. See the seminal works in speech-act theory by J. L. Austin, *How to Do Things with Words,* the William James Lectures delivered at Harvard University in 1965, ed. J. O. Urmson (Oxford: Clarendon Press, 1962), and John Searle, *Speech Acts: An Essay in the Philosophy of Language* (Cambridge: Cambridge University Press, 1969).

whose name had the legal power to suspend the proceedings.[5] At the start of the third public examination, and again during the fifth private one (conducted in her prison cell), she reminds the presiding judge, Pierre Cauchon, that he, too, stands under judgment: "You say that you are my judge; I do not know if you are this, but be well advised that you do not judge poorly, because you would put yourself in great danger."[6]

"You say you are my judge." Joan's language calls Cauchon's authority into question, even as it suggests the presence of another judge, invisible and transcendent, the "God" who, she says, "sent her."[7] On March 17, when asked if she "would submit her words and deeds to the verdict of the church," she had replied, "'I submit myself to God who sent me [*qui me misit*].'"[8]

"Ita missa est," the Latin sentence with which the celebration of the Eucharist ends, ties the very meaning of the Mass *(missa)* to mission, to being sent forth as witnesses, and to final accountability to Christ, the innocent victim, unjustly condemned, who has become the judge. As Saint Peter explained to the people of Caesarea, "They killed him, hanging him on a tree. But God raised him on the third day. . . . He charged us to preach to the people and to testify that he it is who has been appointed by God to be judge of the living and of the dead" (Acts 10:39-42).[9] Saint Paul similarly ties the Eucharist, as a memorial of the passion of Christ, to the theme of judgment in 1 Corinthians 11:27-32, the *locus classicus* for all subsequent discus-

5. See the testimonies of Jean Massieu, Martin Ladvenu, Guillaume Manchon, and Isambart de la Pierre, which were given in the inquest after Joan's death, in *Procès en nullité de la condamnation de Jeanne D'Arc,* 5 vols., ed. Pierre Duparc (Paris: Librairie C. Klincksieck, 1977-88), 1:189, 215, 223, 235, 432.

6. *Joan of Arc, La Pucelle: Selected Sources Translated and Annotated,* trans. Craig Taylor (Manchester, UK: Manchester University Press, 2006), 188 (see also 146); *Procès de condamnation de Jeanne D'Arc,* ed. Pierre Tisset (Paris: Librairie C. Klincksieck, 1960), 1:147-48.

7. *Joan of Arc, La Pucelle,* 197.

8. *Joan of Arc, La Pucelle,* 197; *Procès de condamnation,* 1:166. Karen Sullivan has shown that Joan characteristically refers to "God" and to her "Voices" as the sources of her calling in the early part of the trial proceedings; she only gradually specifies particular saints as her interrogators press her. See Sullivan, *The Interrogation of Joan of Arc,* Medieval Cultures 20 (Minneapolis: University of Minnesota Press, 1999); see also Sullivan, "'I Do Not Name to You the Voice of St. Michael': The Identification of Joan of Arc's Voices," in *Fresh Verdicts on Joan of Arc,* ed. Bonnie Wheeler and Charles T. Wood (New York: Garland, 1996), 85-112.

9. I use *The Holy Bible, Old Testament in the Douay-Challoner Text, New Testament and Psalms in the Confraternity Text,* ed. John P. O'Connell (Chicago: The Catholic Press, 1950).

sions of excommunication: "Whoever eats this bread or drinks the cup of the Lord unworthily, will be guilty of the body and the blood of the Lord. . . . He who eats and drinks unworthily, without distinguishing the body, eats and drinks judgment to himself" (vv. 27-29). Gezo of Tortona (AD 984) typifies this tradition when he writes: "The altar is the tribunal of Christ [*tribunal enim Christi altare est*], and his body with his blood judges those who approach it unworthily."[10]

In the pages that follow, I first examine the early course of Joan's trial, analyzing the way that Joan's judges used the Eucharist strategically as a means to determine the state of Joan's soul. Second, I consider how Joan's transvestism became increasingly linked to the question of her eucharistic devotion and how that combination of concerns came to support (in the minds of her prosecutors and judges) the charge of idolatry against her. Third, I take up the historical questions that surround her last communion, received on the morning of her martyrdom. Finally, I turn to a theo-aesthetical contemplation of that last communion as an act of divine justice and Jehannine beauty. I argue that the course of Joan's trial led from the antagonistic perception of her as an anti-Eucharist (outwardly male, inwardly female and feminine) to the recognition of Joan, even by her prosecutors, as a eucharistic martyr, whose complete loss of an outwardly appearing body in the flames attested to her substantial union with Christ.

Joan's Ordeal of Excommunication

Prior to her capture at Compiègne on May 23, 1430, Joan had been a frequent communicant, a practice that associated her, in the minds of her supporters, with piety and orthodoxy but that also aroused the inimical suspicions of others, those who imputed to Joan an attitude of presumption and disrespect for the Eucharist. The 1455 petition of Joan's mother, Isabelle Rommée, which called for an invalidation of the 1431 verdict against her daughter, mentions that, as a child in Domremy, Joan "received the Eucharist almost every month, even though at an early age, after having duly confessed."[11] This account of Joan's eucharistic piety is corroborated by the testimony that villagers who knew Joan gave during the 1456 inquest. Jean de

10. Gezo of Tortona, *De corpore*, PL 137, col. 391, quoted in Fulton, *From Judgment to Passion*, 56.

11. *Joan of Arc, La Pucelle*, 264; *Procès en nullité de la condamnation*, 1:9.

Nouillonpont and Bertrand de Poulengy, who accompanied Joan on her historic journey from Vaucouleurs to Chinon in January 1429, both testified to her desire to attend Mass on the way: "'If we can hear the Mass,'" she is reported to have said, "'we shall do well.'"[12] In his deposition during the inquest at Orléans, Master Francois Garivel declares of Joan: "This was a simple shepherdess who loved God very much, because she confessed often and frequently received the sacrament of the Eucharist."[13]

The frequency of Joan's communions varied according to the circumstances in which she found herself. The Duke of Alençon reports that "he saw her receive the body of Christ many times, and when she looked at the body of Christ she often shed many tears. She received the Eucharist twice a week and confessed often."[14] The testimony of Jean Pasqueral is similar. "Joan was," he testified, "very pious toward God and the holy Virgin, confessing nearly every day and receiving communion frequently."[15] According to Jean d'Aulon, Joan was a "très dévote créature," who "with great devotion wanted to hear the divine service of our Lord constantly. . . . And she was used to hearing Mass every day, if possible."[16]

Joan's judges at Rouen knew firsthand, as well as by report, of her eucharistic devotion, because she begged them repeatedly to allow her to attend Mass and to receive the sacraments. These ardent requests both preceded the official opening of the trial and punctuated it. On Wednesday, February 21, 1431, shortly before Joan was led in to make her first appearance before her judges, Cauchon explained to the assembly that "the woman had asked to hear Mass first," but that, after consultation "with worthy lords and masters," he concluded that "we should postpone permission for her to hear Mass or attend divine office," because of the grave "crimes of which she was accused and the shameful attire [*difformitate habitus*] she insisted on wearing."[17]

Joan was, in short, formally excommunicated as a suspected heretic from the start. If Joan were, in fact, a heretic — albeit not yet proven to be one — she was already excommunicated, since heresy was a crime that en-

12. *Joan of Arc, La Pucelle,* 272 (cf. 277); *Procès en nullité de la condamnation,* 1:291 (cf. 306).

13. *Joan of Arc, La Pucelle,* 286; *Procès en nullité de la condamnation,* 1:328-29.

14. *Joan of Arc, La Pucelle,* 309; *Procès en nullité de la condamnation,* 1:387.

15. *Joan of Arc, La Pucelle,* 312; *Procès en nullité de la condamnation,* 1:390.

16. *Joan of Arc, La Pucelle,* 347; *Procès en nullité de la condamnation,* 1:486.

17. *The Trial of Joan of Arc,* trans. Daniel Hobbins (Cambridge, MA: Harvard University Press, 2005), 48; *Procès de condamnation,* 1:36.

tailed "automatic excommunication."[18] According to the canon *Si quis suadente,* promulgated at the Second Lateran Council in 1139, the "sentence" of excommunication "took effect immediately after the crime was committed."[19] The offender, in effect, excommunicated him- or herself by breaking faith with the church, its doctrines, its teaching authority, and its sacraments. Joan's judges were allowing for the possibility of excommunication *latae sententiae,* but they were doing more. Elisabeth Vodola explains the significance of the postponement of permission to hear Mass:

> For suspected heretics . . . excommunication was a test: after one year they could be convicted as heretics. Since the sacramental doctrines were emerging as the touchstones of orthodoxy both in the decretals on heresy and in the creed of the Fourth Lateran Council (1215), a willingness to forgo the sacraments for a year or more, quite apart from implying contumacy toward ecclesiastical authorities, *per se,* gave rise to a legal presumption of contempt for the sacraments and therefore of heresy.[20]

Already at the start of the trial, Cauchon had based his decision to excommunicate Joan, at least in part, on her wearing of disgraceful attire. However, her obvious desire for the Eucharist made the accusation that she held the sacrament in disrespect hard to support. As I have noted above, she begged explicitly to be allowed to hear Mass at the commencement of the proceedings. Denied that privilege, she asked Jean Massieu, who was conducting her from her prison cell to a public interrogation, whether "there was some chapel or church en route at which was the *Corpus Christi* [the Eucharist]."[21] When he replied that there was "a chapel situated under the castle where the body of Christ was," Joan begged to be taken there that she might "pay respect to God . . . and pray."[22] When Massieu willingly granted her request, according to his sworn testimony years later, on May 12, 1456, she prayed "on her knees before the chapel . . . very devotedly."[23] Joan was not allowed to enter the chapel, presumably to prevent her from receiving a

18. Elisabeth Vodola, *Excommunication in the Middle Ages* (Berkeley: University of California Press, 1986), 29.

19. Vodola, *Excommunication,* 28-29.

20. Vodola, *Excommunication,* 32.

21. *Joan of Arc, La Pucelle,* 331; *Procès en nullité de la condamnation,* 1:429.

22. *Joan of Arc, La Pucelle,* 331; *Procès en nullité de la condamnation,* 1:429.

23. *Joan of Arc, La Pucelle,* 331; *Procès en nullité de la condamnation,* 1:429.

"spiritual communion" — that is, a sacramental reception through an eating with the eyes, a gaze upon the elevated or exposed host, or even a look upon the tabernacle housing the consecrated host — the kind of communion that involves a directed longing from a distance. She prayed "before the chapel," but the devout proximity of Joan to the sacrament was, in the view of Cauchon, a violation of her formal excommunication, one that seriously undermined its effectiveness as a test for heresy. Massieu reports that "the Lord Bishop was very angry at this and commanded [him] not to allow her to come there to pray in this way."[24]

At the second public examination on February 22, 1431, Joan was asked about her keeping of the church law that required her to confess her sins "each year" and to receive the Eucharist "at Easter." She replied in the affirmative, but she told the interrogator to "move on" when he asked "if she received the Eucharist at other feasts than Easter." She reported having heard Mass at the cathedral in Auxerre on her way to Chinon.[25] At the fourth public examination on Tuesday, February 27, when asked if she had been at Sainte-Catherine-de-Fierbois, where she later directed that a sword be found, "she answered yes, and that she heard three masses in one day there."[26]

Joan's Transvestism and Eucharistic Transubstantiation

At each of the examinations, Joan was asked about her wearing of men's clothes: why she did so, at whose instructions, and under what conditions. Although there were women saints who had disguised themselves as men, there was no precedent for Joan's practice, which did not conceal her feminine identity.[27] The scriptural mandate against cross-dressing in Deuteronomy 22:5 and Saint Paul's opposition to the cutting of women's hair (1 Cor. 11:6) made Joan's masculine attire the object of intense moral scrutiny.

24. *Joan of Arc, La Pucelle,* 331; *Procès en nullité de la condamnation,* 1:429.

25. *Joan of Arc, La Pucelle,* 141-43; *Procès de condamnation,* 1:46-47, 50.

26. *Joan of Arc, La Pucelle,* 155; *Procès de condamnation,* 1:76.

27. On this subject, see Susan Crane, "Clothing and Gender Definition: Joan of Arc," *Journal of Medieval and Early Modern Studies* 26, no. 2 (1996): 297-320; Valerie R. Hotchkiss, "Transvestism on Trial: The Case of Jeanne d'Arc," in *Clothes Make the Man: Female Cross-Dressing in Medieval Europe,* The New Middle Ages 1 (New York: Garland, 1996), 49-68; Susan Schibanoff, "True Lies: Transvestism and Idolatry in the Trial of Joan of Arc," in Wheeler and Wood, *Fresh Verdicts on Joan of Arc,* 49-68.

However, it was only at the sixth public examination on Saturday, March 3, eleven days after the commencement of the proceedings, that the issue of her male clothes was explicitly connected to her eucharistic reception.

> Asked if, when she was going through the country, she often received the sacrament of the Eucharist and of penance, when she was in the towns, she answered yes, from time to time. Asked if she received these sacraments in male clothing, she answered yes, but she did not remember receiving them in armour.[28]

There is in this combination of questions the inference that there was something improper or disrespectful in Joan's receiving communion while so dressed, but a culpable intention of disrespect was, the judges realized, hard to prove. The linkage of Joan's wearing of male clothes to her eucharistic reception suggested a strategy, however, that the judges subsequently followed as they pitted Joan's strong two desires — to dress like a man (thus affirming her fidelity to her special vocation as "the Maid") and to receive the body of Christ — against each other.[29]

The private examination of Joan began on Saturday, March 10. At the seventh of these private examinations, conducted in her prison cell, Joan's explicit request to be allowed to hear Mass prompted a series of questions that allowed her judges to use Joan's excommunication (so painful to her) as a test of her orthodoxy in the Lenten weeks immediately preceding Easter. The transcript of the interrogation, in Craig Taylor's translation, reads as follows:

> Since she had asked to hear mass, she was asked whether it did not seem to her more respectable to wear female clothing [*deferre habitum*

28. *Joan of Arc, La Pucelle,* 171; *Procès de condamnation,* 1:102.

29. Much has been written about Joan's motives for wearing masculine attire from the time she began her mission to save France — that is, from the time she left Vaucouleurs with authorization from Robert de Baudricourt to go to the Dauphin's court at Chinon in February 1429. Joan herself cites different reasons on various occasions, referring to God's will, to the practicalities of her work in the army, and to her concern to protect her virginity in the company of men, both in the field and especially in the prison, where she was guarded by males. Valerie Hotchkiss has usefully suggested that Joan, who also wore masculine attire in the putative safety of the court of Charles VII, may have regarded that attire as analogous to a religious habit, as a sign of her special vocation from God. See Hotchkiss, "Transvestism on Trial," in *Clothes Make the Man,* 51. In the Latin transcript, Joan refers consistently to her male clothes as her *habitus.*

> *muliebrem*]; and she was asked which she would like better, to take the clothing of a woman and to hear mass [*capere habitum muliebrem et audire missam*], or to remain in male clothing and not to hear mass [*manere in habitu virili et non audire missam*]. She replied: "Promise me [*certificetis me*] that I will hear mass [*de audiendo missam*] if I am in the clothing of a woman, and I will give you my answer."
>
> Then the interrogator said to her: "I myself guarantee [*certifico*] that you will hear mass if you are in the clothing of a woman." She answered: "And what do you say if I have promised and sworn [*promisi . . . et iuravi*] to our King not to set aside [*non deponere*] this clothing?"[30]

This first exchange between Joan and her interrogator shows the Maid's distrust of his promise, for which she seeks a legal guarantee, a certification. She opposes his promise of conditional access to the Eucharist to the unconditional promise and vow that she has made to "our King" (a phrase calculated to remind her judge that they have a common obligation and loyalty to God) never to abandon her male dress *(habitus)* and the divine mission it both symbolizes and enables her to fulfill. She understands that putting off *(deponere)* her masculine clothes would amount to a testimony, a deposition, in denial of her calling from God to save France.

Joan's desire to receive communion is so great, however, that she goes on to indicate that she would be willing to wear a "long dress" during Mass, but only for that purpose and occasion: "Nevertheless I reply to you: have a long dress [*tunica longam*] reaching down to the ground made for me, without a train [*sine cauda*], and give it to me to go to mass; and then, on my return, I will put on again my present clothing [*ego iterum capiam istum habitum quem habeo*]."[31] Joan seems to reason that such a time-bound concession to her judges would neither violate her vow nor betray her vocation. The request for a long dress is in keeping with her awareness of her rank and her concern for modest protection. The stipulation "without a train" indicates that she is not asking to be treated like a woman of nobility. She is obviously trying to imagine feminine attire that her judges would regard as appropriate to her social status and respectful of the Eucharist.

However, she remains distrustful of her judges' intentions as they continue to press her for an unconditional response; and she is unsure of the will of her voices in this matter:

30. *Joan of Arc, La Pucelle,* 193; *Procès de condamnation,* 1:156-57.

31. *Joan of Arc, La Pucelle,* 193; *Procès de condamnation,* 1:157.

> Asked again if she would wear the clothing of a woman to go to hear mass, she replied: "I will take counsel [*habebo consilium*] on this and then I will answer you." And then she requested for the honour of God and of Blessed Mary that she be allowed to hear mass in this good town [*bona villa*].
>
> And at this the interrogator told her to put on the clothing of a woman, simply and absolutely [*simpliciter et absolute*]. She answered: "Give me a dress like that of the daughter of a bourgeois, that is to say, a long *houppelande* [a loose-fitting greatcoat], and I will wear it to go and hear mass." She added that she again begged most insistently that she be allowed to hear mass in the outfit that she wore, without changing it [*absque ipsum immutando*].[32]

The relative length of this passage — a sustained probing into a single issue — indicates its importance. Joan's initial request to be allowed to go to Mass gives rise to a series of counterquestions by her judges. The interrogators at this session — Jean de la Fontaine, Nicolas Midi, Gérard Feuillet, Nicolas de Hubent, and Isambart de la Pierre — are trying to force Joan to choose between the Eucharist and her male clothes, the emblem of her vocation, by making the renunciation of those clothes a condition for receiving the Eucharist. Since an annual reception of the sacrament is a Christian's "Easter duty," a matter of obedience to church law, any obedience to her voices that renders her effectively disobedient to the church would manifest the diabolical and idolatrous nature of her voices, her supposed saints, for no true saint would devalue the Eucharist or counsel her to disobedience.

For her part, Joan endeavors valiantly to turn the "either/or" with which they confront her into a "both/and." She is perfectly willing to wear women's clothes, particularly a respectful attire appropriate to her social status, when she receives the Eucharist, if she is indeed given such clothes and such an opportunity, but not to renounce male clothes unconditionally. If no both/and solution to the dilemma can be found, Joan begs simply to be allowed to receive the Eucharist dressed as she is, obedient both to the church and to her voices.

In the eighth private examination (March 17, 1431), held two days later in her cell, Joan was asked again "on the subject of a woman's clothing that was offered to her so that she could go to hear Mass," and she re-

32. *Joan of Arc, La Pucell,* 193-94; *Procès de condamnation,* 1:157-58.

plied that "she still would not take it as long as God liked."[33] On Palm Sunday, March 25, matters came to a head, with Bishop Cauchon demanding that Joan abandon her male clothing in order to be allowed to hear Mass, and Joan begging to be able to attend Mass and receive the Eucharist at Easter in her male clothes. Refusing to answer her directly and making no promises, they asked her "to reply to what she had been asked," namely, "whether she was willing to abandon the clothing of a man if this had been granted her." Pleading, Joan again asked "to hear Mass . . . which she desired to the highest degree," adding that "she could not change her outfit [*habitum mutare non poterat*]." Her judges insisted that she "speak with her voices [*loqueretur cum vocibus suis*] to find out if she could receive [*recipere*] and resume wearing women's clothing in order to receive the Eucharist [*percipere viaticum*] at Easter." Realizing that such a charge effectively put her voices on trial with her, pitting their authority against the will of her judges, Joan repeated that she could not receive communion at the cost of changing her habit *(mutando habitum suum)* and begged for them to permit her "to hear Mass in the clothing of a man, saying that this would not change her soul, and that to wear it was not against the Church."[34]

Joan's comment — "this would not change [*non onerabat*] her soul" — suggests an associational pattern that helps to explain the triadic relationship between her male costume, the Eucharist, and the charge of idolatry. Taylor's translation of *non onerabat* as "would not change" is admittedly tendentious. The Latin verb might be translated as "was not being burdened" or "weighed down" (with guilt?) on account of "carrying" *(portare)* male clothes. However, the notion of a spiritual change is suggested by the context, with its clustering of verbs calling for a change of clothes — *habitum mutare, mutando habitum* — in association with the eucharistic miracle of transubstantiation and by the parallel drawn by the interrogators between Joan's proper receiving *(percipere)* of communion and the reception *(recipere)* of women's clothes.

To choose male clothing (and the obedience to her voices that it symbolized) rather than the Eucharist (especially the annual communion mandated by church law) was, in the understanding of Joan's judges, to

33. *Joan of Arc, La Pucelle,* 198; *Procès de condamnation,* 1:167.

34. *Joan of Arc, La Pucelle,* 205; *Procès de condamnation,* 1:182; *Procès de condamnation,* 1:182; *Procès de condamnation,* 1:183. Earlier in the same interrogation, Joan states that she is not able to receive *(recipere)* women's clothes (see *Procès de condamnation,* 1:182); *Procès de condamnation,* 1:183.

commit idolatry, to worship a false god. This false god was, moreover, viewed as a diabolic mimicry, an anti-Eucharist. The Eucharist, after all, appeared to be one thing — bread — even as it was in reality something else — namely, Christ himself. Jesus had called himself "living Bread" (John 6:51), and bread fittingly symbolized the power of the Eucharist to feed the soul; but the bread itself was only an appearance, not the substance of the sacrament. Joan also appeared to be one thing, for she dressed as a man, but she was in reality something else. Her feminine "soul" *(anima)* was, she declared, "unchanged," "unburdened," even though she had adopted masculine clothes.

The association of Joan's feminine soul and female body, dressed in male clothes, with the Eucharist suggests an underlying fear on the part of Joan's judges of sex and gender change as a diabolical counterpart to eucharistic transubstantiation. God became human, incarnate, at the "fiat" of the Virgin (a mystery frequently compared to that of transubstantiation.)[35] If bread can become Christ's body through consecration, could not a woman become masculine, or a man feminine, while retaining an opposite appearance? Did not Saint Paul declare in Galatians 3:28, "There is neither Jew nor Greek; there is neither slave nor freeman; there is neither male nor female, for you are all one in Christ Jesus"?

Susan Schibanoff has written insightfully that Joan's transvestism was what made her supposed idolatry overt, because, unlike Christian icons and sacramentals, her male clothes were neither simple signs of a true masculinity nor a "true" lie that belied itself by pointing to an unmistakably other, feminine reality. Rather, Joan's male clothes constituted an idolatrous, "false" lie, "for it demanded that the viewer pay it reverence by attending to its corporeality, its accidents and externals."[36] Curiously, Schibanoff does not triangulate her study of transvestism and idolatry in the trial of Joan of Arc to see the specifically eucharistic implications of that pairing. When Joan's judges asked her to choose between her transvestism and her voices, on the one hand, and the Eucharist, on the other, they were clearly casting Joan's male clothes in the role of an idol, an anti-Eucharist, a rival to the sacrament.

Nadia Margolis has pondered deeply the ways that the "mortal body"

35. See James T. O'Connor, *The Hidden Manna: A Theology of the Eucharist,* 2nd ed. (San Francisco: Ignatius Press, 2005), 349-56; Astell, *Eating Beauty,* 58-61.

36. Schibanoff, "True Lies: Transvestism and Idolatry in the Trial of Joan of Arc," in Wheeler and Wood, *Fresh Verdicts on Joan of Arc,* 45.

of Joan of Arc functioned as a "divine proof," a eucharistic "sacramental" for Joan's followers, who discerned in "her body's religious symbolism" outward signs of "God's inward action."[37] Joan's ears heard voices; her eyes saw visions; her body was virginal, untouched. Her lips spoke in prophecy and received communion. "The most profound sacrament, the Eucharist, . . . was fervently practiced by Joan," writes Margolis, and the result was that Joan herself acquired a distinctly eucharistic identity.[38]

A close reading of the eucharistic references in the transcript of the 1431 trial offers additional proof for Margolis's argument, but from an adversarial position. Joan's judges sensed her physical and spiritual closeness to the Eucharist, but they regarded it not as an *imitatio Christi*, a following of Christ, but as a diabolical aping of the sacrament.

Two of the Twelve Articles of Accusation drawn up by Joan's judges and submitted to the theologians and canon lawyers at the University of Paris on April 5, 1431, refer to Joan's obstinate refusal to attend Mass at the cost of wearing a woman's clothing. An excerpt from Article One reads: "She has even chosen not to be present at the office of Mass and to be deprived of the sacred communion of the Eucharist at the times ordained by the Church for the faithful to receive the sacrament, rather than resume the clothing of a woman and abandon the clothing of a man."[39] In Article Five her male clothes are described in detail, along with her claims that she wears such clothes in obedience to God. Her disobedience to God's true commands and express prohibitions has translated, moreover, into disrespect for the sacrament: "And she has frequently received the Eucharist in this garb."[40]

Basing its opinion on these articles, the faculty of theology at the University of Paris concluded: "The said woman is a blasphemer of God and a despiser of God in His sacraments, setting aside divine law, sacred doctrine, and the laws of the Church."[41] The faculty of canon law, citing the "long time" *(per longa tempora)* in which Joan has held to her heretical opinions, declared her condition an *anathema*, the most severe form of excommunication, and noted: "She says she would prefer not to receive the

37. Nadia Margolis, "The Mortal Body as Divine Proof: A Spiritual and Physical Blazon of Joan of Arc," in *Joan of Arc and Spirituality*, ed. Ann W. Astell and Bonnie Wheeler (New York: Palgrave, 2003), 12, 19.

38. Margolis, "The Mortal Body," 12.

39. *Joan of Arc, La Pucelle*, 208; *Procès de condamnation*, 1:291.

40. *Joan of Arc, La Pucelle* 210; *Procès de condamnation*, 1:293.

41. *Joan of Arc, La Pucelle*, 213; *Procès de condamnation*, 1:361.

body of Christ or to confess herself at the time ordained by the Church, rather than to resume woman's clothing after giving up the garb of a man."[42]

On Wednesday, April 18, Joan was ill and in grave danger of death. When Cauchon visited Joan in her cell, accompanied by seven other theologians, she begged to be allowed to receive the sacraments of penance and the Eucharist and to be buried in holy ground.[43] This time the judges did not refer to her male clothes, but made her reception of the sacraments dependent on her renunciation of her voices, in submission to their opinion as representatives of the church militant. Joan refused this disavowal, stating simply that "she loves God, serves him, and is a good Christian."[44]

Afraid of the fire, Joan eventually abjured, publicly submitting on May 24 to the opinion of her judges, who (as she understood) had promised her that she would be taken to an ecclesiastical prison, guarded by women, and allowed to receive communion there, while wearing woman's clothing. When, on Monday, May 28, Joan was found to be wearing men's clothing again, she declared that "she had resumed it because what had been promised to her had not been kept, that is to say that she might go to mass and receive the body of Christ."[45] As for her voices, she declared that she had heard them again, and that they told her that she had committed "a great wrong" *(magnam iniuriam)* in denying them.[46]

On May 29, the judges met with forty clerics and reached a unanimous decision to proceed against Joan for relapse into heresy. On May 30, the judges addressed Joan, who appeared before them in the Old Market at Rouen, denouncing her on multiple counts as "a relapse and a heretic" *(relapsam et hereticam)* who had "fallen again into the sentence of excommunication."[47] Confirming the excommunication, *latae sententiae,* with an official declaration, the judges pronounced her an "excommunicate by

42. *Joan of Arc, La Pucelle,* 215; *Procès de condamnation,* 1:364.

43. *The Trial of Joan of Arc,* trans. Daniel Hobbins (Cambridge, MA: Harvard University Press, 2005), 167; *Procès de condamnation,* 1:329.

44. *The Trial of Joan of Arc,* 169; *Procès de condemnation,* 1:333.

45. *Joan of Arc, La Pucelle,* 220; *Procès de condemnation,* 1:396. If Joan was attacked (and possibly raped) in her cell, as several witnesses indicate, her resumption of male clothes was also self-protective. There is some evidence, too, that she may have been practically forced to resume wearing male clothes through the guards' withholding of her other clothes.

46. *Joan of Arc, La Pucelle,* 221; *Procès de condemnation,* 1:398.

47. *Joan of Arc, La Pucelle,* 222; *Procès de condemnation,* 1:412.

law" *(ipso iure excommunicatam)* and handed her over to the secular authority for punishment.[48]

Joan's Final Communion

That Joan of Arc was permitted by Cauchon to receive communion on the morning of May 30, after having gone to confession to Friar Martin Ladvenu, is, therefore, hard to explain. There are some inconsistencies between and among the subsequent reports, but Joan certainly received the Eucharist in prison on the day of her execution, with the express permission of the bishop of Beauvais, who had denied her this very privilege during the months of her tortuous trial. According to the recollection of Jean Massieu, Friar Martin sent him to Cauchon "to let him know that she had made her confession and was asking to receive the Eucharist."[49] Cauchon consulted with others on this subject and, after some debate, decided that the Dominican friar should grant her the Eucharist and everything that she requested: "Quod sibi traderet eucharistie sacramentum, et omnia quecumque peteret."[50]

Massieu was present at Joan's communion. He reports that the Eucharist was carried to Joan's cell unceremoniously *(multum irreverenter)* by a priest, Peter Maurice, who was wearing neither a surplice nor a stole *(absque superplicio et stola)*, and who came unaccompanied by any acolytes bearing candles *(sine lumine et sine comitiva)*. Massieu himself went to get a stole and candle, and Joan compensated for these truncated rites with her great devotion and tearful reception of the host.[51]

How can we explain this last communion of Joan? One reconstruction of the events entails Joan's final admission and renunciation of heresy as a precondition for her eucharistic reception, while the other account finds in Cauchon's granting of communion to her a tacit acknowledgment of her moral innocence and orthodoxy. According to a dubious report

48. *Joan of Arc, La Pucelle,* 223; *Procès de condemnation,* 1:414.

49. *Joan of Arc, La Pucelle,* 335; *Procès en nullité de la condemnation,* 1:434-35.

50. *Procès en nullité de la condemnation,* 1:435. Massieu's recollection is corroborated by that of Guillaume Manchon, who affirms that Joan received the Eucharist on the morning of May 30, after Cauchon had sought advice from others: "The judges and the counsellors debated whether the sacrament should be given to her at her request, and if she should be absolved during the act of penitence" (*Joan of Arc, La Pucelle,* 330).

51. *Procès en nullité de la condemnation,* 1:210.

composed on June 7, eight days after her death by fire (a report that purports to contain the sworn testimony of seven witnesses), on the morning of May 30, Joan had declared her realization that the voices she had heard were false, were evil spirits. They had deceived her, she reportedly said, promising her a deliverance from prison that was not to occur. She further admitted that she herself was the angel who had brought a crown to the king; there was no other angel. The crown, too, was a fiction. Finally, according to this document of June 7, before Friar Martin gave her the consecrated host, he interrogated her, asking, "Do you believe that this is the body of Christ?" When Joan said yes, he asked her whether she still believed in her voices. She supposedly replied, "I believe in God alone, and I no longer put any faith in these voices, because they have deceived me."[52]

If this posthumous addendum is to be believed, Joan abjured a second time in the presence of seven of her judges on the morning of her death at the stake, denying in unequivocal terms the voices and the sign that had supposedly been given to Charles VII.[53] While such an abjuration would justify the judges' granting of the Eucharist to her as one who was no longer a heretic, it would also make the subsequent public treatment of Joan scandalously inappropriate. As François Meltzer notes, "Had she really repented, she would have publicly disavowed her voices on the scaffold, and there would have been a benediction and an absolution before the burning. Neither of these occurred."[54] Had she in fact abjured a second time, such a denial from Joan's own mouth would surely have been made public prior to her execution as a relapse, to the great rejoicing of her English enemies and the embarrassment of Charles VII.

Moreover, the report of June 7th conflicts with testimony given in the inquest of 1456. Martin Ladvenu, her confessor on the morning of May 30, testified in the nullification trial that "right up to the end of her life, she maintained and asseverated that the voices she heard were of God, and that all that she had done she had done at God's command, and that she did not believe that she had been deceived by her voices, and that the revelations she had received were from God."[55]

The document of June 7th, therefore, is generally regarded as a

52. *The Trial of Joan of Arc*, 207; *Procés de condemnation*, 1:420.

53. For an argument in favor of a second abjuration, see A. E. Jones, *The Trial of Joan of Arc* (Chichester, 1980), 237.

54. François Meltzer, *For Fear of the Fire: Joan of Arc and the Limits of Subjectivity* (Chicago: University of Chicago Press, 2001), 192-93.

55. *Procès en nullité de la condamnation*, 1:444.

clumsy misrepresentation, concocted after Joan's pious, public death by an anxious Cauchon, who was eager to be able to claim that Joan herself had finally denounced her voices. Guillaume Manchon, the official recorder of the trial proceedings, refused to sign it.[56]

If Joan did not abjure a second time on the morning of May 30, her reception of the sacrament can only be interpreted as a surprising charitable concession to her, a final consolation, and a tacit acknowledgment of her religious orthodoxy. Acting as judge and as a means of judgment, the Eucharist finally exonerated Joan of Arc. Among the twenty-seven articles in the interrogatory of May 4, 1452, witnesses of the proceedings at Rouen were asked to affirm or deny Article Twenty-Three: "That although it was abundantly apparent to the judges that Joan . . . was so faithful a Catholic that she was allowed to receive the body of our Lord, nevertheless, out of their excessive zeal for the English, or not wishing to extricate themselves out of fear and pressure, they most unjustly condemned her as a heretic to the pains of the fire."[57]

In Communion with Christ: Joan's Beautiful Justification

The last communion of Joan of Arc on the morning of May 30 and the saintly way in which she, strengthened by the sacrament, suffered her death disrupted the plot of a heretic's trial and aligned the proceedings instead to the passion and death of Christ. According to eyewitness accounts, even those judges who had believed her a heretic and had assented to her death were shaken by the Christlike way in which she endured it.

What was Joan thinking about the Eucharist when she requested again and again — especially at the approach of Holy Week, on her sickbed, and on the day of her death — to be allowed to receive communion? No doubt she knew that the faithful were expected, indeed obliged, to fulfill their "Easter duty" of confession and communion, and that failure to do so would render her culpable. No doubt, too, she sincerely hungered for the sacrament, which she had always before received frequently and with devotion.

56. On the unreliability of this document, see H. A. Kelly, "Saint Joan and Confession: Internal and External Forum," in *Joan of Arc and Spirituality,* ed. Ann W. Astell and Bonnie Wheeler (New York: Palgrave, 2003), 75-76.

57. Quoted in Régine Pernoud and Marie-Véronique Clin, *Joan of Arc: Her Story,* rev. and trans. Jeremy Duquesnay Adams (New York: St. Martin's Press, 1998), 154-55; *Procès en nullité de la condamnation,* 1:195.

The trial records tell us little about her inner life during her imprisonment, but they do suggest an increasing identification with the Eucharist as a memorial of Christ's passion. Even as the *corpus Christi* was kept in the tabernacle in the chapel beneath the castle, so was she, too, a prisoner. On March 14, she related that her voices had spoken to her of her martyrdom *(de martirio tuo)*, which she understood to mean, at the very least, the pain and adversity that she endured in prison. She declared on March 17 that she believed in her voices as firmly as she "believed that Our Lord Jesus suffered His death and passion for us"[58] — a remarkable statement that shocked her judges, which made her witness to her voices equivalent to a creedal witness to Christ.[59] The promises of being able to stay in an ecclesiastical prison and to receive communion, together with her fear of the fire, seems to have been the primary motive for her abjuration. When she realized that those promises, "that she might go to Mass and receive the Body of Christ," were false, she resigned herself to a different sort of spiritual communion with the eucharistic Lord — the way of obedience to God onto death.[60]

François Meltzer argues in *For Fear of the Fire* that what Joan faced — the utter loss of her body, its consumption by flames — is a terrifying image for the loss of a subjectivity, a consciousness, that is mediated precisely by the body and its boundaries, that which distinguishes the individual from the world, from others. Another Christian martyr, Ignatius of Antioch, faced a similar loss prior to his martyrdom, knowing that his body would be eaten by beasts, completely absorbed into the otherness of their bodies. Isambart de la Pierre, a witness to Joan's execution, compares the martyrdom of Joan of Arc explicitly to that of Ignatius.[61] From the midst of the flames, Joan never ceased to call out and to confess the name of Jesus; she pronounced it, Isambart relates, with her last breath, thus "giving a sure sign of the faith in which she was fervent, as we read in the case of Saint Ignatius and many other holy martyrs."[62]

58. *Joan of Arc, La Pucelle,* 189; *Procès de condamnation,* 1:148; *Joan of Arc, La Pucelle,* 197; *Procès de condamnation,* 1:165.

59. The statement by Joan appears in Article 11 of the Twelve Articles of Accusation (April 5, 1431) that were disseminated for comment to theologians at the University of Paris. See *Joan of Arc, La Pucelle,* 212; *Procès de condamnation,* 1:296.

60. *Joan of Arc, La Pucelle,* 220; *Procès de condamnation,* 1:396.

61. Meltzer notes this comparison of Joan to Ignatius, but she does not draw out the eucharistic significance of it. See *For Fear of the Fire,* 192, 199.

62. Testimony of Isambart de la Pierre, in *La Réhabilitation de Jeanne La Pucelle,*

For Ignatius, as for Joan, the hope and the model for a deeper subjectivity, not dependent on having a body but on surrendering it, was the Eucharist. In the host, after all, the body disappeared, had no appearance that was properly its own. The host itself was an improper appearance — no longer bread, but the mere appearance of bread. Comparing the disappearance of his martyred body to that of Christ in the Eucharist, Ignatius says, "I shall be really a disciple of Jesus Christ if and when the world can no longer see so much as my body."[63]

Joan died crying out "Jesus." Her mortal body, reduced to ashes (with the notable exception of her heart), was utterly lost, eradicated. For a body that Nadia Margolis has described as "sacramental," there could be no more profound eucharistic identification than this. Without referring specifically to the Eucharist, Meltzer reaches a similar conclusion when she says: "At its most 'literal' (for example, the martyrdom of a saint), *caritas* entails not only self-overcoming, or the erasure of self-love in the face of the divine, but also the erasure or at least denial of the concept of otherness. What I mean by this is that difference is willfully unrecognized in anticipation of the transparency to be achieved between the soul and divinity through the gift of the body."[64]

Charis, the Greek word for "grace" (Latin: *gratia*) is at the root of both "charity" (in Latin, *caritas*) and "Eu*char*ist" (a word medieval theologians glossed as "good grace").[65] Whereas Joan's judges at Rouen saw her body as an idolatrous anti-Eucharist, when the flames consumed her body, Joan appeared "eucharistic" to many, because of the beautiful way she gave away her body, even as it was taken from her — a body that would never more be embraced, touched, kissed, and venerated in its physicality, a body that would leave no relic of itself, except its heart (and even that would be tossed away, along with her ashes, into the Seine). This eucharistic transformation of the memory and recognition of Joan of Arc (together with its political metaphorical nature)

L'enquête ordonnée par Charles VII en 1450 et le codicille de Guillaume Bouillé, ed. P. Doncoeur, SJ, and Y. Lanhers (Paris: Librairie D'Argences, 1956), 39.

63. Saint Ignatius of Antioch, *The Letters,* in *The Apostolic Fathers,* trans. Gerald G. Walsh, SJ (New York: Christian Heritage, 1948), 109.

64. Meltzer, *For Fear of the Fire,* 36.

65. See my discussion of the "theological aesthetic" of the Eucharist in *Eating Beauty,* esp. 54-58. The Greek root *charis* (like its Latin cognate, *gratia*) never loses the meaning of "beauty," "graciousness," "charm," of an "attractive" and "pleasing" goodness and "comeliness." In the end, Lionel Royer (1852-1926) painted the murals.

grounds the nullification of the 1431 trial and, much later, Joan's canonization process.

The philosopher Jean-Luc Marion has written extensively about how the use of the Eucharist and the icon in combination during the Mass creates a "distortion of the economy that prevents the danger of the idol," for the church "can never identify" the divine nature, facelessly present in the Eucharist, with the painted face of the icon "in a single liturgical performance." Instead, the icon "glorifies itself only by returning all glory to the invisible."[66] In the case of Joan of Arc, her own eucharistic invisibility means that the many icons of Joan — none of which depict her true face, which is forever lost to view — refer to her invisibility as it is incorporated into Christ's.

The eight painted murals in the Basilique Nationale de St. Jeanne d'Arc in Domremy depict scenes from Joan's life in chronological order, with one key, explicitly eucharistic, exception to that rule.[67] In the first mural, Joan, clad in a red dress, kneels on a grassy hillside where sheep are grazing. She reaches out her arms to accept from her three voices (Saints Michael, Catherine, and Margaret) the accoutrements of her mission: a standard, a sword, a helmet. In the second, she kneels before the Dauphin at Chinon, whom she has recognized in his disguise among the courtiers. The third mural depicts Joan on a white horse as she enters Orléans, her hand raised in a blessing that responds to the welcoming, outreached arms of the citizens. The fourth also shows her mounted, this time on a black horse, and carrying her standard, in the midst of the combatants at Patay. In the fifth, she stands at attention, again holding her banner, as the archbishop of Reims crowns a kneeling Charles VII king of France.

The sixth mural (Figure 1) breaks this chronological sequence, hearkening back to Joan's youth in Domremy. It shows her kneeling in the company of other young girls, all of them veiled in long, white veils to receive their first holy communion from the hands of the pastor, Guillaume Fronte. The seventh mural depicts Joan as a kneeling prisoner, darkly clad, as she receives her last communion, her viaticum, from the hands of the

66. Jean-Luc Marion, *The Crossing of the Visible,* trans. James K. A. Smith (Stanford: Stanford University Press, 2004), 77.

67. The basilica was designed by Paul Sedille, built betweem 1881 and 1926, and designated a basilica in 1938. Louis-Maurice Boutet de Monvel (1850-1913) was originally commissioned to create the series of frescoes, but he had to abandon the project due to failing health. In the end, Lionel Royer (1852-1926) painted the murals.

Figure 1. Lionel Royer (1852-1926), Mural 6, First Communion of Jeanne d'Arc, Basilique Nationale de St. Jeanne d'Arc in Domremy. *Photo courtesy of Nora M. Heimann*

Dominican friar, while her three saints look on, their haloes and Joan's in shining contrast to the darkness in the cell. The eighth and final mural portrays Joan's death at the stake, her bound hands folded in prayer, her lips parted. She gazes at the corpus of Christ on the crucifix held out before her, even as her own body is being consumed by flames. The bridal veil Joan wears as a first communicant in the sixth mural thus heightens the spousal quality of her last communion and martyrdom, depicted in the seventh and eighth murals.

The anachronistic ordering of the scenes, which gives a special prominence to the eucharistic moments in Joan's life, seals it as a lived Mass, an incorporation into Christ's own life. Facing the faceless host, the adoring Christ in the sacrament, following him into death, Joan has found her true judge. "The Church's own definition of martyrdom, then — that the crown of martyrdom is given to those who die for and *in* the faith — nullifies any suspicion or taint of heresy in a victim if she dies showing clear signs of faith," writes François Meltzer. "Death does not lie."[68] If the Eucharist as the "food of martyrs" gave Joan the strength, the charity, to die as she did, then Christ can truly be said to have accomplished her justification, understood not only as the nullification of a corrupt legal proceeding but also as a martyr's sanctification.

It is no accident, as Elaine Scarry has taught us, that "a single word, 'fairness,' is used both in referring to the loveliness of countenance and in referring to the ethical requirement for 'being fair,' 'playing fair,' and 'fair

68. Meltzer, *For Fear of the Fire*, 199.

distribution.'"[69] We do not know what the historical Joan of Arc looked like, but in countless works of art, including the murals at Domremy, she appears beautiful in her likeness to Christ, judged innocent by her sacramental communion and moral union with him in her passion and death.[70] What her judges had perceived as a deformity, an incongruity, a mismatch of clothing, body, and soul, was revealed to be a conformity with the pattern of Christ's own life. What judgment could be fairer?[71]

69. Elaine Scarry, *On Beauty and Being Just* (Princeton, NJ: Princeton University Press, 1999), 91.

70. On Joan's depiction in visual art, see Nora M. Heimann, *Joan of Arc in French Art and Culture (1700-1855): From Satire to Sanctity* (Burlington, VT: Ashgate, 2005).

71. I wish to express my personal gratitude to Professor Nora M. Heimann of the department of art and art history at the Catholic University of America for allowing me to reproduce a photo taken by her during her trip to Domremy in the summer of 2010. I thank, too, her assistants, Estevan Portillo and Allison Lipari, for their work in enhancing the image quality.

PART III

Martyrdom Destroys the Church

CHAPTER 6

Persecution or Prosecution, Martyrs or False Martyrs? The Reformation Era, History, and Theological Reflection

Brad S. Gregory

I would like to begin rather unlike a historian (or perhaps as a historian of the very recent past) by noting three important themes in the pontificate of John Paul II: a consistent insistence on religious freedom and denunciation of all forms of violence, including religious persecution; a vigorous promotion of ecumenical relations and interfaith dialogue; and a recognition of the power of Christian martyrdom and its relationship to Christ's suffering and death, from the early church through the twentieth century. On more than one occasion the late pope combined these themes as he praised the witness of non-Catholic Christian martyrs in highly public, official ways. For example, in his 1995 encyclical on ecumenism, *Ut Unum Sint,* he wrote of them that, "despite the tragedy of our divisions, these brothers and sisters have preserved an attachment to Christ and to the Father so radical and absolute as to lead even to the shedding of blood."[1] Even more explicitly, in his homily on the third Sunday of Easter in May 2000, an "Ecumemical Commemoration of the Witnesses to the Faith in the Twentieth Century," the pope praised the witness of Catholic and non-Catholic martyrs as expressions of God's power in the midst of the twentieth century's avalanche of brutality and oppression. On that occasions he said: "The precious heritage which these courageous witnesses have passed down to us is a patrimony shared by all the Churches and Ecclesial Communities. It is a heritage which

1. John Paul II, encyclical letter *Ut Unum Sint,* sect. 83, May 25, 1995: http://www.vatican.va/holy_father/john_paul_ii/encyclicals/documents/hf_jp-ii_enc_25051995_ut-unum-sint_en.html.

speaks more powerfully than all the causes of division. The ecumenism of the martyrs and the witnesses to the faith is the most convincing of all; to the Christians of the twenty-first century it shows the path to unity."[2]

John Paul II singled out and quoted Paul Schneider, an uncompromising Lutheran pastor who was imprisoned, tortured, and killed by the Nazis at Buchenwald in 1939. In taking up the intersection of these themes — the denunciation of persecution, promotion of ecumenism, and the power of martyrdom — the pope acted in ways that were consistent with the pronouncements of the Second Vatican Council. A directive from the Council's Decree on Ecumenism, *Unitatis Redintegratio,* for example, explicitly acknowledges the witness of non-Catholic martyrs: "Catholics must gladly acknowledge and esteem the truly Christian endowments from our common heritage which are to be found among our separated brethren. It is right and salutary to recognize the riches of Christ and virtuous works in the lives of others who are bearing witness to Christ, sometimes even to the shedding of their blood."[3]

How different are these notions from those widespread in early modern Europe. In the Reformation era, martyrdom was the product not of modern dictators but of other Christians — Catholic as well as Protestant — whose views were dramatically at odds with those of the most recent popes. By way of introduction, consider the voices of a few sixteenth-century Roman Catholics who have been officially canonized. Saint Thomas More (singled out by John Paul II as the official patron saint of lawyers and politicians) wrote in the last known letter to his longtime friend Erasmus, less than a year before More himself would be imprisoned in the Tower of London: "As to the statement in my epitaph that I was a source of trouble for heretics — I wrote that with deep feeling. I find that breed of men absolutely loathsome, so much so that, unless they regain their senses, I want to be as hateful to them as anyone can possibly be."[4] Saint Teresa of Avila explained, at the beginning of her *Way of Perfection,* her chief motivation for founding such a strictly cloistered community of reformed female Carmelite religious:

2. John Paul II, "Ecumenical Commemoration of the Witnesses to the Faith in the Twentieth Century," sect. 5, May 7, 2000: http://www.vatican.va/holy_father/john_paul_ii/homilies/2000/documents/hf_jp-ii_hom_20000507_test-fede_en.html.

3. "Decree on Ecumenism *(Unitatis Redintegratio),*" chap. 1, sect. 4, in *Documents of Vatican II,* ed. Austin P. Flannery (Grand Rapids: Eerdmans, 1975), 458.

4. Thomas More to Erasmus [June 1533], in *St. Thomas More: Selected Letters,* ed. Elizabeth Frances Rogers (New Haven: Yale University Press, 1961), no. 46, 180.

> [N]ews reached me of the harm being done in France and of the havoc the Lutherans [in fact, they were Calvinists] had caused and how much this miserable sect was growing. The news distressed me greatly, and . . . I cried to the Lord and begged Him that I might remedy so much evil. It seemed to me that I would have given a thousand lives to save one soul out of the many that were being lost there. . . . As a result I resolved to follow the evangelical counsels of perfection as I could and strive that these few persons who live here do the same. . . . Since we would all be occupied in prayer for those who are defenders of the Church and for preachers and for learned men who protect her from attack, we could help as much as possible this Lord of mine who is so roughly treated by those for whom He has done so much good; it seems these traitors would want Him to be crucified again and that He have no place to lay His head.[5]

As a final example, Saint Robert Southwell, an English Jesuit who would himself be tortured and executed in 1595 for his fidelity to Catholicism, entitled the thirteenth chapter of his *Epistle of Comfort* to fellow Elizabethan Catholics, "That Heretics can not be Martyrs." "Martyrdom cannot be the just punishment of sin," he declares, "but [is] the crown of virtue; and whosoever is justly executed for a true offence, Saint he may be, if he repent him of his fault, and take his death as his just desert; but Martyr he cannot be, though he endure never so many deaths or torments."[6] So Thomas More thought it virtuous to be hateful to Protestants so long as they persisted in their views, Teresa of Avila conceived the prayer of the Discalced Carmelites in Spain as spiritual weapons aiding Catholics against Huguenots in the French Wars of Religion, and Robert Southwell defended the execution of heretics as just punishment and excluded them from the ranks of martyrs.

Many more such examples could be adduced. Such views were commonplace in the sixteenth and seventeenth centuries, and not only among Catholics, but also, *mutatis mutandis,* among Lutheran and Reformed Protestants, who justified the execution of Anabaptists as blasphemers and

5. Teresa of Avila, *The Way of Perfection* [1566; 1583], in *The Collected Works of St. Teresa of Avila,* trans. Kieran Kavanaugh and Otilio Rodriguez (Washington, DC: Institute of Carmelite Studies, 1980), 2:41-42.

6. Robert Southwell, *An Epistle of Comfort, to the Reverend Priestes, and to the Honorable, Worshipful, and other of the Laye sort restrained in Durance for the Catholicke Fayth* (London: n.p., 1587-88), fols. 182-88, quotation on fol. 186v.

of Catholics in England for "treason" during the reigns of Henry VIII and Elizabeth I. The views of both John Paul II and Benedict XVI stand squarely at odds with views widespread in the Reformation era, including those of men and women whom Catholics today believe to be intercessors in heaven.

This juxtaposition of recent papal and conciliar views to those from the Reformation era points out the gulf that exists between recent official Catholic — and, indeed, widespread modern Western — views of religious persecution and martyrdom and the corresponding views of influential early modern Christians. We (meaning contemporary Western people in general) are apt to regard individual freedom of belief, whatever its content, as a fundamental human right, to deplore the persecution of those whose rights in this respect are infringed, and to regard as martyrs those who are killed for their convictions — whatever those convictions might be. Persecution for religious or political beliefs tends to incite Western moral outrage. Among virtually all Christians today, including the current pope and his predecessor, such persecution and violence seems particularly antithetical to Christ's teaching and God's will. What offends is *that* one is persecuted or put to death, not that *for which* one is persecuted or killed.

In the Reformation era, however, this was not so, at least not for many Christians in positions of authority and with significant influence. Persecution was not necessarily unjust — or, in other terms less likely to be misleading today, there was a fundamental difference between persecution and prosecution — and the distinction turned on content, specifically the content of Christian truth. Logically related to this was a distinction between true and false martyrdom: death for the right reasons made one a genuine martyr; the wrong reasons made one a pseudomartyr. Distinct and mutually exclusive martyrological traditions and a corresponding discourse of religious controversy about true and false martyrs were inseparable from the socioreligious divisions of the Reformation era beginning in 1523, when the first executions for the new convictions occurred.[7]

This chapter explores historically these two Reformation-era distinctions alien to widespread modern convictions, namely, the distinction between persecution and prosecution and the distinction between true and

7. For a book-length treatment of the formation of Protestant, Anabaptist, and Roman Catholic martyrological traditions in the sixteenth century, see Brad S. Gregory, *Salvation at Stake: Christian Martyrdom in Early Modern Europe* (Cambridge, MA: Harvard University Press, 1999).

false martyrs. My aim here is to render a bit less simplistic the dismissive sense with which we tend to view the judicial treatment of heterodoxy in early modern Europe, specifically by trying to understand in context those responsible for the actions and articulation of ideas that instinctively strike us as appalling. Denouncing those who lived centuries ago on the basis of our own commitments is easy. Bracketing our own convictions for the sake of understanding contrary ones, whether in the past or present, is not. Because what happened in the Reformation era continues to hamper ecumenical relationships among Christians today, there is a particular temptation — often for morally laudable reasons — to cast sixteenth-century realities in ways that are driven by present yearning for reconciliation. Yet, whatever the attractions of constructing an appealing and usable past in this context, it seems to me that sound theological reflection, as well as ecumenical dialogue in the present, should rely on sound historical comprehension of the past.

The starting point is the presumably uncontroversial assumption that early modern Christians responsible for actions that we find offensive did not regard those actions as morally reprehensible. Otherwise, we must suppose that highly self-conscious, morally serious sixteenth-century Christians were deliberately, repeatedly, and publicly behaving in ways that *they themselves* regarded as gravely sinful. When Southwell made his daily examinations of conscience as a Jesuit, we cannot plausibly imagine him thinking: "I know that Protestants are unjustly persecuted and those who have been executed are martyrs, fellow brothers and sisters in Christ, but I am going to denounce them anyway." But if this is so, then it prompts a serious question: What were the presuppositions and historical realities that made Christians think that it was not only acceptable but dutiful to participate in the execution of other Christians, or to denounce those put to death as false martyrs? Without losing sight of the particularities and individual circumstances that affected specific judicial contexts in different ways, it would seem that we must bear at least eleven such factors in mind in the endeavor to answer this question. They are interrelated, but for the sake of clarity I will enumerate them here individually.

1. Heresy was understood by authorities as a serious crime, and like other crimes, was subject to punishment. The short answer to the basis for the distinction between legitimate and illegitimate persecution, or between persecution and prosecution, is that in the late Middle Ages and Reformation era, heresy was a crime subject to legal sanction. Heresy cases addressed by judicial bodies, such as Holland's Hof in The Hague or parliamentary

courts in France, are interspersed with matter-of-fact banality among the cases of other serious malefactors, a telling indication of heretics' status as criminals among others. To have suggested that in principle heretics should not have been punished would have been analogous to arguing that other criminals should not have been punished either. "For if Emperors do punish theft, murder, rape, adultery, and perjury, why should they not as well punish heresy and sacrilege?" a supporter of Mary Tudor's regime asked in 1556.[8]

On the eve of the Reformation, heresy differed from many crimes because its prosecution ideally required cooperation between ecclesiastical and political authorities. Either episcopally sanctioned inquisitors or papally appointed Dominicans were to investigate whether or not heresy suspects were in fact guilty of deliberate error in matters of Christian doctrine. If so, they were to be given appropriate instruction, ordered to recant their views, subjected to some form of penance or punishment, and received back into the church. Secular authorities were to become involved only if those found guilty refused to abjure their errors, or if previously reconciled heretics relapsed, in which case churchmen turned over to secular officials the heterodox for capital punishment, most often by burning.

It goes without saying that "secular" in this context means "nonecclesiastical," not "nonreligious": political authorities in early modern Europe, whether civic magistrates, territorial princes, or sovereign rulers of emergent nation-states were without exception baptized — and sometimes seriously devout — Christians. Whether sincerely pious or not, their political responsibility was always inflected by religious duty. In France, for example, the coronation oath of the "most Christian king" *(Rex christianissimus)* included a provision that required him to suppress heresy.[9] Political institutions were by no means secular in a modern sense. Between the 1520s and the 1540s, the investigation of religious heterodoxy among Christians was assumed increasingly by secular officials in France, the Low Countries, and England — the three areas in which the largest number of judicial executions of Christians by other Christians occurred.[10]

8. Miles Huggarde, *The displaying of the Protestantes, and sundry their practices . . .* (London: Robert Caly, 1556), fol. 44. For an important recent revisionist account of the prosecution and executions of Protestants in Mary's reign, see Eamon Duffy, *Fires of Faith: Catholic England under Mary Tudor* (New Haven and London: Yale University Press, 2009).

9. William Monter, *Judging the French Reformation: Heresy Trials by Sixteenth-Century Parlements* (Cambridge, MA: Harvard University Press, 1999), 55.

10. See Raymond Mentzer, *Heresy Proceedings in Languedoc, 1500-1560* (Philadelphia: American Philosophical Society, 1984), 2, 10-11, 34, 159; Monter, *Judging the French Reforma-*

2. By the time of the Reformation, the prosecution of heresy had been customary for several centuries in a society deeply traditional in its habits of thought and practice. So habitually averse to "novelty" were late medieval Europeans that even the great innovations of the era — the humanists' disruptive call *ad fontes* ("Back to the sources!") and the Reformation itself — were understood by their proponents as recoveries of an authoritative past that antedated objectionable innovations such as medieval Scholasticism or the assertion of papal authority in the Roman church. Those who sought to rectify perceived injustices, whether aristocrats or peasants, did so by referring to custom and tradition. Given this pervasive cultural reality, it would have been bizarre, at the advent of the Reformation, for either ecclesiastical or secular authorities to have rejected or sought to alter judicial arrangements regarding heresy that had been in place in their basic form since the twelfth century. That was when Gratian had codified in canon law Augustine's notion that heresy entailed deliberate persistence in false doctrine, while in 1148 the Council of Rheims handed heretics over to secular authorities for burning.

Such practices were extended and given greater Roman impetus in the early thirteenth century, when inquisitors were papally commissioned to counter the Cathars in southern France.[11] While Richard Kieckhefer has convincingly argued that there was no unified, institutional "Inquisition" in the High or late Middle Ages analogous to the later Spanish or Roman Inquisitions, there were inquisitorial precedents and practices to enact canon and civil laws.[12] Tradition-minded ecclesiastical and political authorities were not about to ignore those practices in the early sixteenth century with respect to evangelicals or Anabaptists any more than they had with Lollards a century earlier in England. For their part, Zwinglian cities in Switzerland or Lutheran territories in Germany adapted existing

tion, 85-86; Paul E. Valvekens, *De Inquisitie in de Nederlanden der zestiende eeuw* (Amsterdam: De Kinkhoren, 1949), 171-90; Aline Goosens, *Les inquisitions modernes dans les Pays-Bas meridionaux 1520-1633* (Brussels: L'Université de Bruxelles, 1997), 1:47-81.

11. Malcolm Lambert, *Medieval Heresy: Popular Movements from the Gregorian Reform to the Reformation*, 2nd ed. (Oxford: Blackwell, 1992), 44-61, 66-68, 91-146; R. I. Moore, *The Formation of a Persecuting Society: Power and Deviance in Western Europe, 950-1250* (Oxford: Blackwell, 1987), 19-27.

12. Richard Kieckhefer, *Repression of Heresy in Medieval Germany* (Philadelphia: University of Pennsylvania Press, 1979), 1-10; see, more recently, Kieckhefer, "The Office of Inquisition and Medieval Heresy: The Transition from Personal to Institutional Jurisdiction," *Journal of Ecclesiastical History* 46 (1995): 36-61.

laws and practices against Anabaptists and others in the Radical Reformation movement — yet another indication of judicial traditionalism.[13]

3. The traditional association of heresy with sedition was confirmed early in the Reformation era and colored authorities' subsequent views of religious dissent. Because of the degree to which Christianity was interwoven with medieval political institutions, social practices, and cultural assumptions, it was impossible to reject Christian teachings or practices without simultaneously disrupting social relationships and rebelling against political authorities responsible for protecting the church and maintaining order in society. In various ways, this was true of the experience of the Cathars, Waldensians, Hussites, and Lollards between the thirteenth and early sixteenth centuries. Heresy implied subversion and sedition. Already by 1520, Catholic authorities were warning that Luther's criticism of the Roman church would also engender sociopolitical rebellion, and they saw the German Peasants' War of 1524-25 and its proponents' take on "Christian freedom" as dramatic confirmation of their predictions.[14] A decade later, the polygamy and communal ownership of property within the Anabaptist Kingdom of Münster, under the leadership of its prophet-king, Jan van Leiden, added a dramatic coda that horrified authorities throughout Europe and cemented associations of heresy with subversion. Throughout the remainder of the sixteenth century and deep into the seventeenth, rulers and magistrates maintained a keen sensitivity to anything that smacked of religious dissent.

Despite the tendency of some scholars to imagine early modern political regimes as totalitarian in their absolutizing reach, sixteenth-century polities from Spain to Poland were in fact marked by political weakness rather than by powerful and efficient bureaucracies. How could it have been otherwise without professional police forces to suppress local disturbances, without large standing armies that rulers could call on, without any means of rapid communication, without consistent cooperation between central and local authorities? We should be misled neither by the grandiose rhetoric of "absolute rule" nor the grisly displays of public executions, both of which were inversely proportional to the effective exercise of authorities' actual

13. Winfried Trusen, "Rechtliche Grundlagen des Häresiebegriffs und des Ketzerverfahrens," in *Ketzerverfolgung im 16. und frühen 17. Jahrhundert*, ed. Silvana Seidel Menchi (Wolfenbüttel: Harrassowitz, 1992), 11-15.

14. David V. N. Bagchi, *Luther's Earliest Opponents: Catholic Controversialists, 1518-1525* (Minneapolis: Augsburg Fortress, 1991), 98, 108-9; Mark U. Edwards, Jr., *Printing, Propaganda, and Martin Luther* (Berkeley: University of California Press, 1994), 149-62.

power. The repetitious mass of antiheresy legislation in both France and the Low Countries between the 1520s and the early 1560s offers strong, indirect evidence of the ineffectiveness of prosecution.[15] The sedition with which religious dissent was associated, especially after 1525, threatened not all-powerful modern states but rather all-too-vulnerable early modern ones.

4. For the sake of consistency, inherited and contemporary jurisprudence seemed to demand the death penalty for obstinate heretics. Heirs to ancient Roman law, legal theorists and judges in medieval and early modern Europe were well aware of the principle that the punishment must fit the crime. But in medieval and early modern Europe, punitive measures for crimes of all kinds were severe by comparison with the modern era. The public enactment of harsh punishments — a terrifying show of didactic deterrence — was the means by which political authorities attempted to compensate for their conspicuous lack of effective surveillance, swift communication, and powerful technology. It would be anachronistic and arbitrary to abstract the punishment for heresy from this wider judicial context. As Raymond Mentzer has put it, the harsh judicial treatment of crimes against religion was "neither singular nor extreme" in that period when we compare it to the use of the death penalty for felonies such as treason, murder, counterfeiting, arson, and theft.[16] This becomes apparent when we understand the gravity with which heresy was understood. In the words of Saint John Fisher, one of most acute theologians and conscientious bishops of the early sixteenth century, heresy was "the seed of the devil, the inspiration of the wicked spirits, the corruption of our hearts, the blinding of our sight, the quenching of our faith, the destruction of all good fruit, and finally the murder of our souls."[17]

On the eve of the Reformation, heresy had been conceived of as treason against God for more than three centuries, a concept first articulated by Pope Innocent III in 1199.[18] If ordinary traitors received capital punish-

15. For the legislative edicts, see F. A. Isambert, ed., *Recueil Général des anciennes lois françaises, depuis l'an 420 jusqu'a la Révolution de 1789,* vols. 11-15 (Paris, 1827-29), and Ch. Laurent and J. Lameere, eds., *Recueil des ordonnances des Pays-Bas,* 2nd ser., 1506-1700, vols. 2-6 (Brussels: J. Goemaere, 1893-1922).

16. Mentzer, *Heresy Proceedings in Languedoc,* 122, 127.

17. John Fisher, *A sermon had at Paulis by the commandment of the most reuerend father in god my lord legate . . .* (London: Thomas Berthelet, 1526); reprint in *English Works of John Fisher, Bishop of Rochester: Sermons and Other Writings, 1520 to 1535,* ed. Cecilia A. Hatt (Oxford: Oxford University Press, 2002), 147.

18. Lambert, *Medieval Heresy,* 97-98.

ment for their crimes, how could heretics who rejected attempts at correction deserve any less? One might as well have argued that bodily assault should have been punished less seriously than murder. Heresy harmed souls, was concerned with not only temporal realities but eternal salvation, and was a crime committed not simply against human beings but against God. Heretics not only denied in some respect the saving truth revealed by God and maintained by the church, the body of Christ, but through spreading their errors they jeopardized others' salvation as well as their own. Insofar as capital punishment was applied to lesser crimes, it was therefore consistent to apply it to heresy as well.

5. Imprisonment was not a viable form of punishment in early modern Europe. This point concerns not the fact of prosecution for religious heterodoxy, but rather the form it assumed. While the weakness of early modern political institutions and judicial consistency are fundamental to understanding the severity with which religious dissidents were punished, another (less obvious) factor was also critical. We might think that authorities' desire to safeguard truth, honor God, maintain order, and protect other Christians from danger could as well have been served by isolating religious dissidents from others via incarceration, a kind of social death in place of literal execution. But this was not so. Whether for unrepentant heretics or other criminals, imprisonment as a form of punishment was rare in early modern Europe. The facilities were simply lacking; indeed, not until the mid-seventeenth century in certain towns of the Dutch Republic were prisons constructed specifically for the purpose of punishment by isolation.[19] Such prisons as existed during the Reformation era were comparatively small, and they were normally used to hold suspected criminals prior to their trials or convicted criminals before their executions, not to incarcerate wrongdoers for years on end.

In addition, prosecuting criminals even in this way was expensive, as is attested by the meticulous accounts kept for the costs of maintaining, trying, and punishing them. To hold large numbers of criminals serving long-term sentences would have been prohibitively expensive, beyond the financial means of even states such as France or Spain. Like other criminals, heretics were sometimes punished by exile rather than death, but

19. See Edward M. Peters, "Prison Before the Prison," in *The Oxford History of the Prison: The Practice of Punishment in Western Society*, ed. Norval Morris and David J. Rothman (New York: Oxford University Press, 1995), 30-45. For the Dutch innovation, see Peter Spierenburg, "The Body and the State: Early Modern Europe," in Morris and Rothman, *The Oxford History of the Prison*, 72-73.

banishment was fraught with the uncertainty about whether those exiled might return. And when banishment was practiced, it must have seemed to be a provocative kind of antifraternalism: the criminal in question would be sent into a neighboring territory or commonwealth, somewhat like the way Britain would later use Australia, only without the intervening oceans.

6. Biblical passages could be and were taken to sanction the prosecution of religious heterodoxy. Regardless of their specific backgrounds and training, sixteenth-century Catholic and Protestant theologians were aware of passages from Deuteronomy and Leviticus that directly mandated the killing of those among the ancient Israelites who enticed their fellows to follow other gods, blasphemed, prophesied falsely, or disobeyed God's ministers (Deut. 13:1-11; 17:12; 18:20; Lev. 24:14). While such texts were not always interpreted with direct applicability to latter-day Christians, they could be and were readily adapted to heresy, blasphemy, and sacrilege in Christian contexts, as they had been for centuries. Presumably, Christian magistrates had an even greater duty to safeguard God's honor, maintain order, and protect against false religion than did Israelite leaders before Christ's incarnation fulfilled the messianic promises of the Old Testament. Although the New Testament nowhere sanctioned such prosecution directly, Paul warned repeatedly against false teachers and false prophets, and he insisted on obedience to established laws in open-ended ways that were taken to include measures against religious dissent. In his first letter to Timothy, for example, Paul says:

> Now we know that the law is good, if one uses it legitimately. This means that the law is laid down not for the innocent but for the lawless and the disobedient, for the godless and sinful, for the unholy and profane, for those who kill their father or mother, for murderers, fornicators, sodomites, slave traders, liars, perjurers, and *whatever else* is contrary to the sound teaching that conforms to the glorious gospel of the blessed God, which he entrusted to me. (1 Tim. 1:8-11, NRSV; italics added)

Viewed from the perspective of sixteenth-century authorities responsible for upholding God's saving truth and for maintaining order in society, such a passage implicitly supported the prosecution of crimes against religion. Heresy and blasphemy were by definition contrary to the "sound teaching" that conformed to the gospel, however it was understood; and, as

I have already suggested, crimes against religion were regarded as particularly heinous and thus deserving of condign punishment.

7. In practice, suspected heretics were rarely prosecuted for their beliefs as such. To widespread modern sensibilities, one of the most offensive aspects of the prosecution of religious heterodoxy is its ostensible monitoring of the deeply personal and private interior of individual souls in an almost proto-Orwellian fashion. But rarely were people suspected of heterodoxy simply or strictly because of what they believed; nor did authorities have means to detect beliefs per se. In 1536, the Lutheran pastor Urbanus Rhegius rightly noted that if heresy remained unexpressed in people's hearts, it was subject to judgment by God alone.[20] Spiritualist Christians such as the followers of Hendrik Niclaes's Family of Love were rarely prosecuted precisely because they distinguished sharply between internal belief and external behavior, sanctioning outward conformity with the demands of prevailing religiopolitical regimes and thus avoiding detection.[21]

Suspected heretics, by contrast, almost always aroused suspicion because of something they had *done,* such as refusing to attend Mass, refraining from having an infant baptized, publishing a work or circulating a manuscript that contained heretical ideas, sheltering the heterodox, insulting a priest or minister, or dishonoring a religious image. Behavior, not beliefs as such, attracted attention. Of course, such external actions certainly expressed beliefs, and conscientious Catholics, Lutherans, Reformed Protestants, and Anabaptists all assumed, in accordance with many passages in Scripture, that convictions should be manifested concretely in the Christian life. Those who ran afoul of the law, however, did so not because of their convictions as such, but because their convictions were manifested in ways that could be observed and reported by others. It is thus misleading to say that those adjudged heterodox were prosecuted merely for what they believed.

8. Authorities sought to correct rather than kill the heterodox: the ex-

20. Urbanus Rhegius, "Der Leunebergischen bedenken der widertaufer halb, ob die mit dem schwert zu straffen seien," in *Wiedertäuferakten 1527-1626,* ed. Günther Franz, vol. 4 of *Urkundliche Quellen zur hessischen Reformationsgeschichte* (Marburg: N. G. Elwert, 1951), 111.

21. On Spiritualists in the Reformation era, see R. Emmet McLaughlin, "Spiritualism: Schwenckfeld and Franck and Their Early Modern Resonances," in *A Companion to Anabaptism and Spiritualism, 1521-1700,* ed. John D. Roth and James M. Stayer (Leiden: E. J. Brill, 2007), 119-61; on the Familists, see Alastair Hamilton, *The Family of Love* (Cambridge, UK: James Clarke, 1981).

ecution of dissenters was not a victory but a defeat for the regime in question. One of the most common popular stereotypes in all of European history is that of "the Inquisition," conceived of as a bloodthirsty, monolithic, crypto-totalitarian institution that sought ruthlessly to exterminate all who opposed it. (Such a misconception is perpetuated by the continued publication of books with titles such as *Inquisition,* written by scholars who are well aware that the first step in any serious consideration of the topic is to distinguish among medieval inquisitorial practices, the Spanish Inquisition, the Roman Inquisition, and other early-modern inquisitorial institutions and practices in particular European countries.[22])

The judicial practices of the early modern period tend to be seen through the prism of twentieth-century genocides and Foucauldian anachronisms. All laws can be abused by those responsible for implementing them, and the laws against religious heterodoxy in the Reformation era were no exception. But considerable evidence makes clear that, on the whole, legal proceedings against heresy suspects were marked neither by indiscriminate killing nor by the abrogation of legal procedure. The scholarship of John Tedeschi, for example, has revealed the prosecutorial restraint of the Roman Inquisition: its use of evidence and procedural scrupulousness was among the most progressive in Europe at the time.[23] Indeed, the overriding goal of the authorities was not to kill heretics but to save them — as an extension of pastoral concern.[24]

By and large, in judicial proceedings, both ecclesiastical and secular authorities sought not to execute heretics but to convince them of their errors, and so to restore them to orthodoxy and their place in the church. Large numbers of those accused of heresy abjured their views, demonstrating that the process often achieved the intended goal.[25] On many occasions, authorities tried multiple times to persuade those who persisted

22. See, e.g., John Edwards, *Inquisition* (Stroud, UK: Tempus, 1999).

23. See John Tedeschi, *The Prosecution of Heresy: Collected Studies on the Inquisition in Early Modern Italy* (Binghamton, NY: Medieval and Renaissance Texts and Studies, 1991).

24. On the inseparability of inquisitorial activity from pastoral concern among medieval Dominicans, see Christine Caldwell Ames, "Does Inquisition Belong to Religious History?" *American Historical Review* 110 (2005): 11-37.

25. Concerning interrogated Anabaptists, see, e.g., Linda A. Huebert Hecht, "Anabaptist Women in Tirol Who Recanted," in *Profiles of Anabaptist Women: Sixteenth-Century Reforming Pioneers,* ed. C. Arnold Snyder and Linda A. Huebert Hecht (Waterloo, ON: Wilfrid Laurier University Press, 1996), 156-63, and, more generally, the volumes in the series *Quellen zur Geschichte der Täufer,* which provide much evidence for the success of efforts made to secure the recantation of Anabaptists.

to abandon their views, sometimes using family members in their efforts. This would not have been true had they sought simply to slaughter the deviant. The failure of such efforts meant recourse to execution as a last resort, in the dutiful interest of protecting others from harm for the sake of the common good. In effect, if it proved impossible to save heretics from themselves, authorities at least had the duty of saving others from them, "lest they corrupt other good, and honest persons," in the words of Edmund Bonner, the bishop of London under Mary Tudor.[26]

In the Low Countries, where more people were put to death for religion during the reigns of Charles V and Philip II than anywhere else in early modern Europe, well under 1 percent of the population was investigated for suspicion of heresy.[27] Of these, only a small minority were executed, contravening any claim that inquisitors were merciless slaughterers. Some 8-11 percent of those investigated for heresy were put to death during the twenty-year career of the exceptionally active Flemish inquisitor Pieter Titelmans, an average of about six persons per year.[28] Although Titelmans was known for his zeal, in the 1550s he and members of the Council of Flanders actually broke imperial law in order to save penitent Anabaptists, and Titelmans interceded with secular officials trying to prevent the execution of others.[29]

Suspected heretics were tried in order to determine whether they were actually heretics — according to the criteria of a given orthodoxy. Confusion was not heresy, nor was ignorance or superstition, distinctions made by John Calvin and Thomas More.[30] Nor did criticism of the church's shortcomings and corruption — as distinct from its doctrines — constitute heresy. Such criticisms had been part and parcel of the reforming efforts of

26. Edmund Bonner, *Homelies sette forth by the righte reuerende father in God, Edmunds Byshop of London . . .* (London: John Cawood, 1555), fol. 26v.

27. Goosens, *Inquisitions modernes dans Les Pays-Bas* (Brussels: Editions de l'Université de Bruxelles, 1998), 2:190-91.

28. Johan van de Wiele, "De inquisitierechtbank van Pieter Titelmans in de zestiende eeuw in Vlaanderen," *Bijdragen en mededelingen betreffende de geschiedenis der Nederlanden* 97 (1982): 59-61.

29. Johan Decavele, *De dageraad van de Reformatie in Vlaanderen (1520-1565)* (Brussels: Paleis der Academiën, 1975), 1:26, 26n77, 439, 440-42, 449.

30. Thomas More, *A Dialogue Concerning Heresies* [1529], in *The Yale Edition of the Complete Works of St. Thomas More,* vol. 6, pt. 1, ed. Thomas M. C. Lawler et al. (New Haven: Yale University Press, 1981), 416, ll. 23-26; John Calvin, *Declaration pour maintenir la vraye foy que tiennent tous Chrestiens de la Trinité des personnes en un seul Dieu . . .* (Geneva: Jean Crespin, 1554), 48-49.

conscientious men and women since the fourteenth century. Rather, the hallmark of heresy was deliberate and defiant persistence in heterodoxy, an Augustinian view that Gratian had made part of canon law in the twelfth century.[31] For this reason, when torture was used at all in heresy cases (fewer than 10 percent of suspected heretics in Bordeaux, Languedoc, and Paris between 1540 and 1560 were tortured), it was not to coerce suspects to confess to convictions they did not hold but to try to discover the names of fellow criminals, much the way authorities today might seek to learn the names of all those involved in a murder conspiracy.[32]

9. For several centuries prior to the Reformation, the prosecution of heresy had worked. More than merely being traditional in a traditionally minded society, the theological justification and legal machinery for the prosecution of heresy had been largely successful since the thirteenth century. With the possible exception of the Hussites in Bohemia, heterodoxy was corralled and controlled — even though it was not eliminated. Repression had worked before; circa 1520, there was no reason for authorities to think that it would not work again. And in some areas, there were success stories in the sixteenth century: Anabaptists, for example, were essentially eliminated from Bavaria in the late 1520s due to concerted efforts against them, as were the small numbers of Protestants in Spain in the late 1550s and early 1560s.[33] By no means was it a foregone conclusion that repressive measures against religious heterodoxy were bound to fail.[34] Equally plausibly, given the considerable success of their predecessors in late-medieval Europe, rulers might conclude that they should redouble their efforts.

10. Recognition as a martyr depended not on the fact of suffering death, but on the doctrines for which one suffered. Insofar as judicial authorities did not regard just prosecution as tyrannical persecution, they did not believe that, in executing dangerous religious criminals, they were creating Christian martyrs. By contrast and in opposition to this perspective, every celebration of someone as a heroic martyr was a criticism of authorities reviled for unjustly persecuting a holy witness to Christian truth. Hence a distinction between true and false martyrs runs throughout the Reformation era as a correlate of the vast memorialization of Catholic, Protestant, and Anabaptist martyrs. Beginning already in the 1520s, hostile

31. Trusen, "Rechtliche Grundlagen," in Menchi, *Ketzerverfolgung*, 3.

32. Mentzer, *Heresy Proceedings in Languedoc*, 101.

33. For Bavaria, see Claus-Peter Clasen, "The Anabaptists in Bavaria," *Mennonite Quarterly Review* 39 (1965): 244-52.

34. For this point with respect to Marian England, see Duffy, *Fires of Faith*, esp. 7, 79-80.

controversialists attacked each other's claims about who counted as a martyr, denouncing precisely those whom others exalted. Antimartyrology became a discourse, arguably even a genre. Dying for erroneous teachings made one a false martyr, just as dying for God's truth made one a true martyr. Of course, disagreement about "God's truth" was ultimately what divided Christians from one another in the first place, the intractable core of Christianity in the Reformation era. A false martyr could not be a true martyr in exactly the same way that false teachings could not be true. Neither stoic steadfastness at the stake nor impressive courage at the scaffold could transform errors into truths. Had that been the case, as both Catholic and Protestant controversialists argued, then Jews, Muslims, and pagans who died steadfastly would also have to be reckoned true martyrs, a *reductio ad absurdam* insofar as they were not even Christians.[35]

The widespread dispute over true and false martyrs reflected the overwhelming tendency of early modern controversialists to concentrate on issues that divided them. This is exactly the opposite of ecumenical discourse today, which first seeks common ground with an eye toward attaining mutual understanding and eventual reunion. But we should not imagine that the criteria by which people are reckoned martyrs has today become uncontroversial. Most obviously, perhaps, consider the way militant Islamists who kill themselves and others are honored by their sympathizers. That they are denounced by virtually all Westerners and the vast majority of Muslims as terrorists or betrayers of Islam — and are not viewed as martyrs — is exactly the point, namely, that the criteria by which martyrs are recognized remain a matter of dispute. That is, "terrorist" can, in effect, be seen in this instance as a contemporary synonym for "false martyr."

11. The doctrinal criterion for distinguishing between true and false martyrs had a powerful patristic pedigree. Both Catholic and Protestant controversialists repeatedly quoted a dictum that Augustine had used in his struggles with the Donatists in the early fifth century: *Martyrum non est poena, sed causa* ("not the punishment, but the cause, makes a martyr"). When sixteenth-century writers distinguished between true and false martyrs, they were following in the footsteps and invoking the writings of the most important and influential Latin church father, which he had himself used in denouncing the Donatists' celebration of their fallen

35. For a full treatment of the dispute about true and false martyrs in the period, see Gregory, *Salvation at Stake,* 315-41.

fellow believers. In this endeavor Augustine was heir to Saint Cyprian, whose own dictum was also repeatedly invoked and appeared, for example, on the title page of the Roman martyrology in the mid-1580s: *Esse martyr non potest qui in ecclesia non est* ("no one can be a martyr who is not in the church").[36] Since heretics had deliberately separated themselves from Christ's one apostolic church, according to Catholic leaders, they did not belong to it and thus could not be martyrs.

William Tyndale denied that those who died for the pope were martyrs, while the Calvinist Guy de Brès denied that Anabaptists could be martyrs because they refused to obey legitimate magistrates and had separated themselves from the church.[37] Patristic authors, in turn, had worked out their ideas on true and false martyrs through the exegesis of New Testament texts, including what it meant to be persecuted "for righteousness' sake" (Matt. 5:10), the opposite fates of the two thieves crucified with Jesus (Luke 23:39-43), Paul's distinction between those persecuted for living godly in Christ and "wicked people and imposters" (2 Tim. 3:12-13), and Peter's remark that it was praiseworthy to suffer as a Christian but not as a wrongdoer (1 Pet. 5:14-16). Far from concocting a new principle of their own, controversialists in the Reformation era were cleaving to the precedent and invoking the authority of the church fathers, particularly Augustine. To have rejected the centrality of correct convictions in sorting true from false martyrs would have meant flouting patristic authority.

Together, these eleven factors help to account for how and why devout, highly educated, morally scrupulous early modern Christians could consider it their duty to approve of executions for religious heterodoxy and to denounce those put to death as false martyrs. By the early sixteenth century, heresy had been regarded for centuries as a particularly grave crime, one that threatened the souls and the eternal salvation of others as well as the common good and the sociopolitical order. Ecclesiastical — as well as secular — authorities sought not to kill but to correct heretics, among whom those who refused recantation faced execution as a last re-

36. On conflicting martyrological communities in the early church, see Hans Freiherr von Campenhausen, *Die Idee des Martyriums in der alte Kirche*, 2nd ed. (Göttingen: Vandenhoeck und Ruprecht, 1964), 166-75; W. H. C. Frend, *Martyrdom and Persecution in the Early Church: A Study of a Conflict from the Maccabees to Donatus* (Oxford: Blackwell, 1965).

37. William Tyndale, *The obedience of a Christen man and how Christen rulers ought to governe* . . . ([Antwerp], 1528), fol. 119; Guy de Brès, *La racine, sovrce et fondement des Anabaptistes ov rebaptisez de nostre temps* . . . ([Rouen]: A. Clemence, 1565), sig. [a7].

sort. Capital punishment was warranted for the sake of judicial consistency, lest a serious crime be punished more leniently than lesser capital offenses in an era marked generally by penal severity. Such punishment was understood to be consistent with Scripture, and it had been largely successful for three hundred years. The traditional association of heresy with sedition was powerfully reinforced by the Peasants' War of 1524-25 and remained in place throughout the Reformation era. This was especially worrisome to vulnerable early-modern political regimes, a status signaled by their recourse to dramatic public executions as an attempt to deter would-be malefactors. The denunciation of executed heretics as false martyrs was backed by patristic authority, and it was simply a corollary of the difference between true and false doctrines.

Once we have seriously endeavored to understand the assumptions and commitments of early-modern Christians responsible for putting other early-modern Christians to death, we might still wish the early-modern past had been very different from what it was. Intra-Christian violence in the Reformation era certainly makes ecumenical endeavors in the present more difficult. History, however, concerns not the past we wish for, which is an extrapolation of the one we find most "usable," but the one that happened. The practice of history only *begins* when we are confronted with the fact that the past is so stubbornly, unalterably, and radically different from what we wish it would have been. We cannot change what happened in early-modern Christianity, including the drawing of distinctions between persecution and prosecution, or between true and false martyrs. But we can try to understand rather than dismiss the people who made those distinctions and acted on them for reasons they found compelling, just as we act for reasons that we find compelling. Simplistic dichotomies — premodern, intolerant, persecuting, and bad versus modern, tolerant, enlightened, and good — may be flattering, but they do little justice to past or present realities. A sympathetic understanding of past peoples is among the things that historians can offer to theological reflection. What theologians do then is up to them.

CHAPTER 7

Destroying the Church to Save It: Intra-Christian Persecution and the Modern State

William T. Cavanaugh

The most obvious and salient difference between the acts of the early Christian martyrs such as Polycarp and Perpetua and the contemporary accounts John Foxe included in his sixteenth-century *Book of Martyrs* is that in the latter Christians were killed by other Christians, though religious difference was at the source of martyrdom in both instances. In the case of the early Christians, they were put to death for refusing to accommodate themselves to the paganism of the ruling authorities. The problem of Christian martyrdom was solved by the conversion of the Emperor Constantine in 313. By 380, however, Christianity had become the official religion of the Roman Empire, and the Christian church used its considerable political power to enforce conformity to the Christian faith. Church discipline helped keep the civil peace by punishing religious nonconformity.

When the Reformation split the Christian church into rival factions, death for the sake of the one's religious faith became common. For the first time on a large scale, martyrdom in the sixteenth century was an intra-Christian affair. For a while Christians fought vainly to reestablish Constantinian uniformity by military means, under either the Protestant or Catholic banner. Eventually, however, it became clear that the combination of religion with political power was at the root of the problem. If martyrdom is death for the sake of one's religious faith, the only way to solve the problem of martyrdom was to ensure that no religion had the political power required to persecute another. All churches would need to be removed from political power. The modern liberal state, with its separation of church and state and toleration of all faiths, arose as a peacemaking mechanism to end the "Wars of Religion" and thereby close the book on martyrs, at least for Europe. Western society — indeed, the church itself — was saved by the rise of the modern state.

We Westerners never tire of telling this story. It is a wonderfully progressive story that reassures us that the present is better than the past. In doing so it also gives us hope that the future will be even better than the present. The present, we recognize with regret, is still plagued by religious violence of the kind we once overcame. But if it still exists, it must exist as an atavism, a leftover from the past that is doomed to be extinguished by the progressive forces of reason and liberty. The story of the "Wars of Religion," therefore, helps us maintain a temporal dichotomy between us and our past others, that is, between the modern and the medieval. The story also helps us maintain a spatial dichotomy between *us* in the West, who have solved the problem of religious violence, and *them* in the rest of the world, especially Muslims, who have not yet learned that religious passions must be defanged by removing them from the political sphere. We sometimes find it necessary to help them learn this lesson through military means. They, because of their backwardness, will wrongly read our help as religious, not political. They will continue to write their own books of martyrs, unaware that we have done away with martyrdom.

In this chapter I question this story by looking at the historical record. As we will see, the case is not as simple as the standard story implies. Christians certainly did kill each other, marking a signal failure of the church's discipleship. But the transfer of power from the church to the state was not simply a remedy for the violence. Indeed, the transfer of power from the church to the state predated the division of Christendom into Catholics and Protestants and in many ways was at the cause of the violence of the so-called Wars of Religion. The shift from medieval to modern — from church-power to state-power — was a long and complex process — with gains and losses. Whatever it was, it was not a simple progressive march from violence to peace. The gradual transferal of loyalty from international church to national state was not the end of martyrdom in Europe but the shift to a new kind of martyrdom: dying for one's country — and, we must hasten to add, killing for one's country.

Religion and Politics

For the standard story to be true, all of the following must obtain: (1) religious difference must be the primary cause of the wars; (2) the primary cause of the wars must be religious, not political, economic, or social; (3) religion, therefore, must be at least analytically separable from political, economic, and social causes in these wars; (4) the separation of religion from power by the state must be a response to, not a cause of, the wars; and (5) this separation must have produced a peaceful Europe. Let us examine each of these five claims in turn.

(1) The first thing we notice about the historical record is the many instances in which religious difference was *not* a factor in the so-called religious wars.

- Between the time that Martin Luther nailed his 95 Theses to the church door at Wittenberg in 1517 and the outbreak of the first "religious war" — the Schmalkaldic War of 1546-47 — almost thirty years would pass. The Catholic prosecutor of the Schmalkaldic War, Holy Roman Emperor Charles V, spent much of the decade following Luther's excommunication in 1520 at war not against Luther, but against the pope. As Richard Dunn points out, "Charles V's soldiers sacked Rome, not Wittenberg, in 1527, and when the papacy belatedly sponsored a reform program, both the Habsburgs and the Valois refused to endorse much of it, rejecting especially those Trentine decrees which encroached on their sovereign authority."[1] The wars of the 1520s were part of the ongoing struggle between the pope and the emperor for control over Italy and for control over the church in German territories.[2]
- The early decades of the Reformation saw Catholic France in frequent wars against the Catholic emperor. The wars began in 1521, 1527, 1536, 1542, and 1552; most of them lasted two or three years.[3] Charles V was at war for twenty-three of the forty-one years of his reign, sixteen of them against France.[4]
- Starting in 1525, Catholic France made frequent alliances with the Muslim Turks against Catholic Emperor Charles V.[5]

1. Richard S. Dunn, *The Age of Religious Wars, 1559-1689* (New York: Norton, 1970), 6.

2. Dunn, *The Age of Religious Wars,* 6-7; see also James D. Tracy, *Emperor Charles V, Impresario of War: Campaign Strategy, International Finance, and Domestic Politics* (Cambridge: Cambridge University Press, 2002), 45-47, 306.

3. Wim Blockmans, *Emperor Charles V, 1500-1558* (London and New York: Arnold Publishers and Oxford University Press, 2002), 77. These wars were essentially a continuation of French attacks on the Holy Roman Empire in 1494 and 1498.

4. Blockmans, *Emperor Charles V,* 139.

5. Blockmans, *Emperor Charles V,* 41; Tracy, *Charles V, Impresario of War,* 307.

- Until the Schmalkaldic War of 1546-47, the Protestant princes of the Holy Roman Empire generally supported the Catholic emperor in his wars against France. In 1544, Charles granted wide control to the Protestant princes over the churches in their realms in exchange for military support against France.[6]
- The first "religious war" of Charles V against the Schmalkaldic League found a number of important Protestant princes on Charles's side, including Duke Moritz of Saxony, the Margrave Albrecht-Alcibiades of Brandenburg,[7] and the Margrave Hans of Küstrin (Maltby, 62). The Protestant Philip of Hesse had already signed a treaty to support Charles against the Schmalkaldic League, but he reneged in 1546 (Maltby, 56). Wim Blockmans observes: "The fact that a number of Protestant princes joined Charles's army shows that the entire operation was based on sheer opportunism" (Blockmans, 94).
- Catholic Bavaria refused to fight for the Habsburg emperor in the Schmalkaldic War, though Bavaria did provide some material assistance (Maltby, 58). Already in 1531, Bavaria had allied with many Lutheran princes in opposing Ferdinand's election as king of the Romans, and in 1533, Bavaria had joined Philip of Hesse in restoring Württemburg to the Protestant Duke Ulrich (Maltby, 53).
- The popes were equally unreliable. In January 1547, Pope Paul III abruptly withdrew his forces from Germany, fearing that Charles's military successes would make him too strong (Blockmans, 95). As Blockmans notes, "the pope found a few apostates in northern Germany less awful than a supreme emperor" (Blockmans, 110). In 1556-57, Pope Paul IV went to war against another Habsburg monarch, the devoutly Catholic Phillip II of Spain (Maltby, 112-13).
- In alliance with Lutheran princes, the Catholic King Henry II of France attacked the emperor's forces in 1552 (Maltby, 62-64). The

6. Klaus Jaitner, "The Popes and the Struggle for Power During the Sixteenth and Seventeenth Centuries," in *1648: War and Peace in Europe*, vol. 1, ed. Klaus Bussmann and Heinz Schilling (Münster: Veranstaltungsgesellschaft 350 Jahre Westfalischer Friede, 1998), 62.

7. Tracy, *Charles V, Impresario of War*, 209-15. Both would later ally with the Schmalkaldic League in March 1552; William Maltby, *The Reign of Charles V* (New York: Palgrave, 2002), 63. Several months later, however, Albrecht-Alcibiades was back on Charles's side in an attempt to recover the towns of Lorraine for the empire (Blockmans, *Emperor Charles V*, 75). Hereafter, page references to these works appear in parentheses in the text.

Catholic princes of the empire stood by, neutral, while Charles went down to defeat. As Richard Dunn observes, "the German princes, Catholic and Lutheran, had in effect ganged up against the Habsburgs" (Dunn, 49). As a result, the emperor had to accept the Peace of Augsburg, which granted the princes the right to determine the ecclesiastical affiliation of their subjects. Dunn notes that the German peasantry and urban working class "were inclined to follow orders inertly on the religious issue, and switch from Lutheran to Catholic, or vice versa, as their masters required" (Dunn, 50-51).

- Most of Charles's soldiers were mercenaries, and they included many Protestants. Some of Charles's favorite troops were the High German *Landsknechte,* who commanded a relatively high wage but were good fighters, despite the prevalence of Lutheranism among them (Tracy, 32-34, 46, 33n47).
- The French Wars of Religion, generally dated 1562-98, are usually assumed to have pitted the Calvinist Huguenot minority against the Catholic majority. The reality is more complex. In 1573, the governor of Narbonne, the baron Raymond de Fourquevaux, reported to King Charles IX that the common people believed the wars were rooted in a conspiracy of Protestant and Catholic nobles together.[8] Other contemporary accounts confirm that this view was widespread (Heller, 63). Though such a grand conspiracy is doubtful, there were many examples of nobility changing church affiliation at whim, and many examples of collaboration between Protestant and Catholic nobles (Heller, 63-65).
- Instances of Protestant-Catholic collaboration among the nobility were generally aimed at asserting the ancient rights of the nobility over against the centralizing efforts of the monarchy. In 1573, the Catholic Henri de Turenne, duke of Bouillon, led the Huguenot forces in upper Guyenne and Périgord.[9]
- In 1574, the Catholic royal governor of Languedoc, Henri de Montmorency, sieur de Damville, who had previously fought against the Protestants, joined forces with the Huguenot nobility to support a

8. Henry Heller, *Iron and Blood: Civil Wars in Sixteenth-Century France* (Montreal and Kingston: McGill-Queen's University Press, 1991), 53, 61-62.

9. J. H. M. Salmon, *Society in Crisis: France in the Sixteenth Century* (New York: St. Martin's Press, 1975), 198. Salmon reports that Turenne almost converted to Protestantism two years later, but did not for fear it would impede his future advancement. He did become a Calvinist later in life.

proposed antimonarchical constitution.[10] He led the anticrown military forces in the west and south against the forces of Jacques de Crussol, duke of Uzès, former Huguenot destroyer of Catholic churches (Salmon, 197-98).

- In 1575, the Catholic duke of Alençon, King Henry III's brother, joined the Huguenots in open rebellion against the monarchy's oppressive taxation (Holt, 103). In 1578, as duke of Anjou, he would seek the hand of the staunchly Protestant Elizabeth I of England in marriage, in an attempt to secure an English-French alliance versus Spain (Holt, 117-19).
- A number of Protestants joined the ultra-Catholic duke of Guise's war of 1579-80 against the crown. J. H. M. Salmon comments: "So strong was the disaffection of the nobility, and so little was religion a determining factor in their alignment, that a number of Huguenot seigneurs in the eastern provinces showed a readiness to follow Guise's banners" (Salmon, 204-5).[11]
- In 1583, the Protestant Jan Casimir of the Palatinate joined forces with the Catholic duke of Lorraine against Henry III (Salmon, 234).
- Catholic nobles Conti and Soissons served the Protestant Condé in the 1587 campaigns (Salmon, 244).
- The crown was not above making alliances with the Huguenots when it served its purposes. In 1571, Charles IX allied with the Huguenots for an anti-Habsburg campaign in the Low Countries (Salmon, 183-85).
- Henry III joined forces with the Protestant Henry of Navarre in 1589 (Salmon, 257; Holt, 130-32).
- The Catholic kings also made alliances with Protestants beyond France's borders. In 1580, Anjou offered the French crown's support to Dutch Calvinist rebels against Spanish rule. In return, Anjou would become sovereign of the Netherlands, if the revolt were to succeed (Holt, 117-18).[12]

10. Mack P. Holt, *The French Wars of Religion, 1562-1629* (Cambridge: Cambridge University Press, 1995), 99; see also Salmon, *Society in Crisis,* 176, 197.

11. Salmon notes that even Huguenot champion Henri de Condé considered an alliance with the Duke of Guise (204).

12. Holt, *The French Wars of Religion,* 117-18. German Catholics also supported Dutch Protestants against the Spanish. The Catholic Duke Wilhelm of Jülich, Cleves, and Berg actively supported William of Orange in his armed rebellion that began in 1568. William of Orange also exercised flexible ecclesiastical politics. In the period 1576-85, when he needed the

- The fluidity of the nobles' and the crown's ecclesiastical affiliations is captured by Salmon in the following passage:

  > If the shift from feudal obligation to clientage had intensified the spirit of self-interest among the nobility of the sword, it was never more evident than in the years immediately before the death of Anjou in 1584. Ambition and expediency among the princes, magnates, and their followers made a mockery of religious ideals. Huguenot and Catholic Politiques had co-operated in Anjou's service in the Netherlands, just as they had at Navarre's petty court at Nérac. Montpensier, once a zealous persecutor of heretics, had deserted the Guisard camp to advocate toleration. Damville had changed alliances once more and abandoned his close association with the Valois government to effect a *rapprochement* with Navarre. For political reasons Navarre himself had resisted a mission undertaken by Epernon to reconvert him to Catholicism. Not only his Huguenot counselors, Duplessis-Mornay and d'Aubigné, urged him to stand firm, but even his Catholic chancellor, Du Ferrier, argued that more would be lost than gained by a new apostasy. More surprising was a covert attempt by Philip II to secure Navarre as his ally, coupled with a proposal that the Bourbon should repudiate Marguerite de Valois to marry the Infanta. (Salmon, 234)

- Collaboration between Protestants and Catholics of the lower classes was also widespread in the French "Wars of Religion," mainly in an effort to resist abuse by the nobility and the crown. In Agen in 1562, the Catholic baron François de Fumel forbade his Huguenot peasants from conducting services in the Calvinist manner. They revolted, and were joined by hundreds of Catholic peasants. Together they seized Fumel's château and beheaded him in front of his wife. Holt comments: "The episode shows above all how difficult it is to divide sixteenth-century French men and women into neat communities of Protestants and Catholics along doctrinal or even cultural lines" (Holt, 50-51).
- In 1578, the Protestant and Catholic inhabitants of Pont-en-Roians

support of Catholic nobles in the southern provinces of the Netherlands, he defended Catholicism and suppressed Calvinism in the south, while supporting Calvinism and proscribing Catholicism in the north (Jonathan Israel, "The Dutch-Spanish War and the Holy Roman Empire [1568-1648]," in Bussmann and Schilling, *1648: War and Peace in Europe*, 112-14).

acted together to expel the Protestant captain Bouvier, who had refused to abide by the terms of the treaty of Bergerac (Heller, 95).

- In 1578-80, the widespread "Chaperons-sans-cordon" uprising united Catholics and Protestants against the crown's attempt to impose a third levy of the *taille* tax in a single year. In 1579, an army of Catholic and Protestant artisans and peasants based in Rome destroyed the fortress of Châteaudouble and went on to capture Roissas. The combined forces moved throughout the region, occupying seigneurial manors. They were finally trapped and slaughtered by royal troops in March 1580 (Heller, 209-11).
- In 1579, Catholic and Protestant parishes actively collaborated in the revolt in the Vivarais against the violence and corruption of the ruling classes. In the spring of 1580, the Protestant François Barjac led a combined Catholic and Huguenot force from the Vivarais against the troops stationed at the fortress of Crussol (Heller, 91-92).
- In 1586, Catholic and Protestant villages collaborated in an attack on Saint Bertrand de Comminges (Heller, 127). In 1591, the peasant federation of the Campanelle, based in Comminges, joined Catholics and Protestants together to make war on the nobility (Salmon, 277).
- In the Haut-Biterrois in the 1590s, a league of twenty-four villages of both Protestants and Catholics arose to protest taxes and set up a system of self-defense and self-government (Heller, 126).
- In 1593-94, Protestant and Catholic peasants joined in dozens of uprisings in the southwest of France. Some of these consisted of a few hundred peasants, while others gathered up to 40,000 (Holt, 156-57). The most famous of these revolts was that of the Croquants, whose articles of association required the ignoring of ecclesiastical differences (Salmon, 282-91).
- If Protestants and Catholics often collaborated in the French civil wars of 1562-98, it is also the case that the Catholics were divided into two main parties, the Catholic League and those called Politiques, who often found themselves on opposing sides of the violence. The Queen Mother, Catherine de Medici, promoted Protestants such as Navarre, Condé, and Coligny to positions of importance in order to counter the power of the ultra-Catholic Guises. In May 1588, the Guise-led League took Paris from the royal troops, and Henry III fled the city. In December of that year, Henry III had the duke and cardinal of Guise killed, and he made a pact with the Protestant Henry of Navarre to make war on the Catholic League. Henry III himself was

assassinated in August 1589 by a Jacobin monk. With Henry of Navarre as successor to the throne, Catholics split into royalists, who supported him, and Leaguers, who led a full-scale military rebellion against him and his supporters (Salmon, 243-57).

- The black legend of the religious wars presents the Thirty Years' War as one widespread unified conflict pitting Europe's Protestants against its Catholics. There was indeed an attempt in 1609 to expand the Protestant Union, which was created by eight German principalities, into a pan-European alliance. However, only the counts of Oettingen and the cities of Strasbourg, Ulm, and Nuremburg responded. The elector of Saxony, King Christian of Denmark, and the Reformed cities of Switzerland — in short, the majority of Protestant princes and regions — refused to participate in the Protestant Union.[13] When the Protestant estates of Bohemia rebelled against Emperor Ferdinand II in the opening act of the Thirty Years' War, they offered the crown of Bohemia to Frederick V of the Palatinate, one of the founders of the Protestant Union. The other members of the Protestant Union refused to support him, however, and the union disbanded two years later.[14]
- The Protestant Union attracted some Catholic support. The now-Catholic Henry IV of France sent troops to support the Protestant Union's intervention in the succession crisis in Cleves-Jülich in 1610, but he demanded as a condition of support that the union sever all contact with French Huguenots (Parker, 29-33). The Catholic prince Carlo Emanuele I of Savoy made an alliance with the Protestant Union in 1619 because the Austrian Habsburgs had failed to solve the succession crisis in Monferrato in a way favorable to his interests. After the Bohemian Protestants were defeated at the Battle of White Mountain, Carlo Emanuele switched his support to the Habsburgs.[15]
- The Lutheran elector of Saxony, John George, helped Emperor Ferdinand II reconquer Bohemia, in exchange for the Habsburg province Lusatia (Dunn, 71). In 1626, the elector of Saxony published

13. The Swiss Reformed cities refused to join the Protestant Union because of their alliance obligations to the Swiss Confederation's Catholic regions; Kaspar von Greyerz, "Switzerland During the Thirty Years' War," in Bussmann and Schilling, *1648: War and Peace in Europe,* 135.

14. Geoffrey Parker, ed., *The Thirty Years' War* (London: Routledge, 1984), 59-64.

15. Robert Oresko, "The House of Savoy and the Thirty Years' War," in Bussmann and Schilling, *1648: War and Peace in Europe,* 143-44.

a lengthy argument in which he tried to persuade his fellow Protestants to support the Catholic emperor. According to John George, the emperor was fighting a just war against rebels, not a crusade against Protestants; what the emperor did in Bohemia and Austria was covered by the principle of *cuius regio, eius religio.* Those who opposed the emperor were guilty of treason. The elector of Saxony even cited Luther's admonition to obey the powers that be (Parker, 94). John George would later throw in his lot with the Swedes against the emperor (Parker, 136).

- Catholic France supported Protestant princes from early on in the war. France supported the Protestant Grisons in Switzerland against the Habsburgs in 1623 (Oresko, 144-45). In 1624, the minister for foreign affairs, Charles de la Vieuville, made alliances and promises of aid to the Dutch and to multiple German Protestant princes. He also opened negotiations with England to restore Frederick to the throne of Bohemia (Parker, 70-71).
- Cardinal Richilieu replaced Vieuville later in 1624 and demanded English and Dutch help in repressing the Huguenots. When such help was not forthcoming, Richilieu abandoned plans for an alliance with England; the Dutch, however, did send a fleet to aid in the defeat of the Huguenot stronghold La Rochelle in 1628 (Parker, 76).
- While the Calvinist Dutch were helping the French defeat the Calvinists at La Rochelle, Catholic Spain was supporting the Protestant duke of Rohan in his battle against the French crown in Languedoc.[16]
- The principal adviser of the Calvinist elector of Brandenburg, George William, was a Catholic, Count Adam of Schwarzenberg (Collins, 115).
- One of the leading commanders of the imperial army under Albrecht von Wallenstein, Hans Georg von Arnim, was a Lutheran. Historian R. Po-Chia Hsia observes: "To build the largest and most powerful army in Europe, Wallenstein employed military talent regardless of confessional allegiance."[17]
- Wallenstein's foot soldiers included many Protestants, including — ironically — those fleeing because of the imposition of Catholic rule

16. James B. Collins, *The State in Early Modern France* (Cambridge: Cambridge University Press, 1995), 29.

17. R. Po-Chia Hsia, *Social Discipline in the Reformation: Central Europe 1550-1750* (London: Routledge, 1989), 85.

in their home territories. In April 1633, for example, Wallenstein gained a large number of Protestant recruits from Austria, who had left because of Emperor Ferdinand's policy of re-Catholicization there (Parker, 194).

- Private mercenary armies of flexible allegiance helped perpetuate the Thirty Years' War. Soldiers of fortune sold the services of their armies to the highest bidder. Ernst von Mansfield worked first for the Catholic Spanish, then for the Lutheran Frederick V, and subsequently switched sides several more times (Dunn, 71-72). Protestant Scots and English served as officers in Catholic armies, especially in France. Some, such as Captain Sidnam Poyntz, switched sides several times. Sir James Turner acknowledged that he "had swallowed, without chewing, in Germanie, a very dangerous maxime, which military men there too much follow, which was, that soe we serve our master honestlie, it is no matter what master we serve" (quoted in Parker, 195).
- Sweden's King Gustavus Adolphus is sometimes presented as the champion of the Protestant cause upon his entry into the war in 1630. However, Gustavus found it difficult to gain Protestant allies. When Swedish troops landed in Germany, their sole ally in the empire was the city of Stralsund. Over the next few months, the Swedish gained only a few more small principalities as allies (Parker, 123). The most powerful of the Protestant imperial diets saw the Swedish invasion as a threat. They met in the Convention of Leipzig from February to April 1631 in order to form a third party that would be independent of Swedish and imperial control.[18] After the initial Swedish victories in 1631, however, many formerly neutral territories were forced to join the Swedes. With Swedish troops approaching in October 1631, the Margrave Christian of Brandenburg-Kulmbach, who had avoided any military engagement up to that point, swore his allegiance to Gustavus and agreed to quarter and subsidize his troops. The common people endured many hardships due to the presence of the Swedish troops. When the Lutheran peasants attempted to drive out the Swedes in November 1632, they were massacred (Parker, 127-28).
- France under Cardinal Richilieu signed a treaty with Sweden in Jan-

18. Herbert Langer, "The Royal Swedish War in Germany," in Bussmann and Schilling, *1648: War and Peace in Europe*, 189.

uary 1631, in which France agreed to subsidize heavily the Swedish war effort (Parker, 127-28).[19] Cardinal Richilieu also made a pact with the Protestant principality of Hesse-Kassel.[20] The French began sending troops to battle imperial forces in the winter of 1634-35, and the latter half of the Thirty Years' War was largely a battle between Catholic France, on the one hand, and the Catholic Habsburgs, on the other (Parker, 142).

- In March 1635, the troops of fervently Catholic Spain attacked Trier and kidnapped the Catholic archbishop elector. Catholic France subsequently declared war on Catholic Spain (Parker, 142; Oresko, 146).
- In May 1635, the Protestant principalities of Brandenburg and Saxony reconciled with the emperor in the Peace of Prague. Not only did hostilities between the parties cease, but the armies of the Protestant principalities were absorbed into the imperial armies. Within months, most Lutheran states made peace with the emperor on the same terms, and proceeded to direct their energies against the Swedes (Parker, 142-43). By 1638, the Scottish Presbyterian Robert Baillie could observe, "For the Swedds, I see not what their eirand is now in Germany, bot to shed Protestant blood" (Parker, 182).
- The pope, on the other hand, refused to support the Holy Roman Emperor, instead giving his approval to the Swedish-French alliance. Pope Urban VIII's main interest lay in weakening Habsburg control over the Papal States in central Italy.[21]
- In 1643, Lutheran Sweden attacked Lutheran Denmark. King Christian IV had long harassed Swedish shipping in the Baltic and had given asylum to political enemies of Sweden. When word reached Stockholm that Denmark was negotiating an alliance with the emperor, Sweden decided to make a preemptive strike. The conflict lasted two years. Despite the Catholic emperor's aid, Denmark was defeated and forced to sue for peace (Parker, 174).

19. Richilieu did stipulate that Catholic worship should be tolerated in territories conquered by Sweden, but as Parker points out, he had no way of forcing Sweden to comply (Parker, 124, 262n6).

20. Konrad Repgen, "Negotiating the Peace of Westphalia: A Survey with an Examination of the Major Problems," in Bussmann and Schilling, *1648: War and Peace in Europe*, 355.

21. Jaitner, "The Popes and the Struggle for Power," 65. As Jaitner suggests, the pope's "call to fight against heretics and heresies in the Empire was merely rhetorical with no concrete consequences."

- If the above instances of warmaking — in which members of the same church fought each other and members of different churches collaborated — undermine the standard narrative of the Wars of Religion, the *absence* of war between Lutherans and Calvinists also undermines the standard tale. If theological difference tends toward war, we should expect to find Lutheran-Calvinist wars; in actual fact, we find none. Although there were internal tensions in some principalities between Lutheran princes and Calvinist nobility, or Calvinist princes and Lutheran nobility, no Lutheran prince ever went to war against a Calvinist prince.[22] The absence of such wars cannot be attributed to the similarity of Lutheranism and Calvinism. There were sufficient theological differences to sustain a permanent divide between the two branches of the Reformation. Such differences were serious enough to produce sporadic attempts by the civil authorities to enforce doctrinal uniformity. In the decades following Phillip Melanchthon's death in 1560, there was an effort to root out "crypto-Calvinists" from the ranks of Lutheranism. The rector of the University of Wittenberg, Caspar Peucer, was imprisoned for crypto-Calvinism from 1574 to 1586; Nikolaus Krell was executed for crypto-Calvinism in Dresden in 1601. Many crypto-Calvinists among the Lutherans were forced to relocate to regions friendlier to Calvinism, such as Hesse-Kassel.[23] However, the fact that Lutheran-Calvinist tensions played no part in the "Wars of Religion" indicates at minimum that significant theological differences in the public realm did not necessarily produce war in sixteenth- and seventeenth-century Europe.

The above list contains examples of Catholics killing Catholics, and Catholics collaborating with Protestants in these wars. Undoubtedly, historians of this period could add more instances of war between members of the same church, as well as collaboration in war among members of different churches. It is also undoubtedly true, however, that we could compile an even longer list of acts of war between Catholics and Protestants in the sixteenth and seventeenth centuries. May we not simply conclude that this list

22. Such was the case in the Palatinate and Brandenburg-Prussia; Eric W. Gritsch, *A History of Lutheranism* (Minneapolis: Fortress Press, 2002), 110-11.

23. Herbert J. A. Bouman, "Retrospect and Prospect," *Sixteenth-Century Studies* 8, no. 4 (1977): 84-104; David C. Steinmetz, *Reformers in the Wings: From Geiler von Kayserberg to Theodore Beza,* 2nd. ed. (Oxford: Oxford University Press, 2001).

contains *exceptions* to the general rule that war was between different "religions" during this era, but that the standard narrative of the "Wars of Religion" still holds?

There are two immediate reasons why this would not be an adequate response. First, the list contains more than just a few isolated instances. In the case of the Thirty Years' War, for example, one could characterize the latter half of the war as primarily a struggle between the two great Catholic powers of Europe: France, on the one hand, against the two branches of the Habsburgs, on the other. Second, the above list contains more than just exceptions: if the wars in question are indeed "Wars of Religion," then the instances above are *inexplicable* exceptions. Why, in a war over religion, would those who share the same religious beliefs kill each other? Why, in a war over religion, would those on opposite sides of the religious divide collaborate?

Imagine I am writing a history of World War I. I am telling the standard story of the war as a struggle between two sets of nations, fueled by complex national aspirations, when I uncover a startling fact: the English counties of Somerset, Kent, Durham, Shropshire, Norfolk, Suffolk, and Cornwall entered World War I on the side of the Kaiser. Leaders in each of these counties declared their allegiance to the German cause, and thousands of troops were sent by ship to Hamburg to join the German forces fighting on the Western front. I could respond to this discovery by noting these odd exceptions, but pointing out that the majority of English counties fought for the Allied powers, so the basic plotline of the war is unaltered. If I were a good historian, however, I would most likely drop everything and try to find a narrative that would take these cases into account. What motivated the leaders of these counties? Did the troops from these counties go out of conviction or desperation? What grievances did these counties have against London that made them unwilling to fight for the king? What other factors besides nationalism were at work in this war?

(2) In the actual case of the sixteenth- and seventeenth-century wars, historians generally deal with the facts from the list above by acknowledging that other factors besides religion were at work in the "Wars of Religion" — political, economic, and social factors. The question then becomes one of the relative importance of the various factors. Are political, economic, and social factors important enough that we are no longer justified in calling these wars "of religion"? The above list contains acts of war in which religion as a principal motivating factor must *necessarily* be ruled out. But

once religion is ruled out as a significant factor from these events, the remainder of acts of war — those between Protestants and Catholics — become suspect as well. Were other factors besides religion the principal motivators in these cases as well? If Catholics killed Catholics for political and economic reasons, did Catholics also kill Protestants for political and economic reasons?

Historians take different positions on this question. Opinions range from those who think that religion was an important factor among other significant factors to those who think that religion was not important, except as a cover for underlying political and economic and social causes. This divide is apparent if we look at twentieth-century historiography of the French wars. For much of that century, historians downplayed the role of religion in favor of supposedly more fundamental political, economic, and social causes. In 1909, James Westfall Thompson wrote: "Although the purposes of the Huguenots were clandestinely more political than religious, it was expedient to cloak them under a mantle of faith."[24] Henri Drouot's 1937 work on the Catholic League in Burgundy saw religious factors as merely a cover for class tensions. Druout observes: "Classes were more clearly defined, and above all, social tensions arose and festered, social tensions that religion could disguise in its own colors and intensify with fanaticism, but which were really the basis of local tensions at the time of the League."[25] Such opinions predominated in twentieth-century historiography, and continue to be found in figures such as Henry Heller, who writes that the French civil wars of the sixteenth century were "from start to finish . . . a kind of class war from above."[26]

In recent decades, however, this view has been challenged. Natalie Zemon Davis's 1973 article "The Rites of Violence" is considered a watershed for bringing religious factors back into the study of the French wars. Davis objects to the standard practice of reducing religious factors to, for example, class conflict, and she identifies the cause of popular riots in sixteenth-century France as "ridding the community of dreaded pollution," a factor she identifies as "essentially religious." For Catholics, the

24. James Westfall Thompson, *The Wars of Religion in France, 1559-1576: The Huguenots, Catherine de Medici, Philip II*, 2nd ed. (New York: Frederick Ungar, 1957), 142.

25. Henri Drouot, *Mayenne et la Bourgogne: Etude sur la Ligue (1587-1596)*, 2 vols. (Paris and Dijon: Auguste Picard, 1937), 1:33, quoted in Mack Holt, "Putting Religion Back into the Wars of Religion," *French Historical Studies* 18, no. 2 (Autumn 1993): 529.

26. Heller, *Iron and Blood*, 136, as quoted in Holt, "Putting Religion Back into the Wars of Religion," 545.

rites of violence promised the "restoration of unity to the body social"; for Protestants, the goal was the creation of a new kind of unity in the body social.[27] In his 1993 review article entitled "Putting Religion Back Into the Wars of Religion," Mack Holt identifies a number of other recent attempts to take religious factors seriously. According to Holt, the older Weberian approach is being supplanted by a more Durkheimian influence; rather than see material causes as more fundamental than religion, Durkheim identified religion with the rituals necessary to bind adherents to the social group. Holt sees this influence at work in works by Denis Crouzet, Barbara Diefendorf, Denis Richet, and Michael Wolfe, the last of whom argues, "Although politics certainly had its place, as did questions of social interest and economic competition, these bitter conflicts were primarily religious wars."[28]

So we have one group of historians who dismiss religion as an important factor in the French civil wars of the sixteenth century and another group who want to reclaim religion as an important driving force in these conflicts. What are we to conclude? Barbara Diefendorf asks an apt question: "Must we go from an overly political interpretation of the period to one that seems to offer very little room for politics, at least as traditionally viewed?" Should we, as Diefendorf says she is trying to do, seek "middle ground" between political and religious interpretations? Or is there a problem with the way politics and religion have been, in Diefendorf's phrase, "traditionally viewed"? She hints at such an answer when she says, "[F]rom my perspective, at least, religious and secular motives were inseparable."[29] According to Diefendorf, processions of the eucharistic host, which sometimes served as the occasion of violence, were not purely religious events, but were opportunities to reinforce social bodies and ask God's intervention in "secular affairs." These processions show how "Catholic beliefs, monarchical politics, and civic identity were mutually reinforcing elements of Parisian culture."[30]

27. Natalie Zemon Davis, *Society and Culture in Early Modern France* (Stanford: Stanford University Press, 1975), 157, 164, 160. Chapter 6 of this book originally appeared as "The Rites of Violence: Religious Riot in Sixteenth-Century France," *Past & Present* 59 (May 1973).

28. Michael Wolfe, *The Conversion of Henry IV: Politics, Power, and Religious Belief in Early Modern France* (Cambridge, MA: Harvard University Press, 1993), 5.

29. Barbara Diefendorf, *Beneath the Cross: Catholics and Huguenots in Sixteenth-Century Paris* (New York and Oxford: Oxford University Press, 1991), 6.

30. Diefendorf, *Beneath the Cross,* 38.

(3) In order for the black legend of the religious wars to be true, "religion" must be at least analytically separable from "politics," "economics," and so forth. That is, even if things seem to be quite complex on the ground, and people act from a variety of motives, we must be able at least on paper to identify which motives are religious and which political. Though historians disagree on which factors predominated, many historians exude the same confidence that religious factors can be picked out from the other factors. Surely, when eucharistic doctrine is involved, the motivation can be labeled "religious"; when it is a matter of extending or protecting the power of the monarchy over the lesser nobility, then the motivation is clearly "political." What happens, however, if, as Diefendorf says, the Eucharist creates a "social" body? What if, as Crouzet says, the monarchy is "sacral"?

In a 1991 essay entitled "Unrethinking the Sixteenth-Century Wars of Religion," John Bossy calls Davis's essay "The Rites of Violence" "the most important contribution to understanding the wars of religion made in our time." What Bossy likes about Davis's work is that she studiously avoids the category of *society,* and thus does she avoid an anachronistic reduction of religion to social causes. Bossy puts some distance here between his own view and that of Durkheim. "The fact about society is that there is good reason to suppose that no such thing existed in the sixteenth century. I suspect that there was no such thing because there was no such concept. . . . There was nothing we could refer to which [a sixteenth-century person] would not recognize as falling under the heading 'Commonwealth,' or under the heading 'Church' or 'Christianity.'" There was no abstraction called "society" that remained once religion was bracketed off. According to Bossy, the supreme embodiment of Christian "social" reality was the Eucharist.[31]

To fully grasp this point, we should recall what Bossy says elsewhere about "religion": there was also no such concept in the sixteenth century, or at least it was not fully formed until about 1700. Bossy says that the development of the modern idea of society was "a successor effect of the transition in 'religion,' whose history it reproduced. One cannot therefore exactly call Religion and Society twins; but in other respects they are like the sexes according to Aristophanes, effects of the fission of a primitive

31. John Bossy, "Unrethinking the Sixteenth-Century Wars of Religion," in *Belief in History: Innovative Approaches to European and American Religion,* ed. Thomas Kselman (Notre Dame, IN: University of Notre Dame Press, 1991), 278-80.

whole, yearning towards one another across a great divide."[32] In other words, in the sixteenth century there simply was no coherent way yet to divide "religious" causes from "social" causes; the divide is a modern invention. If this is true, then Davis has not entirely escaped anachronism when she claims that the riots were "essentially religious." Indeed, if we follow Davis in seeing that the goal of the rites of violence was either to restore a lost unity of the body social (Catholics) or create a new unity of the body social (Protestants), then there is no reason at all for calling the violence "essentially religious," as opposed to social, political, or economic. Rival visions of the social order were at stake, and there is simply no way to separate out religious factors from other factors that are supposedly more mundane and rational. Davis and Bossy are right to criticize earlier historiography's attempts to see political, social, and economic factors as more real and more basic than religious factors. But we are not therefore licensed to reach the opposite and equally invalid conclusion that there is something called "religion" lurking behind more mundane factors that is responsible for the fury of these wars. Nor do we solve the problem simply by seeking middle ground, for example, assigning equal shares of responsibility to political, religious, economic, and social causes.

The Rise of the State

(4) Where does this leave the standard narrative about the wars of religion? It means that there is no way to pinpoint something called "religion" as the cause of these wars and excise it from the exercise of public power. The standard narrative says that the modern state identified religion as the root of the problem and separated it out from politics. In fact, however, there was no separation of religion and politics. What we see in reality is what Bossy describes as a "migration of the holy" from the church to the state,[33] or, as John Neville Figgis put it, "the religion of the State has replaced the religion of the Church, or, to be more correct . . . religion is becoming individual while the civil power is recognised as having the paramount claims of an organized society upon the allegiance of its members."[34] This alle-

32. John Bossy, *Christianity in the West, 1400-1700* (Oxford: Oxford University Press, 1985), 170-71.

33. Bossy, *Christianity in the West,* 153-61.

34. John Neville Figgis, *From Gerson to Grotius, 1414-1625* (New York: Harper Torchbook, 1960), 124.

giance most pointedly includes the requirement to participate in war. Carolyn Marvin says: "[I]n the West the power to compel believers to die passed from Christianity to the nation-state, where it largely remains."[35] Ostensibly, the holy is separated from politics for the sake of peace; in reality, the emerging state appropriates the holy to become itself a new kind of "religion."

The sacralization of early modern monarchs was one of the most visible signs of the migration of the holy to the state. In France, monarchs freely borrowed from the rituals of the feast of Corpus Christi to express sacred solidarity with the crown. Charles VIII was welcomed to Rouen with the titles Lamb of God, savior, head of the mystical body of France, guardian of the book of the seven seals, and deified bringer of peace.[36] By 1625, the General Assembly of the Clergy of France could proclaim not only that the French kings were ordained by God, but "they themselves were gods."[37]

The "Wars of Religion" were not ended by the secularization of the state. On the contrary, the seventeenth and eighteenth centuries saw the sacralization of the state and the quasi divinity of monarchs reach new heights. It is crucial to see, however, that the later secularization of the state was in some respects not a contrary movement to the sacralization of the state. As John Wolf has written in his study of Louis XIV, "the deification of the person of the king in this theocentric era was accomplished in much the same way and with the same intentions that secular societies of the nineteenth and twentieth centuries have deified the state."[38] The eventual development of the idea of religion and politics as two essentially separate realms of human endeavor served to augment the "religion of the state." As Quentin Skinner points out, the idea of politics as an independent branch of moral philosophy depends on the rise of the modern state.[39] The modern idea of religion as a realm of human activity inherently separate from politics likewise depends on a new configuration of Christian societies in which many legislative and jurisdictional powers and claims to power — as well as claims to the devotion and allegiance of the people — were pass-

35. Carolyn Marvin and David Ingle, "Blood Sacrifice and the Nation: Revisiting Civil Religion," *Journal of the American Academy of Religion* 64, no. 4 (1996): 769.

36. Bossy, *Christianity in the West,* 154-55.

37. Holt, *The French Wars of Religion,* 9.

38. John B. Wolf, *Louis XIV* (New York: Norton, 1968).

39. Quentin Skinner, *The Foundations of Modern Political Thought* (Cambridge: Cambridge University Press, 1978), 2:349-50.

ing from the church to the new sovereign state. The new conception of religion would help to "purify" the church of powers and claims that were not its proper function. The new concept of religion helped facilitate the shift to state dominance over the church by distinguishing inward religion from the bodily disciplines of the state. The new subject is thus able to do due service to both church and state — without conflict.

Early modern theorists of the state presented their attempts to separate civil government from religion not as the creation of something new but as an attempt to clarify and separate two essentially distinct types of human endeavor that had somehow gotten mixed up together. John Locke writes:

> [T]he church itself is a thing absolutely separate and distinct from the commonwealth. The boundaries on both sides are fixed and immovable. He jumbles heaven and earth together, the things most remote and opposite, who mixes these two societies, which are in their original, end, business, and in everything perfectly distinct and infinitely different from each other.[40]

In fact, however, the advent of the modern state, with its concept of sovereignty and its absorption of many of the powers of the old ecclesiastical regime, was proving that the boundaries were anything but fixed and immovable. The centralizing power of the modern state that was asserted over against medieval privileges was met with fierce resistance by those for whom the state was indeed something new and unwelcome. The creation of separate realms of religion and politics was not simply the solution to the violence that racked Europe in the sixteenth and seventeenth centuries; it was itself a cause of the violence. What we have is not the solution to violence by its secularization, but a "migration of the holy" from church to state, and thereby the creation of a new kind of martyrdom.

The idea that the transfer of power from the church to the state was the solution to the wars of the sixteenth century is implausible, as the process of state-building, begun well before the Reformation, was inherently conflictual. Beginning in the late medieval period, the process involved the internal integration of previously scattered powers under the aegis of the ruler, and the external demarcation of territory over against other, foreign states. Heinz Schilling writes:

40. John Locke, *A Letter Concerning Toleration* (Indianapolis: Bobbs-Merrill, 1955), 27.

> The internal process of state-building was no different to the external one and the accompanying birth of the early modern Europe of the great powers was accompanied by massive disruption. Internally the rulers and their state elites used violent means against the estates, cities, clergy and local associations which laid claim to an independent, non-derived right of political participation which the early modern state could no longer grant under the principle of sovereignty. Externally in addition to the above-mentioned tendencies of territorial adjustment between the states, conflicts were mainly over "rank," since at this stage there was no generally acknowledged system of states. Therefore, at the end of the middle ages, Europe entered a long phase of intense violent upheaval both within and between states.[41]

Much of the violence of the fifteenth through seventeenth centuries can be explained in terms of the resistance of local elites to the centralizing efforts of monarchs and emperors. Charles V's campaigns against Protestant princes, with some Protestant help, were largely attempts to make of the decentralized Holy Roman Empire a modern state with a single church and administration. Resistance from both Protestant and Catholic princes, with the help of Catholic France, was intended to both thwart Charles's attempts at state-building and consolidate the princes' own control over the churches in their realms. The Peace of Augsburg — whose principle of *cuius regio, eius religio* gave each prince the power to determine the religion of his subjects — was not the state's solution to religious violence, but instead represented the victory of one set of state-building elites over another. In the Peace of Augsburg, as Richard Dunn notes,

> [t]he German princes, Catholic and Lutheran, had in effect ganged up against the Habsburgs. They had observed, correctly enough, that Charles V had been trying not only to crush Protestantism but to increase Habsburg power and check the centrifugal tendencies within the empire. The princes, both Lutheran and Catholic, had also been trying to turn the Reformation crisis to their personal advantage, by asserting new authority over their local churches, tightening ecclesiastical patronage, and squeezing more profit from church revenues.[42]

41. Heinz Schilling, "War and Peace at the Emergence of Modernity: Europe Between State Belligerence, Religious Wars, and the Desire for Peace," in Bussmann and Schilling, *1648: War and Peace in Europe*, 14.

42. Dunn, *The Age of Religious Wars*, 49.

The French "Wars of Religion" pitted the French crown's determination to unite France under "une foi, une loi, un roi" against the nobility who resisted such threats to their power and privileges. Both the Calvinist Huguenots and the Catholic League fought the monarchy in an attempt to resist the centralization of power. While the crown's propagandists, such as Michel de L'Hôpital, strove to establish continuity between the crown and an idealized medieval monarchy, Huguenot propaganda idealized the nobility as those who defended ancient custom and the political body of France against the usurpations of the growing royal bureaucracy.[43] The manifesto of the Catholic League likewise committed its members not only to restoring the dignity of the Catholic Church, but to recovering the "perfect freedom" to which the nobles were entitled and abolishing "new taxes and all additions since the reign of Charles IX."[44] Robert Descimon and Eli Barnavi have described the Catholic League as "a reaction of the body social against absolutizing centralism."[45] The French civil wars ended when the nobility allied with the crown to put down popular unrest. The absolutist state was realized in seventeenth-century France by co-opting the nobility into the centralizing project of the crown.[46]

Similar comments could be made about the state-building projects that led up to the Thirty Years' War, which began in German lands and spilled out across Europe. Heinz Schilling sees the Thirty Years' War as the confluence of two major trends in Europe, both of which had begun well before Martin Luther: the rise of the state and the reform of the church.[47] R. Po-Chia Hsia comments on early seventeenth-century Germany: "Confessional struggles often reflected the contest between the centralizing state and the traditional forces of a society based on estates and established privileges."[48]

The point of all this is *not* that these wars were really about politics and not really about religion; nor is the point that the state caused the wars and the church was innocent. The point is that the transfer of power

43. Salmon, *Society in Crisis*, 168-69; see also Donna Bohanan, *Crown and Nobility in Early Modern France* (Basingstoke, UK: Palgrave, 2001), 27-32.

44. Quoted in Salmon, *Society in Crisis*, 238.

45. Elie Barnavi and Robert Descimon, *La Sainte ligue, le juge et la potence* (Paris: Hachette, 1985), quoted in Heller, *Iron and Blood*, 106.

46. Bohanan, *Crown and Nobility*, 29-32; see also James B. Collins, *The State in Early Modern France* (Cambridge: Cambridge University Press, 1995), 1-2, 13.

47. Schilling, "War and Peace," 13.

48. Hsia, *Social Discipline in the Reformation*, 36.

from the church to the state was not the solution to the violence of the sixteenth and seventeenth centuries, but was at the cause of those wars. The church was deeply implicated in the violence, for it became increasingly identified with and absorbed into the state-building project. Beginning in the fifteenth century, rulers looked to expand their powers by absorbing the powers and revenues of the church. In France and Spain, a series of concessions wrung from the papacy over the course of the fifteenth century and into the first decades of the sixteenth century transferred many church revenues and appointments from the pope to the crown. After the Concordat of Bologna in 1516 gave the French king unfettered license to make ecclesiastical appointments, Francis I packed the episcopacy with his clients, largely nobles of the sword who had no theological training whatsoever.[49]

In the late fifteenth century, the civil authorities in Sweden, England, Denmark, and Germany tried — with only partial success — to limit clerical exemptions from civil courts, limit the power of ecclesiastical courts, and transfer church appointments, revenues, and lands to the secular rulers. As Quentin Skinner points out, the Reformation failed in France and Spain, where the monarchies had largely absorbed the church into their clientage systems, and therefore had an interest in maintaining the status quo, and the Reformation succeeded in England, Scandinavia, and many German principalities, where breaking with the Catholic Church meant that the church could be used to augment the power of the civil authorities. To cite one example, King Gustav Vasa welcomed the Reformation to Sweden in 1524 by transferring the receipt of tithes from the church to the crown. Three years later he appropriated the entire property of the church.[50]

This is not to say that rulers were insincere in their embrace of the Reformation. It is to say, however, that the building of the modern state was not simply a response to religious divisions but was itself deeply implicated in the production of such differences. This connection is confirmed by the "confessionalization thesis," which since the 1970s has redefined historical scholarship on Germany and much of the rest of Europe during the sixteenth and seventeenth centuries. The building of strong confessional identities among Protestants and Catholics during that period was part of the state-building project. Luther Peterson summarizes it this way:

49. Salmon, *Society in Crisis*, 80-82.
50. Skinner, *Foundations*, 2:58-64.

> The confessionalization thesis is a fruitful instrument in explaining the transformation of medieval feudal monarchies into modern states, in particular how the new states changed their inhabitants into disciplined, obedient and united subjects. According to the thesis, a key factor in that change is the establishment of religious uniformity in the state: the populace was taught a religious identity — Catholic, Lutheran, or Calvinist — through doctrinal statements (confessions and catechisms) and liturgical practices. This distinguished "us" as a religious and political community from "other," often neighboring, religious-political societies. The ruler was sacralized as the defender and — in Protestant lands — leader of the church, rightfully overseeing the church of his land. These state-led churches also aided state development by imposing moral discipline on the communities.[51]

(5) If the rise of the modern state did not in fact produce a more peaceful Europe, it did produce a shift in what people were willing to kill and die for. The migration of the holy was accompanied by a migration in the meaning of the term "martyrdom." Ernst Kantorowicz has documented that, as early as the thirteenth century, the language of martyrdom on behalf of the celestial *patria* had begun to shift to martyrdom on behalf of the earthly *patria*. Meanwhile, the *communis patria* was redefined from either one's locality or Christendom as a whole to the emerging protonational state. The more advanced national monarchies such as France were appropriating liturgical symbolism from the church such that the emerging state was a mystical body politic and source of *caritas* that bound one to one's compatriots. Martyrdom *pro fide* was eclipsed by or included in martyrdom *pro patria*, which was extolled as a work of *caritas* on behalf of one's countrymen.[52]

While the future was assured for the praise of death for one's country, Christian martyrdom would be strictly delimited by the theorists of the modern state. Thomas Hobbes assumed the fittingness of dying for the "mortal god" Leviathan. Christian martyrdom, however, he restricted only to those who died for proclaiming one single article of faith: "Jesus is the Christ." Those who oppose the laws of the civil state for any other doctrine

51. Luther D. Peterson, "Johann Pfeffinger's Treatises of 1550 in Defense of Adiaphora: 'High Church' Lutheranism and Confessionalization in Albertine Saxony," in *Confessionalization in Europe, 1555-1700: Essays in Honor of Bodo Nischan*, ed. John M. Headley, Hans J. Hillerbrand, and Anthony J. Papalas (Aldershot, UK: Ashgate, 2004), 104-5.

52. Ernst H. Kantorowicz, *The King's Two Bodies: A Study in Medieval Political Theology* (Princeton, NJ: Princeton University Press, 1957), 232-72.

do so for private ambition and deserve their punishment. A person can only be a martyr, or witness, if he or she proclaims that Jesus is the Christ to infidels. There can be no martyrs in a Christian commonwealth, for one cannot witness to those who already believe.[53] In eliminating any possibility of civil disobedience to the state, Hobbes eliminates the possibility of martyrdom for Christ.

Conclusion

If we grant that the migration of power from the church to the state was not as innocent of violence as the standard narrative would have it, we might still object that the early modern state was not yet secularized. We have now learned that violence can be tamed by privatizing religion. The problem with Hobbes's state was its failure to separate church and state.

This objection continues to see politics and religion as two essentially different human activities that can be — and should be — sorted out. As the history above indicates, however, the process is most accurately seen as the migration of the holy from church to state, not the sorting out of religion from politics. Those who say that nationalism is the modern religion, as Carlton Hayes does, are not far off the mark.[54] It would be foolish to expect that, once the state had claimed the holy, it would dispose of its power. If that were the case, we would expect that martyrdom would have faded from human history, at least in the West. However, as the poet Wilfred Owen would say during World War I, "The old Lie: Dulce et decorum est/Pro patria mori" would carry more weight than ever in the twentieth century and into our time. As Eric Hobsbawm has pointed out, ours is an unliturgical age in most respects, with one enormous exception: the public life of the citizen of the nation-state. "Indeed most of the occasions when people become conscious of citizenship as such remain associated with symbols and semi-ritual practices (for instance, elections), most of which are historically novel and largely invented: flags, images, ceremonies and music."[55] Benedict Anderson has said that in modernity the nation re-

53. Thomas Hobbes, *Leviathan; or, The Matter, Forme, and Power of a Commonwealth Ecclesiasticall and Civil* (New York: Collier Books, 1962), 363-66.

54. Carlton Hayes, *Nationalism: A Religion* (New York: Macmillan, 1960).

55. Eric Hobsbawm, "Introduction: Inventing Traditions," in *The Invention of Tradition*, ed. Eric Hobsbawm and Terence Ranger (Cambridge: Cambridge University Press, 1983), 12.

places the church as the primary institution that deals with death. Nations provide a new kind of salvation; my death is not in vain if it is for the nation, which lives on into a limitless future.[56] According to Carolyn Marvin and David Ingle, the nation not only gives death meaning, but sacrifice for the nation-state provides the glue that binds a liberal social order together.

> Americans generally see their nation as a secular culture possessed of few myths, or with weak myths everywhere, but none central and organizing. We see American nationalism as a ritual system organized around a core myth of violently sacrificed divinity manifest in the highest patriotic ceremony and the most accessible popular culture.[57]

For this reason Marvin and Ingle declare, "nationalism is the most powerful religion in the United States, and perhaps in many other countries."[58]

There is good reason to be skeptical of the standard narrative of religious wars. That narrative assures us that the modern state stepped in to save us from zealotry and fanaticism by removing religion from access to power. It is more likely the case, however, that what we have witnessed is the migration of the holy from the church to the state, and the substitution of one kind of martyrdom for another. More than just a history lesson, this gives us reason to be skeptical about the way Western nations deal with the non-Western world. We claim that our wars are peacemaking efforts to spread the blessings of liberalism to backward countries like Iraq, countries that have not yet learned to separate the baneful influence of religion from politics. It may be, however, that there is less difference between dying and killing for Allah and dying and killing for the U.S. flag than we usually prefer to believe.

56. Benedict Anderson, *Imagined Communities: Reflections on the Origin and Spread of Nationalism,* rev. ed. (London: Verso, 1991), 9-12.

57. Carolyn Marvin and David W. Ingle, *Blood Sacrifice and the Nation: Totem Rituals and the American Flag* (Cambridge: Cambridge University Press, 1999), 3.

58. Marvin and Ingle, *Blood Sacrifice and the Nation,* 767.

CHAPTER 8

Martyrs and Antimartyrs: Reflections on Treason, Fidelity, and the Gospel

MICHAEL L. BUDDE

Introduction

Political authorities, in punishing the transgressors whom the church would narrate as "martyrs," have not generally described their actions as making martyrs. Those on the sharp side of the sword frequently found themselves condemned as traitors — to the empire, the clan, the state, or the people. Historian Lacey Baldwin Smith draws attention to the frequent and close links between martyrdom and treason, even as the distinctions between them often seem arbitrary.[1] Martyrs "recognize a higher allegiance and on occasion are happy to betray the loyalties that lesser men and women hold sacred. . . ."[2]

Joyce Salisbury, among others, suggests that the earliest Christians were turned in by their neighbors for reasons that were "shockingly simple."

> Christians were perceived by their pagan neighbors to be antisocial in the deepest meaning of the word. They were creating their own society within the Roman one, and their loyalties were to each other rather than to the family structures that formed the backbone of conservative Roman society. Their faith led them to renounce parents, children, and

1. Lacey Baldwin Smith, *Fools, Martyrs, Traitors: The Story of Martyrdom in the Western World* (New York: Knopf, 1997), 6.

2. Smith, *Fools, Martyrs, Traitors,* 15.

spouses, and Romans believed this actively undermined the fabric of society. In fact, it did.[3]

It may well be that the charge of treason weighed less heavily on the consciences of Christians in the first centuries of the church than it did on later ones. While Christians under Rome prayed for the emperor and avoided outright rebellion, they harbored no sense that it was *their* empire, that they had a crucial stake in sustaining and empowering the regime through their participation and support. The empire was a fact of life that sometimes — like the weather — brought them good or ill, but seldom did the early Christians lose sight of the fact that they were part of a more important community, a polity with claims on their loyalty and conduct far deeper than those of the caesar. The church was their true polity, a community called out from the diversity of human cultures to be a foretaste and harbinger of the kingdom of God. Their citizenship rested in heaven rather than in Rome; having the empire accuse one of treason might be unpleasant, but it was not seen as surprising, nor did it often engender the sort of inner turmoil typical of deeply divided loyalties.

The Constantinian/Theodosian settlement removed wholesale persecution of the church from the equation, but it sharpened rather than resolved the tensions within Christian thought and practice on political authority, obedience, and Christianity. Such tensions inhered in the odd reality of texts often read as counsels to political subservience and obedience being written by persons themselves often imprisoned for disregarding imperial and local orders (Rom. 13:1-7; 1 Pet. 2:13-14). How could Peter and Paul have ever become martyrs if they had acted in accord with the sort of mandatory obedience later Christians derived from their New Testament texts?

Since Constantine, Christians have long been confused about what to do when presented with evil or unjust regimes. Some authorities, on scriptural and/or natural law grounds, maintained that believers were to submit meekly even to the worst of regimes. Others argued that regimes that violated the church or minimal standards of justice had thereby voided the rule of obedience owed by Christians, while others counseled submission until power holders at other levels (e.g., local magistrates) moved against those in power. The legacy of this confusion grew even

3. Joyce Salisbury, *The Blood of Martyrs: Unintended Consequences of Ancient Violence* (New York: Routledge, 2004).

more complex during the modern era, with the addition of considerations of just revolution (derived from just-war theory) and liberation pushing against the conservative biases of earlier accommodations and norms. Neither the counsels of obedience nor the defense of revolution, for the most part, saw the church as a people or polity in its own right, distinct from clan, state, social movement, or nation. Those within the church who maintained this kind of ecclesiology were marginal in their communities, or else they were prosecuted by their coreligionists on charges of treason.[4]

Nevertheless, martyrs continue to call the church back to a stronger sense of its own uniqueness and distinctiveness. Just as Christians have long studied and venerated the lives of the martyrs in order to deepen believers' journeys of discipleship, so may other lessons and exemplars emerge from reflecting on what I call "antimartyrs," persons who put other loyalties above their membership in the body of Christ, who refused martyrdom in favor of personal advantage or accommodation. Antimartyrs may be of several types. Some are those whose primary loyalties are to a state, ideology, or movement rather than to the gospel of Christ. Others are those who betray their Christian brothers and sisters in exchange for inducements, incentives, or advantages. I would exclude from this category persons who abjure the faith as a result of torture or extreme fear: such people testify to human finitude and weakness rather than to an affirmative privileging of an identity superior to that of being a Christian. While such distinctions may become obscured in the messiness of human conflict, I believe that they retain value as interpretive categories.

In this chapter I explore some twentieth-century examples of martyrdom — and antimartyrdom — in order to offer some observations about discipleship, secular allegiances, and membership in the transnational body of Christ. In doing so, I hope to contribute to a disarming of the power of "sedition" or "treason" as an accusation leveled against Christians. For too long Christians have sought to deflect charges of treason, bending over backward to prove their loyalty and reliability to rulers of all kinds. Instead, I think the integrity of the church and its faithfulness to the gospel are better served by resituating "treason" as an irremovable possibility of a robust ecclesiology that "seeks first the kingdom of God." It is likely the case that Christians understand "treason" in ways distinct from how it is understood in conventional political terms. If Christians can

4. Brad Gregory, *Salvation at Stake: Christian Martyrs in Early Modern Europe* (Cambridge, MA: Harvard University Press, 1999).

overcome the squeamishness attached to accusations of disloyalty, they may find themselves more favorably positioned to be better followers of Christ and able to serve "the welfare of the city" in ways the city needs but refuses to accept (Jer. 29:7). That is always important, but perhaps especially so in our era, marked as it is by fluctuating ideas on obligation and loyalty, and shallow modern and postmodern confidence in multiple, overlapping, and hybridized identities and allegiances.

A Tale of Two Archbishops

No one envisioned that the cautious and bureaucratic Oscar Romero, the "safe" choice to lead the archdiocese of San Salvador in 1977, would soon be proclaimed a martyr by Christians worldwide. Indeed, that is part of the Romero lore in the stories told about him.

Romero became archbishop during a dark period in El Salvador's one-sided civil war, in which government and affiliated military groups did the vast majority of killing in a conflict that led to tens of thousands of deaths. The regime and its death squads targeted anyone seen as sympathetic to reform efforts that would benefit the poor, whether in urban or rural contexts: union organizers, advocates for land reform, human-rights workers, religious educators, and church leaders defending the dignity and priorities of the poor. The death squads that pushed Romero into public opposition to the regime, a stance that included weekly homilies describing atrocities and abuses,[5] canceling all Masses except for the funeral Mass of a Jesuit murdered by the government, and more — those death squads also killed Romero. On March 24, 1980, Romero was gunned down while saying Mass, executed by a death squad run by a graduate of U.S. military training (Roberto D'Aubuisson, founder of the conservative ARENA party and championed by several right-wing groups in the United States). The assassin's bullets killed Romero a day after he had called on soldiers to stop the repression of the poor, and after he had issued a public appeal to U.S. President Jimmy Carter to cut off all funding to the Salvadoran military.

In 2005, timed to coincide with the twenty-fifth anniversary of

5. Chris Kraul and Tracy Wilkinson, "Assassinated Archbishop to Join Beatification Path," *Los Angeles Times*, March 30, 2005. This report drew ratings higher than any radio broadcasts except World Cup soccer.

Romero's assassination, the Vatican announced the opening of beatification proceedings on the archbishop's case, the first step toward possible formal proclamation of sainthood in the Catholic tradition. The beatification of Romero, as well as his being proclaimed a martyr for the faith, has been politically charged from the moment of his murder.

The Salvadoran government has consistently resisted characterizing Romero as a martyr, claiming instead that he died as a leftist partisan in the civil war. Many elements of the Salvadoran elite then and now have viewed Romero as a communist sympathizer who, far from being a witness to the Christian faith, subverted church and state alike. Similarly, most of Romero's fellow bishops (and Vatican officials such as Cardinal Alfonso Lopez Trujillo) maintained that Romero did not die for the faith but rather because of his misguided leftist sympathies.[6] Indeed, during his brief time as archbishop, many of Romero's fellow bishops — as well as the Vatican nuncio to El Salvador — sought to silence or replace him.

Among the majority of Christians in El Salvador and elsewhere, however, Romero died as a martyr rather than as an ideologue. Throughout the region, at the level of popular piety, Romero has been received as a pastor whose defense of his flock led him to embody Christ's sacrifice anew. Romero was no mere propagandist for the political left (whom he critiqued and about whom he harbored significant misgivings); rather, he was someone who testified to the power of Christian love and discipleship in life and death.

Ironically, despite efforts by Vatican bureaucrats to derail or slow the process of Romero's canonization, the slain leader has enjoyed the support of two significant figures: Pope John Paul II and Pope Benedict XVI. As Paul Jeffrey has noted, "John Paul clearly believed Romero died a martyr for his faith." During a 2000 celebration commemorating twentieth-century martyrs, John Paul was upset not to find Romero's name on the list of Christian martyrs compiled by Vatican officials. So he wrote in Romero's name himself, and he added that Romero was "killed during the celebration of the Holy Mass."[7] The former Joseph Ratzinger, now Pope Benedict XVI, told reporters in 2007 that Romero merits beatification (the first step in canonization) and acknowledgment as a martyr for the faith.[8]

6. Paul Jeffrey, "After 25 Years, 'St. Romero of the World' Still Inspires," *National Catholic Reporter,* April 15, 2005.

7. Jeffrey, "'St. Romero of the World' Still Inspires."

8. Nicole Winfield, "Religion in the News," *Associated Press,* August 3, 2007.

Halfway around the world, another Catholic archbishop faced another dictatorship willing to kill clergy and lay leaders it considered to be subversive. His story ended very differently, the last act being played out on a world stage with a surprise ending. At the start of the Mass installing him as archbishop of Warsaw in January 2007, Stanislaw Wielgus stunned the dignitaries packing his cathedral — and viewers watching the live broadcast — by resigning from the position. Two days earlier, after weeks of denial and evasion, he admitted to having worked with the Polish secret police for many years during the communist era.

Wielgus had agreed to become an informant after he had requested permission to study abroad in the late 1970s. While Wielgus insisted that he turned over no information of value to the secret police, a church commission concluded that "numerous essential documents exist that confirm Rev. Stanislaw Wielgus' willingness for conscious and secret cooperation with the security organs of Communist Poland."[9] Polish newspapers reported that he informed on dissidents and priests for more than twenty years, and perhaps met with police more than fifty times in one five-year period.[10]

Despite the Catholic Church's opposition to communism in Poland and the Eastern bloc, Wielgus was not the only church leader to have collaborated with internal security forces. Father Tadeusz Isakowicz-Zaleski, a priest who attempted to organize a Solidarity chapter in his seminary before being stopped by his superiors, was tortured by Polish secret police (who videotaped the session for subsequent instructional purposes). Twenty years later, when reading the 500-page file the police had compiled on him, Zaleski learned that two priests were among those who informed on him.[11] When his superiors refused to look into the matter, Zaleski began his own research about church leaders who collaborated with the secret police.

What he found in secret police files once believed to have been destroyed was that between 10 and 15 percent of clergy in the archdiocese of Krakow were police informants or collaborators. While the information in such files is notoriously uneven in reliability — the police often included rumor or outright falsehoods in attempts to discredit people or boost their

9. "Warsaw Archbishop Says He Leaves His Fate with Pope Amid Scandal over Communist Collaboration," *Associated Press/International Herald-Tribune*, January 5, 2007.

10. Craig Smith, "Ties to Communist Secret Police Snare Polish Bishop," *New York Times*, January 6, 2007.

11. Tom Hundley, "Tortured Priest's Tenacity Exposes Betrayal in Church," *Chicago Tribune*, February 26, 2007.

own image of effectiveness — Zaleski identified thirty-nine members of the clergy (five of them bishops) whom he believed cooperated with the regime. Historians familiar with the Polish case estimate that 10 to 15 percent of clergy nationally were informants or collaborators, comparable to Zaleski's figures for Krakow.[12]

After having attempted to inhibit discussion of clergy collaboration, the Polish bishops established their own commission to review secret police files. While noting the unreliability of the files and the need to corroborate information in them, the bishops' commission noted that, of 132 bishops living in 2007, "about a dozen were registered by the security services of communist Poland as "secret collaborators" or "operational contacts," with one described as an "agent of the intelligence agency."[13] The commission's report was forwarded to the Vatican for review.

While the existence of collaborators does not detract from the church's reputation for having resisted the communist regime, it does raise questions in at least some respects. Not all collaboration was extorted via force or blackmail (despite recent revisionist attempts to attribute nearly all cases to brute coercion). Denying someone permission to study abroad does not compare with torture and beatings used to elicit collaboration. It is possible that at least some collaboration was by those who believed it was their civic duty to cooperate with the official organs of government. Ironically, the regime's most successful period of recruitment seems to have been during the 1980s, the era of Solidarity and the papacy of Karol Wojtyla, who was spied on by several priests over a period of years.[14]

The Sacristan and the Priest

On October 26, 2007, the Catholic bishop of Linn (Austria) and the archbishop of Innsbruck announced the formal beatification of Franz Jaggerstatter, whom they described as a "martyr" and "a prophet with a global view and a penetrating insight."[15] However, these bishops' predeces-

12. Hundley, "Tortured Priest's Tenacity."

13. "Polish Church Reports Secret Police Ties," *Associated Press,* June 27, 2007.

14. Jonathan Luxmoore, "The Secret Policemen's Bishop," *The Tablet,* January 13, 2007.

15. Ludwig Schwarz and Manfred Scheuer, *Franz Jagerstatter: A Shining Example in Dark Times* (Linz, Austria: Diocese of Linz, 2007), "Foreword" by Erna Putz. Available at: http://www.dioezeselinz.at/redaktion/index.php?action_new=Lesen&Article_ID=39496.

sors had a very different view of Jagerstatter and his witness; indeed, the church's about-face on this Austrian farmer testifies to the power of even the most seemingly useless of gospel-based witness. Had Jagerstatter's case not come to the attention of the church worldwide, thanks largely to the scholarly work of the late Gordon Zahn — in other words, had his memory remained within the confines of the Austrian church alone — it is difficult to see this parish sacristan as someone who would later be praised as a martyr and candidate for sainthood.

What Jagerstatter did, he did in the face of opposition from all sides — from his mother and wife and family, his friends and neighbors, his parish priest and bishop, and, of course, from his government leaders. After returning home from basic military training in 1941, Jagerstatter vowed not to return, refusing to help advance the Nazi cause as a member of the Austrian military (Austria had been annexed by Germany in 1937). He considered Nazi Germany to be an evil regime wholly incompatible with Christianity; he described its wars as unjust plunder and the savaging of its neighbors, which his Christian conscience would not allow him to support in any way. Despite repeated efforts on all sides, Jagerstatter refused to change his mind. He was arrested and finally executed by beheading in 1943.

While Jagerstatter's position rested on the duty to follow Christ rather than an evil regime bent on the destruction of the innocent (as well as of the church), his pastors emphasized that such decisions were not the responsibility of laypeople. Rather, they said, Christians were to obey civil authority in accord with Romans 13 and similar texts; they also emphasized Jagerstatter's duty to provide for his family, who would be made to suffer if he continued to refuse military service to the Nazis.

In one of his letters, Jagerstatter observed:

> If people took as much trouble to warn men against the serious sins which bring eternal death, and thus keep them from such sins, as they are taking to warn me against a dishonorable death, I think Satan could count on no more than a meager harvest in the last days. Again and again, people stress the obligations of conscience as they concern my wife and children. But I cannot believe that just because a man has a wife and children, he is free to offend God by lying (not to mention all the other things he would be called upon to do). Did not Christ Himself say, "He who loves father, mother, or children more than me is not worthy of My love"? Or, "Fear not those who can kill the body but

> not the soul; rather fear much more those who seek to destroy body and soul in hell"?[16]

In his research on Jagerstatter, including interviews with his family and neighbors, Zahn describes the community's general sense about Jagerstatter, both during his lifetime and when his witness began gathering international attention after more than a decade of silence.

> [T]he community continues to reject Jagerstatter's stand as a stubborn and pointless display of essentially political imprudence, or even an actual failure to fulfill a legitimate duty. It is to be explained and forgiven in terms of an unfortunate mental aberration brought about, or at least intensified, by religious excess. The question of whether his action was morally right is, for the most part, set aside. While some of the villagers were quite willing to accept the possibility that he might someday be formally acknowledged as a saint, this possibility was not considered at all incompatible with the community's general disapproval of his action. (p. 146)

Zahn notes that, for the most part, Jagerstatter's contemporaries tried to avoid talking or thinking about him: they did not tell his story to their children, and most seemed to hope the story would go away on its own (pp. 146-48, 150). When it came to Catholic leaders, Zahn notes that, while "they could congratulate him for his unswerving commitment and give him assurances that he would not be committing a sin . . . none had been able or willing to tell him that *he was right*" (p. 162). In fact, many in the Austrian hierarchy after the war had difficulty discussing Jagerstatter's case in ways that didn't reflect poorly on their support for the war effort (pp. 164-65). Emblematic in this respect, to Zahn, was Bishop Joseph Fleisser of Linz, who after the war could describe Jagerstatter as a "martyr to conscience" but not as an example worthy of imitation.

> I consider the greatest heroes to be those exemplary young Catholic men, seminarians, priests, and heads of families who fought and died in heroic fulfillment of duty and in the firm conviction that they were fulfilling the will of God at their post just as the Christian soldiers in the armies of the heathen emperor had done. (pp. 164-65)

16. Gordon Zahn, *In Solitary Witness: The Life and Death of Franz Jagerstatter* (Springfield, IL: Templegate Publishers, 1964), 97-98. Hereafter, page references to this work appear in parentheses in the text.

Jagerstatter, then, was a rather curious martyr, one whose witness was "a stand *against* his fellow Catholics and their spiritual leaders who were wholeheartedly committed to, or at least willing to acquiesce in, the war effort" (pp. 162-63). This powerful and improbable witness dramatized what one English bishop (during the Vatican II discussion of what would become the Pastoral Constitution on the Church in the Modern World, *Gaudium et Spes*) described as "the major scandal of Christianity," namely, that "almost every national hierarchy in almost every war has allowed itself to become the moral arm of its own government, even in wars later recognized as palpably unjust" (Zahn's preface). How ironic, then, that Bishop Fleisser's successor would be among the bishops describing Jagerstatter as "a prophet with a global view and a penetrating insight . . . an advocate of non-violence and peace."[17]

A generation later, thousands of miles away — but in a place itself touched by Nazi immigrants and fugitive war criminals — another Catholic presented a witness quite different from Jagerstatter's refusal to cooperate with an evil regime. His came during the dark years and military repression of Latin America, which saw the entire region after 1954 fall to dictatorship, death squads, and authoritarian civilian regimes. In many countries the Catholic Church and its leaders resisted such United States–backed regimes and their policies.

Such was not the case in Argentina, however, where almost all church leaders supported the dictatorship and its "dirty war" between 1976 and 1983. During this period, tens of thousands were abducted, tortured, murdered, or disappeared. Argentine bishops provided information to the regime about their own priests and lay leaders, defended the regime publicly against international and internal criticism, and called on the Christian faithful to support the regime in its fight against godless communism.[18]

In October 2007, a Catholic priest received a life sentence for aiding the junta in seven murders, thirty-one cases of torture, and forty-two kidnappings. Christian von Wernich served as a police chaplain during the dirty war; and while he is the first priest prosecuted for human rights violations in Argentina, human rights groups suggest he was far from alone in committing such violations. Witnesses in von Wernich's trial testified that

17. Schwarz and Scheuer, *Franz Jagerstatter.*

18. Emilio Mignone, *Witness to the Truth: The Complicity of Church and Dictatorship in Argentina* (Maryknoll, NY: Orbis, 1988). Hereafter, page references to this work appear in parentheses in the text.

he listened to the confessions of prisoners, turning over to interrogators the names of persons mentioned during the sacrament of reconciliation. In addition, von Wernich questioned detainees, was present during torture sessions, and dealt with and misled family members searching for persons abducted by the state.

He also provided moral support to the torturers and killers among the Argentine military and death squads. As one officer said, "Father von Wernich saw that what had happened had shocked me and [he] spoke to me, telling me that what we had done was necessary; it was a patriotic act and God knew it was for the good of the country."[19]

The "patriotic acts" of torture and murder defended by von Wernich were directed, in most cases, against persons who shared his (and the torturers') Catholic faith. In siding with the state over against his coreligionists, he even violated the absolute confidentiality of sacramental confession. In a church unable to distinguish between the body politic and the body of Christ, von Wernich was loyal to the former and a traitor to the latter. In this von Wernich reflected the view of many Catholic dictators throughout the region: that is, that the church had become infested by Marxist subversives and dupes. In killing and torturing church leaders, the faithful Catholics in the government, military, and death squads believed they were purging the church of anti-Christian elements that had corrupted it. In other words, they were persecuting the church in order to save it.

In this, the Argentine (and other) dictators were joined by many members of the Argentinian Catholic hierarchy. Archbishop Adolfo Tortulo, head of the military vicariate and president of the Argentine Bishops' Conference, took time during episcopal meetings to justify torture on theological grounds that he derived from medieval sources. His successor as head of the military vicariate, Bishop Jose Medina, concurred in his defense of torture (Mignone, 4, 7, 9). Beyond their defense of torture and other atrocities, according to attorney Emilio Mignone, the military vicariate provided other essential services that describe a general practice that was to play out in the particulars of von Wernich's case:

19. Jeremy McDermott, "'Interrogator in a Cassock' Given Life," *The Scotsman,* October 11, 2007; David Usborne, "Argentina's Disappeared," *The Independent,* October 11, 2007; Hilary Burke, "Argentine Priest Conviction Puts Church in Hot Seat, *Reuters,* October 10, 2007; Alexei Barrionuevo, "Argentine Church Faces 'Dirty War' Past," *The New York Times,* September 17, 2007.

> Above and beyond [particular abusive incidents], the main role of the chaplains — who took their orders from the military vicariate — was to distort and soothe the conscience of repressors, by legitimating violations committed against the dignity of the human person. "When we had doubts," Admiral Zaratiegui has said, "we went to our spiritual advisors, who could only be members of the vicariate, and they put our minds at ease." They went so far as to compose sacrilegious prayers. One of them goes, "Impart skill to my hand, so the shot will hit the mark." (Mignone, 11)

Not only did the junta derive consolation from church chaplains like von Wernich, it also drew ideological support from bishops like Victoria Bonamin, to whom the world was divided between "atheistic materialism" and "Christian humanism" — the latter defended by the dictatorship.

> The antiguerrilla struggle is a struggle for the Argentine Republic, for its integrity, but for its altars as well. . . . This struggle is a struggle to defend morality, human dignity, and ultimately a struggle to defend God. . . . Therefore, I pray for divine protection over this "dirty war" in which we are engaged. (Mignone, 6)

Both Persecutor and Martyr? The Strange Case of Gabino Olaso

In an October 12, 2007, column, noted Catholic journalist John Allen describes the unusual background of Father Gabino Olaso Zabala, an Augustinian priest and one of 498 martyrs of the Spanish Civil War beatified by the Vatican in October 2007. What makes the martyred Olaso distinctive is that, forty years earlier, he had committed heinous deeds in the service of the Spanish Empire. In 1896, Olaso participated in the torture of Fr. Mariano Dacanay, a Filipino priest thought to be sympathetic to the anti-Spanish *insurrectos* in the Philippines. Dacanay was held in the Augustinian seminary in Vigan and tortured by guards, who received encouragement and assistance from Olaso. According to Dacanay's subsequent account (generally accepted as credible, according to Allen), Olaso himself kicked Dacanay in the head, rendering him semiconscious.[20]

While Catholic theology does not require that persons proclaimed as

20. John Allen, "Torture in his History Taints Spanish Martyr's Beatification," *National Catholic Reporter,* October 12, 2007.

martyrs must have lived pious lives — dying for the faith was not restricted exclusively to moral exemplars in life — Olaso does represent some rather strong contrasts. Unlike Saul, the persecutor whose allegiance to Christ made possible Paul the martyr, Olaso's nationalist allegiances remained unchanged throughout his life. What he was willing to torture for, he was apparently willing to die for, a consistency that raises as many questions as it answers. Saint Augustine, in whose name Olaso served as a priest for decades, famously proclaimed that Christian martyrs are distinguished not by their manner of death but by the cause for which they died (noble pagans can die bravely under adversity, but to Augustine only dying for the true faith makes a Christian martyr). One wonders, in that case, about interpretations of the "cause" capable of justifying the torturing and martyring of a fellow priest (in a seminary, no less) and the subsequent martyrdom of the torturer himself. Also, one cannot help wondering whether Olano lived a defective notion of Christian discipleship, distorted by the toxin of nationalism, or whether he was a faithful modern follower of Augustine, the church father who defended the torture of the Donatists as an act of charity aimed at saving them from perdition — or whether the two positions are identical.

Learning from Martyrs and Antimartyrs

In diverse ways, these cases offer insights to persons concerned about Christian discipleship in our day. By pushing against the legacy of a presumed identity between Christianity and political loyalties, these exemplars contribute to greater clarity in vision and practice.

As noted by many scholars, the power of martyrdom generally requires the existence of a church or community capable of receiving that witness — to name and affirm it, reflect on and disseminate it, to use it as a model of Christianity well lived that is taught to others.[21] In the cases of Romero and Jagerstatter, such a church was missing in part (El Salvador) or altogether (Austria) during the martyr's lifetime. It took the larger church — transnational, not beholden to a single set of national allegiances or commitments — to recognize and receive the martyrs' witness. Such may well be a structural commonplace in the era after modernity, with the worldwide character of the body of Christ sliced into national

21. Salisbury, *Blood of Martyrs,* 2-3.

fragments. Tied so closely in many places to nationalist fusions of faith and political identity, such churches may be less capable of recognizing martyrdom in their midst (unless persecution comes from the outside, targeting the "patriotic believer" on both grounds).

Jagerstatter provides a martyr's witness against Austrian Catholicism nearly as much as against Nazism. His refusal of military service asks uncomfortable questions of ecclesiastical, political, and cultural forces that chose to cooperate with the Nazis. And while Romero was immediately proclaimed a martyr by popular voices within the Salvadoran church, that view was rejected by most of his fellow bishops, the papal nuncio, and powerful Catholics tied to the Salvadoran regime and its backers in the United States. Left to themselves, the churches in Austria and El Salvador would probably have suppressed or rewritten these martyrs' stories such that their witness would have either remained invisible or been rendered harmless. To counteract the structural shortcomings of national churches requires the entire church's ability and willingness even to proclaim some people martyrs as a means of fraternal correction of local churches.

One thing distinguishing suicide from martyrdom, according to Craig Hovey, is that while suicides often try to control the meaning and power of their death, martyrs entrust themselves

> to the church's memory with no guarantee that the church will discern the meaning of their death in its continued existence. This is not because they might be betrayed by the church but because even in death they openly subject themselves to the church's discipline. After all, the way the church narrates the past is a work of disciplining its tendencies toward self-deception and learning to speak truthfully, especially about those things at which it has failed.[22]

Having stood for the Christian way even in the face of substantial church opposition, in other words, Jagerstatter and Romero also bought their brothers and sisters a chance to repent and speak truthfully even at a remove of several decades.

For many people, some of these cases pluck the strings of a moral intuition long thought dormant or diminished in an egalitarian age. For some, the heinous acts of von Wernich and Olaso (and the betrayal by Wielgus) are worse because they were ordained clergy; similarly, the sacri-

22. Craig Hovey, *To Share in the Body: A Theology of Martyrdom for Today's Church* (Grand Rapids: Brazos, 2008).

fice of Jagerstatter is all the more remarkable because he was a layman, not a cleric. Whether a remnant of the dual-ethic thinking of Christendom or residual clericalism, these cases invert our moral anticipations: we find martyrdom more consistent with the totality of commitment presumed by the clerical vocation, and we expect the willingness to torture to be more likely among laypeople, whose vocations more frequently legitimate the use of lethal and coercive force.

The wrong way to engage this moral intuition is to ascribe it to a presumption of innate virtue among clerics as opposed to those of the lay state. More appropriate, I believe, is to recognize in it the stirrings of a guilty ecclesial conscience left over from the compromise with lethal force in Christendom (in which laypeople could kill when necessary, but such was eventually considered to be incompatible with the ordained state). The shock we feel when we see clergy as killers, torturers, and collaborators, whatever else it does, forces us to ask why we feel as much disquiet over the status of the doer compared with the deed itself. Is torture by lay Christians a lesser offense than that of Olaso or von Wernich? If so, why?

Similarly — and despite the more recent celebrations — Jagerstatter's choice disquiets one in ways that similar choices by a cleric would not. Jagerstatter's refusal was not in the midst of a life of clerical celibacy and limited personal obligations, but rather in the midst of all the "natural" responsibilities of fatherhood, marriage, community, and locality — all the things, in other words, that historically have "excused" laypeople from following the way of the cross unto death if necessary. Priests and nuns can give their life for Christ because they do not have spouses, children, and neighbors who depend on them (married Protestant clergy represent an interesting category of persons pulled in opposite directions). A milder version of discipleship has been seen as appropriate for laypeople, in which being reasonable and cautious is both appropriate and legitimate. Jagerstatter's isolated witness upends this comfortable compromise, bringing back Jesus' unambiguous words on family and discipleship to all Christians — ordained and lay, married and single, young and old.

Hovey is correct in noting the deep continuities between martyrdom and the spiritual/ecclesial practices and disciplines that attach to all Christians who understand their baptism.

> [M]artyrdom is not at the far end of a continuum marked out by various degrees of self-denial. It is not asceticism to the extreme, penitence with greater intensity, the most uncomfortable hair shirt imaginable.

> Instead, "deny yourself" is related to "take up your cross and follow me" as means to end. The former is necessary to accomplish the latter. The way of Jesus requires the unseating of those modes of behavior, ways of life, desires, and thoughts that are conditioned on scales of self-preservation, self-protection, and security for one's life. The church upholds its commitment to the way of Jesus when it helps members undergo the discipline necessary to resist the lure of wealth and cultivate the imagination required to reject vanity, the humility to ignore temptations to feed the acquisition of power, the patience to wait for justice when wronged, and the courage to withstand harm without the soothing consolation of revenge. The virtues necessary to be a martyr are no different from the virtues necessary to be a faithful Christian. This means that martyrdom is not a special calling for a select few but the commitment of every Christian and the responsibility of every church. Even though not every individual Christian will be killed, there is no way to distinguish those who will from those who will not. Even though not every Christian will be remembered as a martyr, every church that locates its identity in the cross is obligated to cultivate those virtues necessary to enable all of its members to die for the cause of Christ. Every Christian is a member of a martyr-church.[23]

The scandal of the antimartyrs raises another question: Which is the worse offense, treason against the state or treason against the church? Not only did the three antimartyr pastors explored here (Olaso, von Wernich, Wielgus) serve their respective regimes, they did so in ways that targeted their coreligionists. They informed against their brothers and sisters in Christ, used their sacramental roles against the faithful, and put national allegiance over the ties of baptism. In this they were joined by the murderers of Romero and other church leaders, for whom the state represented the true protector of Christian values against a church rendered unworthy of respect or allegiance.

This question of betrayals chosen — state or church — may in the future present itself more frequently and in more diverse forms than one might imagine. For example, the use of government informants and spies in congregations is likely to increase as a result of some church leaders' refusal to cooperate with laws affecting ministry and pastoral care among undocumented immigrants, an example of what one conservative commentator calls "philanthropic lawlessness" as a gentler substitute for the

23. Hovey, *To Share in the Body*, 59-60.

term "treason.'"[24] More plain-speaking patriots decry what they see as "aiding and abetting the criminal invasion of America by Mexicans."[25] The infiltration of churches, as well as congregants informing on one another and on pastors, are foreseeable both because of the more pronounced anti-immigrant views of white Christians in the United States (compared to church leaders) and because of the longtime fusion of Christianity and nationalism in the U.S. church.[26] Being loyal citizens in these cases will be a more powerful motivator than inhibitions against betraying fellow Christians; indeed, so deep is the presumed identity between Christianity and nationalism in American culture that the possibility of betraying fellow believers is denied in principle by most people. Standing with "America" cannot mean standing against the church, only against a misguided and corrupt version of Christianity temporarily in charge. The affinities between U.S. and Latin American rationalizations of antichurch religious nationalism (subverting the corrupt church and its leaders in order to protect "true" Christianity) are unmistakable.

Conclusion: The Peculiarities of Christian Treason

Christian treason is a most unusual sort of thing, at least when compared with traditional political and secular understandings of the term. Christian treason does not arise from fealty to another state or worldly sovereign, but to the Prince of Peace, whom the Bible portrays as a contrast to all worldly principalities and powers. In this, the children of darkness may perceive more accurately than do the more optimistic children of light; the more optimistic persist in thinking that kings and rulers, regimes of all types, actually might want what Christ wants if only they were more enlightened.

There is no simple formulation or rule that will suffice for dictating when Christians must obey God rather than human authority; searching for such a rule or checklist itself adds to the problem by removing the discernment of situations and choices from the gathered body of the church.

24. Brooke Levitske, "Illegal Immigration and the Church: Philanthropic Lawlessness," *The Acton Institute,* July 11, 2007.

25. Ralph Ovadal, "Romanizing America Through Illegal Immigration" (n.d.); available at pcc.monroe.org.

26. Gregory Smith, "Attitudes Toward Immigration: In the Pulpit and Pew," *Pew Forum on Religion and Public Life,* April 26, 2006.

For churches that take themselves seriously as forerunners of God's new creation, as an eschatological community whose common life and witness to the kingdom of God is something distinct from the capacities of the nations, the consistency of their corporate existence likely makes state action the variable factor at issue. In a way, Ronald Reagan's explanation of his move from the Democratic Party to the Republicans provides an imperfect analogy: he didn't leave the Democrats, he said; rather, the party left him by changing its priorities and commitments. That may well describe the ebbs and flows of when discipleship becomes treasonous for churches with a sense of themselves: their life and practice remains the same, but secular power holders keep moving the goalposts separating acceptable and unacceptable conduct and thought in accord with state needs and aspirations. What is unexceptional in one context — loving one's enemy, naming the names of killers, offering help to the poor — becomes subversive when the lines separating secular loyalty and disloyalty are moved by the powerful.

Too much emphasis on "treason" itself can obscure the more important point that, for Christians, the more fundamental category is one of loyalty — to the gospel, to continuing Jesus' work as the kingdom of God continues to unfold, to the brothers and sisters in the church, and to those whom Jesus calls us to love in spite of the world's logic to the contrary. What the world narrates as treason is merely a season in the larger story of Christian allegiance to something larger, deeper, and more real than the political claims of states and sovereigns. If the Resurrection ultimately deprives death of its sting (1 Cor. 15:54-56), perhaps the creation of the church at Pentecost will ultimately deprive accusations of treason of the power to undermine ecclesial solidarity and Christian practice.

PART IV

Martyrdom and the Future Church

CHAPTER 9

Is Anything Worth Dying For? Martyrdom, Exteriority, and Politics After Bare Life

D. Stephen Long and Geoffrey Holdsclaw

Introduction

"What is worth living for?" Can this question be answered if we fail to ask the correlative question, "What is worth dying for?" And once we pose this question, how can we avoid a similar, disturbing question, which in one sense remains close to this, yet in another is far from it: "What is worth killing for?" For many, to live well requires knowing what is worth dying for. But once we confess this, how can we avoid asking what we might kill for in order to live well? If the question "What is worth dying for?" inevitably leads to "What is worth killing for?" then isn't the question itself too dangerous? Perhaps we are better off not asking questions with such depth — or such height. Modern, secular politics begins with this fear. If we ground politics in some transcendent goal for which persons should be willing to die, then we may produce a militaristic society grounded in martial values.

Modern democracies attempt to avoid this by grounding politics in an "exclusive" humanism. It bases politics in human life as it is, without reference to transcendent goals and thus without attempting to create a society of virtuous persons. As Madison, Hamilton, and Jay argued in *The Federalist Papers,* the danger to political society is an excessive attachment to antiquity or to a desire for some golden age where political society primarily sought to produce virtuous persons. A commercial republic will avoid the militaristic temptation that such political societies produced. "Commercial republics like ours will never be disposed to waste themselves in ruinous contentions with each other. They will be governed by mutual interest, and will cultivate a spirit of mutual amity and concord."[1]

Of course, Hegel thought a thoroughgoing commercial republic would produce a "city of sows," who would lose heroic virtues. For this reason, a virtuous politics requires war to prevent people from being satisfied solely with the pursuit of mutual interest. If people were not confronted with the possibility of dying or killing for the nation, then they would become self-indulgent and incapable of a well-lived life. In his critique, Hegel recognizes that modern political arrangements were founded less on a question "What is worth dying for?" than on the question "How can we combine people so that they are less interested in what they might die for and more in how they might live in mutual amity and concord?" The bare affirmation of life becomes the basis for politics. It is the basis that most inhabitants of Western democracies have become so comfortable with that we can hardly fathom calling it into question. But has it made us less militaristic, less violent? Is there any way out of such a political configuration?

Politics According to Exclusive Humanism

Among the many innovations of modern political thought — such as seeking general rules through historical investigation (Machiavelli), postulating a scientific foundation for politics (Hobbes), outlining a theory of private property (Locke), or expressing the "general will" of the people (Rousseau) — the innovation that most interests us here is the idea that each person is most concerned with preserving his or her own life. Mark Lilla traces this development of the purely human as the foundation for a modern, secular politics. Lilla describes how a shift to a "new approach" to politics takes place in the seventeenth and eighteenth centuries. Hobbes is the main character in this story, for he is "the first thinker to suggest that religious conflict and political conflict are essentially the same conflict."[2] If we can defuse religious conflict, then we will defuse political conflict. This is accomplished by separating politics from theology, or rather, by cordoning off questions of theological and moral truth to a private domain and

1. *The Federalist Papers* (New York: Penguin Books, 1987), 106.

2. Mark Lilla, *The Stillborn God: Religion, Politics, and the Modern West* (New York: Knopf, 2007), 80.

recasting politics as a matter of public survival. The "divine nexus" that allowed previous Christians to think of politics came to an end as Hobbes cut against the grain of all received opinions, either classical or medieval, and their attending metaphysical assumptions. The old — and theological — questions of goodness, truth, and beauty were "replaced by a new approach to politics focused exclusively on human nature and human needs. A Great Separation took place, severing Western political philosophy decisively from cosmology and theology. It remains the most distinctive feature of the Modern West to this day."[3] This exclusive humanism becomes the foundation of modern, secular politics, whether it be of the social-contract variety or of the broadly pragmatist tradition.

This foundation, for Hobbes, is that every person always acts — in the fear of a violent death — out of the interest of preserving his or her own life. All other sources of politics based in opinion (religious, metaphysical, moral) lead to disputes causing violence. These disputes, caused by the unruly, idiosyncratic, and excessive passions, must be held in check by a totally rational foundation. Therefore, against all other passionate dogmas about what constitutes a "good" life or a "true" doctrine, the only rational, dogmatic position from which to begin political thought is that of the preservation of life.[4] This stripping of life from goodness and truth leads to a reduction of life as mere biological life. Human biological life that is not coordinated by social, political, religious, or cosmic life is what Giorgio Agamben calls "bare life." As Agamben notes, modern, secular politics begins with "bare life" in search of a common "form of life" because a priori it disallows a common good based in anything besides biological existence.[5]

Modern, secular politics begins from the lowest common denominator of biological existence and builds from this a political existence, rather than allowing humanity to be defined as political from the beginning, as Aristotle did. In this way the preservation of biological life simultaneously gives direction to modern political thought and hinders reference to a "beyond" or "exterior," which, when not agreed on, would lead to disputes and violence. Therefore, politics is not part of our human natures, but rather is a product of seeking to preserve bare life. For Hobbes, the preservation of

3. Lilla, *The Stillborn God,* 58.

4. See Hobbes, *Leviathan,* chaps. 4-6, 10-17.

5. Giorgio Agamben, *Homo Sacer: Sovereign Power and Bare Life,* trans. Daniel Heller-Roazen (Stanford: Stanford University Press, 1998), 9.

bare life becomes the only impetus for leaving the state of nature (where every person has the right to defend his life by any means deemed necessary) by entering into the commonwealth, where all agree to lay down the right of preserving their own lives by giving this right to the sovereign, who will rule over them in order to best preserve all their lives.[6] By this the state of nature, while it seems to be exterior to, is incorporated within the commonwealth as its very center because the sovereign retains the rights of nature. In this way, bare life as "exteriority — the law of nature and the principle of the preservation of one's own life — is truly the innermost center of the political system,"[7] and what seemed initially excluded is now included as the very foundation of the commonwealth, for "life in the state of nature is defined only by its being unconditionally exposed to a death threat . . . and political life . . . is nothing but this very same life always exposed to a threat that now rests exclusively in the hands of the sovereign."[8]

Agamben notes that, while in modern political thought, this notion of bare life is particularly emphasized, its roots begin at the margins of political life in ancient Rome. He puts it this way: "[T]he production of bare life is the originary activity of sovereignty," creating a space between natural law and divine law such that sovereignty can kill without the act being homicide (a violation of natural law) nor a sacrifice (a fulfillment of divine law), and therefore grasping a region of power for itself.[9] This production of bare life beginning in ancient Rome, and given full force in modernity, is in fact the process of "capturing" life within the bonds of sovereignty under the name of "preserving life." This production of "bare life," followed by the sovereign assuming exclusive responsibility for preserving such life, is the basis of our current political order. Any explication of another politically grounded conception of life is at best dismissed as metaphysically pernicious or religiously irrelevant, and at worst pathologically oriented toward terrorism. If, for Aristotle, only wild beasts and the gods dwelt outside the city, for modernity only terrorists and psychopaths dwell outside the sovereign nation-state. Anything exterior to this foundation breeds violence.

Therefore, once politics becomes grounded solely on human nature and human needs as bare life, it no longer asks what is worth dying for. Instead, a different question emerges in the formation of a humanist politics:

6. *Leviathan,* chaps. 17-18.

7. *Leviathan,* 37.

8. Giorgio Agamben, *Means Without Ends: Notes on Politics,* trans. Vincenzo Binetti and Cesare Casarino (Minneapolis: University of Minnesota Press, 2000), 11.

9. Agamben, *Means Without Ends,* 6, 83.

"How do we avoid dying?" "How do we decrease suffering and increase pleasure for the most people possible?" "How do we eliminate questions of goodness and truth and focus on 'bare life'?" Hobbes's exclusive humanism yields a politics less concerned about what we might die for and more with how we might live and avoid the question altogether.[10] And modern, secular politics allows for nothing external to this exclusively humanist foundation.

Politics as Exterior to Bare Life

If modern, liberal politics assumes an exclusive humanism producing an immanent politics of bare life, then this politics refuses to concede any exterior place to a different kind of politics. If the only thing worth dying for is the preservation of the conditions for a politics where nothing is worth dying for, then how do we get outside this contradictory political order? Where would we find an exteriority to such a politics? Kenneth Surin notes that with the domination of the global capitalist economy comes the decline of the noble citizen-subject engaged with public affairs, tutored in the habits of democracy by a nation-state worth living and dying for. In its place arises the consumer-subject engaged in private pursuits, tutored by Disney and Nintendo, coddled by a nation-state whose primary purpose is to protect markets and compete with other nation-states for resources. The rational sovereign subject of political representation and its coordinated rational sovereign state have given over to the consumer-subject and the competitive-state.[11] This new situation has adjusted the coordinates of the

10. This poses difficulties for Hobbes in arguing why persons should go to war. Because political society exists in order for me to serve those interests grounded in my human nature as it is, the only thing for which I might be called to die is what challenges my ability to pursue those interests. But it will never be in my interest to die in order to pursue those interests. For this reason, Hobbes argued that society should tolerate alternatives to military service. He says: "[A] man that is commanded as a soldier to fight against the enemy, though his sovereign have right enough to punish his refusal with death, may nevertheless in many cases refuse, without injustice; as when he substituteth a sufficient soldier in his place: for in this case he deserteth not the service of the commonwealth." Thomas Hobbes, *Leviathan* (London: Fount Paperbacks, 1983), 211.

11. Kenneth Surin, "Rewriting the Ontological Script of Liberation: On the Question of Finding a New Kind of Political Subject," in *Theology and the Political: A New Debate*, ed. Creston Davis, John Milbank, and Slavoj Žižek (Durham: Duke University Press, 2005), 240-51. Hereafter, page references to this essay appear in parentheses in the text.

"previous politics," which kept capitalism in check through the real differences between the politics of the right and the left, as well as the real possibility of radically readjusting the existing political arrangements. But through the absorption of both the right and left into the maintenance of capitalism, and the demise of communism as an alternative socioeconomic possibility, our current situation allows for no exteriority to the liberal-democratic constellation. Therefore, "politics today is post-political precisely to the extent that there is no such exteriority to the political as it actually exists," no point from which to pose serious questions, or even "overturn the system in its entirety" (p. 253). In light of this, current struggles for liberation must once more find an exteriority from which to coordinate action.

Four Exteriorities — and a Fifth

Surin submits four possible options for opening an exteriority beyond the existing framework. First is a "politics of difference," or multiculturalism. As Surin notes, such a politics mirrors the typical liberal framework and thus does not offer a sufficient exteriority. His second option, the "politics of subjectivity," is based in the reciprocity of a subject and its other, articulated most ably by Derrida. But he deems this too paralyzing in the face of actual existing exploitation, unable to articulate a course of action or come to any concrete decision, fearing that it might in some way violate the Other as transcendental coordinate. This achieves only an immobilizing exteriority. The third option is a "politics of the Event" based in the militant fidelity to a singular political process, triggered by an "event" that is exterior to — yet fundamentally reordering of — the current political order, offering a hoped-for universality. For Surin, however, this is too romantic and too elusive as a basis for mobilizing a broad-based political movement. It is an ambiguous exteriority at best (pp. 254-57).

The fourth option, and Surin's preference, is the "politics of the multitude," which centers on the margins of the ordinary connections, interactions, and potentialities of people and collectives, displacing the need to postulate a "general will," or cohesive political body, because the multitude is "structurally autopoetic" according to its own powers and history. This is an immanent exteriority (somehow, that is not a contradiction) (p. 257). Surin contrasts this last exteriority to the Christian option of exteriority based in the *analogia entis*. But even if lured for a moment by the call of transcendence as political exteriority, Surin faults theology for having a hierarchy of being and a preestablished harmony not compatible with radical, democratic equality. Therefore, in contrast to Thomistic *analogy,* Surin proposes the multitude based in Scotist *univocity* as an exteriority based in immanence rather than transcendence (pp. 257-63).

Alongside these four hastily summarized exteriorities, there is a fifth, which we will call "excessive humanism." Against the grain of modern — and even postmodern — political theory, enshrined in our liberal-democratic system, Slovenian philosopher and cultural critic Slavoj Žižek dares to ask this scandalous question: "What if we are 'really alive' only if and when we engage ourselves with an *excessive intensity* that puts us beyond 'mere life'? What if, when we focus on mere survival . . . what we ultimately lose is life itself?" Žižek is questioning the basis of bare life in modern political discourse; he provocatively focuses these questions for us when he asks: "What if the Palestinian suicide bomber on the point of blowing himself (and others) up is, in an emphatic sense, 'more alive' than . . . a New York yuppie jogging along the Hudson river in order to keep his body in shape?" Challenging the assumption that the affirmation of bare life is itself sufficient to live well, Žižek probes the limits of our current political system. For Žižek, what makes "life worth living is the very *excess of life,*" for only those who know there is more to life than bare life are really alive.[12] Life only has meaning when its coordinates are beyond mere survival. But, of course, modern secular theorists will counter that this *excess of life* always leads down the path of *excessive death.* For those offering this critique, the "Holocaust serves as a warning of what the ultimate result of the submission of Life to some higher Goal is."[13]

This, then, is the continuing paradox of our current political situation. In its denial of life beyond any transcendent causes, it risks losing really being alive; but it also claims that every affirmation of the excess of

12. Slavoj Žižek, *The Puppet and the Dwarf: The Perverse Core of Christianity* (Cambridge, MA: MIT Press, 2003), 94-95 (italics added).

13. Žižek, *Puppet and Dwarf,* 99. Despite his compelling narrative of humanism and modern political theology, Lilla repeats this modern fear. He worries that Rosenzweig's and Barth's apocalyptic theology could not give us an adequate political alternative to liberal theology even though the latter was a dead end. All their theology could offer was "a kind of negative political theology" where "politics cannot redeem us" (Lilla, *The Stillborn God,* 275-76). Such an apocalyptic theology is too exterior. The result was that "neither Rosenzweig, who died in 1929, nor Barth, who lived until 1968, recognized the connection between the rhetoric of their theological messianism and the apocalyptic rhetoric that was beginning to engulf German society" (278).

life reverts into its opposite as death. If we identify with something beyond life for which we are willing to die, have we not at the same moment identified something that we are tempted — perhaps even obligated — to kill for? And does an affirmation of the excess of life establish a sufficient exteriority to move beyond a modern, secular politics?

Exteriority as Transgressing or Traversing

In this regard, Žižek alerts us to a lure awaiting us even in these realms exterior to modern, secular politics. For Žižek, as for many postmodern theorists, the excessive nature of life constitutes what makes "life" worth living, beyond the mere preservation of life. These theorists agree that there exists an excessive dimension to life that has been violently suppressed in modernity in the name of preserving life and peace. These theorists, in an inversion of Hobbes, claim that the passions of the people must be reinscribed into the political sphere rather than rationally circumscribed by it. In this way an ever-broadening and inclusive political field will emerge through an endless renegotiation and rearticulation, such that no one person will be excluded or oppressed but will be allowed to fully express her or his own private lifestyle. By this, each private lifestyle is given its own "form of life," and every subject is affirmed within the political order.[14] And, of course, this seems perfectly reasonable and desirable. Against a modern, secular politics of exclusive humanism, this is a postmodern *excessive* humanism seeking inclusion of all others.

The problem with giving free rein to all excessive individual or corporate identities and lifestyles, usually marked by their transgressive nature, is that it exactly mirrors the processes of global capitalism. Kenneth Surin points out above that our postpolitical situation is caused not only by the suppressive nature of modern nation-states but by the assumption of the political by the economic, creating the consumer-subject and the competitive-state. We live in a postpolitical age because everything has become economy oriented (perfectly articulated in *The Federalist Papers*). And the market revels in transgressing every rule and crossing every line, all in an effort to create new markets for selling new products to new consumer-subjects. And yet Žižek complains — against Surin — that those promoting the "politics of multitude" as a broadening of the politi-

14. Slavoj Žižek, *The Ticklish Subject* (New York: Verso, 1999), chap. 5.

cal field through transgressive rearticulations exactly mimic the machinations of global capitalism. For "the subject of late capitalist market relations is perverse" in its attempt to transgress all limits, yet in its very perversion maintains itself as a version of capitalism.[15] Therefore, a political orientation seeking to broaden the political field through transgressive rearticulation fails in achieving or producing an exteriority to our current postpolitical milieu, and it only reaffirms the consumer-subject dressed up as a political activist.

Why is this? Perversion, which Žižek uses in a technical sense drawing from psychoanalysis, stays within the political order, albeit in the seemingly exterior form of transgression. Perversion as constant transgression, in the name of the excess of life previously suppressed by the political order, enters into a morbid (con)fusion of what counts as life and death by claiming that (political and subjective) life functions as transgression and that (political and subjective) death comes from the law (whether they are the political laws of the land or the subjective laws of civility, sociality, and even rationality). This morbid confusion of life and death is perfectly articulated by Saint Paul in Romans 7, exegeted for psychoanalysis by Lacan, and applied to cultural and political theory by Žižek. This mutual implication of the existing political order and its own transgression allow for a *reasonable* form of resistance within the political order.

In seeking to affirm both the excess of life and the possibility of meaningful politics, transgression seeks to move within the political order as a broadening, reordering, and rearticulation of current and future "forms of life." It must do this in the form of transgression because to truly move beyond, rather than merely transgress within, the political order would mean to lose all contact with reality, all systems of meaning and significance, and thus the possibility of reasonable political action. But Žižek contends that this ultimately fails as a true exteriority to our postpolitical system because it is trapped in (because it mirrors) an economic system that feeds on the excess of life. In this way Žižek claims that not all affirmations of the excess of life automatically move us beyond modern political theory or its late-capitalist postpolitical instantiation.

As a result, the prevailing postpolitical system cannot be transgressed but only *traversed*.[16] Rather than transgressing the political order in vain attempts at rehabilitating it, Žižek proposes traversing the political order

15. Žižek, *Ticklish Subject*, 248.
16. Žižek, *Ticklish Subject*, 265-69.

through a radical "subjective destitution." Rather than seeking "subjective affirmation" *from* (indicating source/origin) the political order, one ought to enact a "subjective destitution" *from* (indicating separation/removal) the sociosymbolic order. The figure of this "subjective destitution" is death. Only in what we might call a "psychic suicide," where one is biologically alive, yet dead to the sociosymbolic coordinates of social, political, and economic life, is one placed in a true exteriority to the postpolitical system, standing in "the suicidal outside of the symbolic order."[17] This outside of the political order, of the system of meaning and significance, is also outside the management of "bare life" by the nation-state. But it is only gained through the passage of death, a death many political theorists are unwilling to entertain because it seems simultaneously too *excessive* in its stepping outside the bounds of rationality, reasonability, and all other figures of political "realism," and too *moderate* in its apparently disinterested posture toward the current state of affairs. These theorists would claim that such a radical break makes it impossible to transform the political order because one is so utterly beyond it, so utterly detached, and too "heavenly minded to be any earthly good."

But this is exactly Žižek's intention when he speaks of "subjective destitution" as death, for only when one considers oneself dead to the existing order will one be able to actually *act* freely with regard to it. Only then will one move from piecemeal forms of transgressive resistance against the existing order toward creating the possibility of another order altogether. This "subjective destitution" is a radical reformation through a traversal of the existing order, rather than a gradual transformation through a transgressional reappropriation of the existing order. Only this excessive humanism as traversal, says Žižek, can offer an exteriority to our postpolitical situation.

In this traversing as "subjective destitution" to all political manipulations and ultimatums, to all figures of political realism, we recover the possibility and significance of martyrdom. But while Žižek holds out this possibility, he can never quite tell us why we would want to subject ourselves to this "psychic suicide." Moreover, he cannot adequately distinguish between martyrdom and suicide because he does not offer us an account of goodness or truth for which we must be willing to die — but not as an act we exercise upon ourselves. It is an act that occurs indirectly only through our witness to a good that cannot be relinquished. Without this kind of a

17. Žižek, *Welcome to the Desert of the Real* (New York: Verso, 2002), 99.

vision of what is good and true, we lack any cause or movement that would inspire such devotion. Suicide is not the equivalent of martyrdom. The former cannot sustain an appropriate humanism, but the latter can. Suicide, unlike martyrdom, too easily leads to homicide. It is more than problematic that the figure of excessive life is a suicide bomber who believes he is a martyr. In these ways, while Žižek's appeal to the excess of life and his call for traversal rather than transgression significantly loosen the grip of *exclusive* humanism, his excessive humanism ultimately cannot secure an exteriority that would not reinscribe violence.

Martyrdom and a Postsecular, Postimmanent Politics: Immanent Humanism

Therefore, if excessive humanism remains tied to exclusive humanism, how might martyrdom function as an exterior to modern, secular politics? Or rather, how can a postpolitical politics understand itself properly as a postsecular politics? To answer these questions, we must return to the initial trajectories of modern political thought so that we might properly plot a different course. In a contrasting manner to Mark Lilla, Charles Taylor charts the rise of the exclusive humanist politics through a complex change in the "social imaginary." Whereas prior to the sixteenth century it was impossible to envision the good life apart from "God," now it is impossible to conceive of "God" as more than one option among many for securing a good life. Secularism does not mean the inevitable death of God; rather, it means that God becomes one preference among others, which means that we can always think of the good life without God even if we still affirm that God is essential for it. Taylor charts these changes less through major thinkers such as Hobbes, Rousseau and Kant (as Lilla does) and more through movements that give rise to social "cross pressures" in culture, politics, and economics. A key turning point occurs once "providential deism" takes hold. It affirms God as maker, but in such a way that the order God creates is "impersonal" and primarily found in a "natural religion" that became "obscured by accretions and corruptions" in the doctrinal developments in the church. But we can get behind these to pure natural religion because we know God has one goal for us: "mutual benefit."[18] Once this becomes our

18. Charles Taylor, *A Secular Age* (Cambridge, MA: Belknap Press, 2007), 221. Hereafter, page references to this work appear in parentheses in the text.

true end, of course, we do not need God for anything but to secure the conditions for the possibility of our pursuit of "bienfaisance." The result is that "we have moved from a world in which the place of fullness was understood as unproblematically outside of or 'beyond' human life, to a conflicted age in which this construal is challenged by others, which place it (in a wide range of different ways) 'within' human life" (p. 15). If Taylor is correct, the question "What is worth dying for?" makes little sense, for such a question presupposes a fullness that exceeds life itself. In a secular age, death is always loss, never gain — even if it is necessary.

Discontentment with such an exclusive humanism produces both a romantic and antihumanist reaction against it (or what we have been calling excessive humanism). Yet Taylor offers an interesting twist on the antihumanist reaction, a reaction we see in postmodern political discourse. It colludes with the humanism it supposedly stands against because it cannot conceive of a good that exceeds it except ironically. The antihumanism that opposes the humanist politics remains a species of it because the "anthropocentric turn" characterizes both. Antihumanism picks up on earlier religious themes of reducing suffering and valuing ordinary life and makes them a "crucial strand" that eventually becomes all it can offer. This is a humanism that assumes an immanence where "the affirmation of ordinary life" becomes the sole purpose for social and political existence (p. 370). Taylor notes that a form of primarily Protestant Christian piety inspired this affirmation of life.

> This affirmation, which constitutes a major component of our modern ethical outlook, was originally inspired by a mode of Christian piety. It exalted practical agape, and was polemically directed against the pride, élitism, one might say, self-absorption of those who believed in "higher" activities or spiritualities. Consider the Reformers' attack on the supposedly "higher" vocations of the monastic life. These were meant to mark out élite paths of superior dedication, but were in fact deviations into pride and self-delusion. The really holy life for the Christian was within ordinary life itself, living in work and household in a Christian and worshipful manner. (p. 370)

His analysis suggests that the move to an immanent humanist politics, traced so well by Lilla, has antecedents in a Christian piety even if it could never have gone as far as Hobbes or Rousseau.

Taylor then recognizes that the "immanent counter-Enlightenment," with its antihumanism, cannot finally exceed this affirmation of ordinary life by exclusive humanism. Nietzsche, the father of antihumanism, "rebelled against the idea that our highest goal is to preserve and increase life, to prevent suffering," but he did so not by pointing to any eschatological or transcendent purpose that would disrupt the basic contours of exclusive humanism. He merely took the exclusive humanism to its logical conclusion. Death, suffering, violence are inescapably part of what it means to live. Asking the question "What is worth dying for?" wrongly assumes that we have some alternative. Because life necessarily entails death, to affirm life is to affirm death. Taylor notes:

> So this move remains within the modern affirmation of life in a sense. There is nothing higher than the movement of life itself (the Will to Power). But it chafes at the benevolence, the universalism, the harmony, the order. It wants to rehabilitate destruction and chaos, the infliction of suffering and exploitation, as part of life to be affirmed. Life properly understood also affirms death and destruction. To pretend otherwise is to try to restrict it, tame it, hem it in, deprive it of its highest manifestations, what makes it something you can say "yes" to. (p. 373)

To affirm death as necessary for life may do nothing to escape the "biopolitics" that grounds life in bare survival. Here the antihumanists need the immanent humanist world as much as anyone else. In fact, have we not all become comfortable with such a political foundation even if we react against it?

A secular politics grounded in an exclusive humanism gives our lives security. We fear those who would question it. This secular politics has the oddest ardent defenders, from evangelical theologians deeply committed to the integrity of secular law to modern-day atheists who suggest that we must be ready to kill religious people to preserve our secular security. It is why we fear religion even when we cannot live without it. There is a common assumption today that persons committed to orthodox doctrines — Jewish, Christian, or Islamic — are somehow searching for certainty in an era of insecurity. But this is exactly backwards. The retrieval of orthodoxy against the deadening effects of liberal or progressive revisionism is no effort to find certainty in insecure times; instead, it is an effort to destabilize what has become so certain that it cannot even be questioned without its many defenders, secular and religious, closing ranks and making certain nothing gets destabilized. An immanent secular politics either keeps us from asking questions about transcendent goals for which we might live and die, or it tempts us to ask them solely in a way that affirms that same politics. Therefore, this politics must manage martyrdom but never be a martyrdom. It does this by way of celebrating soldiers as martyrs, and even frames the victims of 9/11 as national martyrs, whose deaths must be rendered intelligible by securing the possibility that no such taking of life can ever be repeated — even if it requires taking the lives of others.

Genuine Humanism

To do more than play with the question "What is worth dying for?" we will need something more than the paradox of the excessive humanist humanism; we will need a religious believer who knows his or her convictions are true. David Novak, a rabbi of Orthodox Judaism, rightly argues that neither Jews nor Christians can accept any account of truth that relativizes their convictions and subordinates them to an immanent humanism. "Relativism," he notes," is "dangerous" to any profound ecumenical dialogue, for it "denies" what both Jews and Christians affirm: "some things are true all the time everywhere for everyone." Novak observes:

> Indeed, these claims, like "God elects Israel" or "God is incarnate in Jesus," are what Judaism and Christianity are all about. In fact, Judaism requires Jews to die as martyrs rather than exchange Judaism for anything else, even something as similar to Judaism as Christianity. Christianity makes a similar claim on Christians. Martyrs are willing to die for what they believe to be the highest truth one could possibly know in this world, because without a commitment to the existence of truth, one cannot affirm the truth of God.

Novak also notes an "excess of life" that alone accounts for life. But in order to affirm this excess, he must invoke "truth." If we are not bound to the truth of our doctrines, there can be no excess of life.

> In truth, Žižek also recognizes this, and he recognizes — following Chesterton — that only such a commitment to orthodoxy can sustain a genuine humanism. He writes, Chesterton's basic matrix is that of the "thrilling romance of orthodoxy": in a proper Leninist way, he asserts that the search for true orthodoxy, far from being boring, humdrum

and safe, is the most daring and perilous adventure (... how much less risk and theoretical effort, how much more passive opportunism and theoretical laziness, is in the easy revisionist conclusion that the changed historical circumstances demand some "new paradigm"!).[19]

Žižek then offers a compelling Chesterton quote that those "who begin to fight the Church for the sake of freedom and humanity end by flinging away freedom and humanity if only they may fight the Church."[20] G. K. Chesterton recognized what Taylor identifies, that an exclusive humanism does not oppose antihumanism, but produces it. Jesus himself said something along these lines: those who seek to save their lives will lose them. Those who lose their lives for his sake will save them.

These kinds of claims are precisely what an immanent secular politics fears. If it asks you to die or kill, it will be to prevent any political realization of such claims; for they are the standard explanation for why violence occurs in the modern era. Are we allowed to die for anything today other than Western liberal democracies? Has it become our only possible politics, such that any other kind of politics beyond secularism will not be permitted?

Isn't Western liberal democracy the political embodiment of this domineering immanence? The standard political assumption is that if we strive for something true or good, we might get saints, but we will more likely get fascists who impose their account of truth or goodness on the rest of us. So democracy is, as Churchill so aptly put it, "the worst form of government — except for all the others." Without a doubt, there is great truth contained in this sentiment. Who would not prefer living under a democratic realm over a fascist regime, where each individual's life can only be defined in reference to the totality of the regime? Liberal democracies are supposed to protect us from that kind of totalization.

This occurs when they cannot tolerate what Rabbi Novak noted as essential to persons of faith, or, to put it as it is declared in the Christian Gospels: "We must obey God rather than men." Of course, this does create political problems. It could be cited by Oliver North while he was running covert military operations against a nation's perceived enemies or by Martin Luther King writing his letter from a Birmingham jail. How can we dis-

19. David Novak, "What to Seek and What to Avoid in Jewish-Christian Dialogue," in *Christianity in Jewish Terms*, ed. Tikva Frymer-Kensky et al. (Boulder, CO: Westview Press, 2000), 4.

20. Žižek, *Puppet and Dwarf*, 35-36.

criminate between such uses of religion as a politics-transcending form of politics? Isn't it safer to follow the route of liberal democratic politics and police against all such postsecular politics? This brings us to the furor Archbishop Rowan Williams caused by suggesting just such a postsecular politics.

The trouble Williams stirred up by suggesting the possibility that modern Western democracies might make a place for some such political alterity as Sharia law reveals that, across the theological spectrum (liberals, evangelicals, high church, low church), secular liberalism has become the only possible political entity for which one should give one's life. Yet this makes no sense to anyone faithful to Islam, Christianity, or Judaism. For the difficulty with liberal democracies is that they require — at least to this point — the relativizing of Christian, Jewish, or Islamic truth claims to a "public reason" that alone allows for political acts of testimony.

Anyone who has followed Rowan Williams's work with care would not be surprised by his suggestion that a secular, liberal democratic society should make space for alternative religious forms of political governance, even including some aspects of Sharia law. This has been a common theme in his Episcopal opposition to secularism. For instance, after his visit to China, he wrote the following:

> So the ideal of a society where no visible public signs of religion would be seen — no crosses around necks, no sidelocks, turbans or veils — is a politically dangerous one. It assumes that what comes first in society is the central political "licensing authority," which has all the resource it needs to create a workable public morality. Few places have tried as systematically as China to set this in stone; and now there is a tacit admission of defeat. Here in the UK, the daily reality of faith in ordinary communities is bound up with the maintenance of civil society, with enabling citizens to ask constructively critical questions of the State and to co-operate with statutory bodies to meet urgent needs. We could do with some common sense and realism about this. It would be something of a paradox if we had to look to the emerging China to find it.[21]

Williams challenges the simple political space where the only thing worth living for, and consequently worth dying for, is that space. He fears

21. "Both Crosses and Veils Must be Allowed," *The New York Times*, October 27, 2006: http://www.archbishopofcanterbury.org/660.

that it is a space of pure power and thus one that could not finally resist fascism. He writes: "To the extent that popular liberal and pluralist thought assumes with blithe unawareness a basic model of meaningful action in terms of assertion, it assumes a final social unintelligibility, an ultimate inability to make sense of each other's actions (which involves understanding so as to query and reexpress) — and thus raises the specter of the purest fascism, an uncriticizable exercise of social power in the name of a supposed corporate assertion."[22]

Is he suggesting that what we need is simply more "identities" represented in the public realm? If so, then this would be no profound alternative to Western liberal democracies. It would simply be its latest version of multiculturalism. But Williams assumes that Christians, Muslims, and Jews can do something secularists cannot do: they can present their claims in terms of truth, and this allows their claims to be adjudicated. The adjudication will not be based on some neutral universal reason overseen by exclusive humanism, but by others who also recognize that the particularity of orthodox faith claims demands universal truth claims. This would make for a complex political arrangement where persons could live under overlapping laws, which prompted him to say:

> I think at the moment there's a great deal of confusion about this; a lot of what's been written whether it was about the Catholic church adoptions agencies last year, sometimes what's written about Jewish or Muslim communities; a lot of what's written suggests that the ideal situation is one in which there is one law and only one law for everybody; now that principle that there's one law for everybody is an important pillar of our social identity as a Western liberal democracy, but I think it's a misunderstanding to suppose that that means people don't have other affiliations, other loyalties which shape and dictate how they behave in society and the law needs to take some account of that, so an approach to law which simply said, "There is one law for everybody and that is all there is to be said, and anything else that commands your loyalty or your allegiance is completely irrelevant in the processes of the courts." I think that's a bit of a danger.

The danger is precisely that one universal law, not grounded in any particular truth or loyalty, polices — even violently — all the dogmatic truth

22. Rowan Williams's "Introduction," in Davis, Milbank, and Žižek, *Theology and the Political*, 2.

claims that humans know they are called to adhere to — even at the expense of life itself.

Anyone interested in a postsecular politics can only applaud such thinking. But it is not mere multiculturalism. It can only be affirmed given Williams's deep commitment to Christian orthodoxy. This gives him a politics that does not begin with the question of evil, but of goodness and truth, and inevitably requires an exteriority, a postsecular politics that can still find a place for others because of the confidence in the universality of its own truth. This universal truth and its correlative goodness then forms the basis for politics. When the problem of evil is the first political question, then the only thing worth dying for is the prevention of some account of truth or goodness from dominating public discourse. Those who make such claims can only be viewed as a threat to be policed. When the question of the true or the good is our first political question, then we can make a place for others precisely because we are convinced of our own truth commitments. That others have such convictions is not a problem. Williams's postsecular politics assumes a universality grounded in the truth of dogmatic Christian convictions. This is the reason he must make room for others, even those who might find it necessary to practice certain forms of Sharia law. But this same universality will provide limits on what can be practiced.

What is surprising is not that the archbishop suggested this, but the responses on both the left and the right that quickly closed ranks to make sure no alterity to secular politics would emerge. For instance, the former evangelical archbishop of Canterbury, George Carey, declared: "There can be no exceptions to the laws of our land which have been so painfully honed by the struggle for democracy and human rights."[23] That this statement will not cause alarm and outcry among evangelicals when Williams's statement did shows how thoroughly evangelicals have made their peace with liberal, secular democracy. Notice how Carey's sentiment gets echoed on the liberal website "episcopal life," where Gary Fletcher writes:

> I suggest a better headline would have been: "Archbishop of Canterbury Loses His Mind." Why in the world would the leader of the Church of England advocate for the imposition of Islamic law in Britain? So profound a misunderstanding of the proud English and British heritage from the leader of the Church of England is incomprehensi-

23. http://www.newsoftheworld.co.uk/1002_sharia.shtml.

> ble. Ironically, his comments demonstrate either ignorance of or hostility toward the historic commitment of the British people to freedom and self-determination. The first nation to emerge from the political chaos of the Middle Ages, the defiant victor over the militarily superior Spanish Armada in the 16th century, the last bastion in Europe against the forces of fascism in the century past, the people of the United Kingdom surrender their autonomy to no foreign power, secular or religious. Surrender is precisely what the Archbishop now says is "unavoidable."[24]

Freedom, self-determination, immanent human rights, a single secular law that allows no exceptions — this is the secular politics that always closes ranks in order to ensure that no account of truth or goodness will escape this simple political space. It gives us stability by permitting no exteriority. But this will never work, because people of faith know that, having found the pearl of great price, they must sacrifice all for its sake. Exclusive humanism produces only one form of protest: a violent excess that commits suicide in order to refuse its interiorization. In clinging to life without asking what might be worthy of death, it loses life and accentuates death. A postsecular politics that affirms politics must emerge from some account of what is true will be willing to die for those dogmas. Oddly enough, in being willing to lose its life, it may find the only way to preserve it — even to preserve a genuine humanism.

24. http://www.newsoftheworld.co.uk/1002_sharia.shtml.

CHAPTER 10

"Threatened with Resurrection": Martyrdom and Reconciliation in the World Church

Emmanuel M. Katongole

There is something here with us
Which doesn't let us sleep,
Which doesn't let us rest,
Which doesn't stop pounding
Deep inside. . . .
What keeps us from sleeping
Is that they have threatened us with Resurrection.

Julia Esquivel

Introduction

We live in a world not only marked by war, poverty, injustice, and all kinds of destructive conflicts. Ours is also a world in which the social programs we have to address these problems seem ineffective, or in some cases even end up exposing deeper social divisions. Therefore, it is not surprising that in the face of what seem to be intractable challenges of poverty, violence, and injustice, there is a growing sense of despair and cynicism about goodness and peace in the world. Many try to mask this cynicism by adopting a posture of pragmatic realism: the world is the way it is, and nothing much can be done about it. All one has to do is maximize any good one can gain or exploit the opportunities there are in the world for one's own survival or for the well-being of one's loved ones. But this pragmatic individualism is itself another form of hopelessness.

If we are to avoid this kind of hopelessness, we need not simply more strategies and skills that purport to "fix" the brokenness of the world (important as these might be), but more stories worth living for — and therefore worth dying for — in the midst of the world's brokenness. It is such a story that Paul points to in 2 Corinthians 5:17:

> So, whoever is in Christ, there is a new creation. The old world has passed away. The new is here. All this is from God, who has reconciled us to himself through Christ and given the ministry of reconciliation.

For Paul, the hope of the story — which reconciliation names — is not a static state of peace, whatever that might mean, but an invitation to a journey. Moreover, as is clear from the above biblical text, the invitation to this journey is not limited to a few individuals; rather, it is to all who have been baptized ("anyone who is in Christ . . ."). In fact, elsewhere Paul shows that the journey is not even limited to Christians, but that all human beings, indeed the whole of God's creation, is on this journey and "awaits with eager longing" the freedom of God's new creation (Rom. 8:19-23).

In this chapter I would like to show that Christian martyrs, in their lives and deaths, provide the most concrete, dynamic, and exemplary case of the journey of reconciliation. More specifically, I would like to show that the journey that the martyrs exemplify provides the church and the world with a dangerous hope in that it is a hope that both invites and threatens the church into a life of vigil, a life of social struggle, and a new and resurrected community. Without these gifts, Christians would not know what it means to live as a people of hope in a broken and violent world.

Martyrdom: A Dangerous Hope

In naming martyrs, the church declares men and women who have lived in an exemplary way and have paid the ultimate sacrifice to be *living* witnesses — that is, witnesses who, though dead, are still with us. One must be careful not to romanticize the martyrs' "being with us." Their presence with us is a fact to be at once celebrated and feared. For, on the one hand, to the extent that they are with us still, they are "our friends" — part of the cloud of witnesses (Heb. 11) who inspire, support, encourage, and journey with us. On the other hand, their being in our midst also "threatens" us with resurrection and constantly keeps us from sleeping.

Those familiar with the life of Guatemalan dissident Julia Esquivel might immediately recognize that I am drawing from her poem "Threatened with Resurrection." Since her poem provides a very helpful way of exploring the odd presence that martyrs are in our midst, and thus the dangerous hope they exemplify, I believe it will be helpful to quote her at length.

A school teacher forced into exile from her native Guatemala, Julia Esquivel composed this poem:

There is something here with us
Which doesn't let us sleep,
Which doesn't let us rest,
Which doesn't stop pounding
Deep inside,
It is the silent, warm weeping
of Indian women without their husbands,
it is the sad gaze of the children
fixed there beyond memory,
in the very pupil of our eyes
which during sleep,
though closed, keep watch
with each contraction
of the heart,
in every awakening

Now six of them have left us,
And nine in Rabinal,
And two, plus two, plus two,
And ten, a hundred, a thousand,
a whole army
witnesses to our pain,
our fear,
our courage,
our hope!

What keeps us from sleeping
Is that they have threatened us with Resurrection.[1]

1. Julia Esquivel, *Threatened with Resurrection* (Elgin, IL: The Brethren Press, 1982), 59-61.

In his discussion of this work, Parker Palmer notes that it is not immediately clear from the poem who "threatens us with resurrection." On the one hand, Esquivel seems to be speaking of the killers — the "demented gorillas" who have killed hundreds of peasants in Rabinal and who threaten those who are still alive. On the other hand, however, it seems the threat of resurrection comes not from the killers but from the dead themselves. In the end, as Parker Palmer suggests, "the poem imitates life, in which the 'threat of resurrection' comes both from those who dispense death and from those who have died in the hope of new life."

The implications for this observation, Palmer says, are significant:

> If it is true that both killers and the killed threaten us with resurrection, then we are caught between a rock and a hard place. On the one hand, we fear the killers, but not simply because they want to kill us. We fear them because they test our convictions about resurrection; they test our willingness to be brought into a larger life than the one we now know. On the other hand, we fear the innocent victims of the killers, those who have died for love and justice and peace. Though they are our friends, we fear them because they call us to follow them in the "marathon of Hope." If we were to take their calling seriously, we ourselves would have to undergo some form of dying.

Palmer continues:

> Caught between the killers and the killed, we . . . huddle together in a conspiracy of silence, trying to ignore the ambiguous call of the new life that lies beyond death. Julia Esquivel is trying to break up our little huddle, I think, trying to inspire our active lives, calling us to engage the demented gorillas as well as our martyred friends, calling us to walk into our fear of resurrection and to open ourselves to the life on the other side.[2]

I find Parker's observations about Esquivel's poem particularly helpful in understanding the dangerous hope exemplified by the martyrs. The odd gift that martyrs are to the church and to the world lies precisely in their ability to break our little huddles of fear. In doing so, they keep the church from sleeping, as the constant "pounding" of their memory

2. Parker Palmer, *The Active Life* (San Francisco: Jossey-Bass, 1990), 139-57. I am grateful for Palmer's work, which first drew my attention to Esquivel's poem.

reenergizes the church into a life of struggle, and invites Christians into a new communion — a resurrected community on the other side of death. That is why the church can offer no more determinative sign of hope than to name and celebrate the memory of martyrs. For in so doing the church draws attention to at least three critical gifts: vigilance, social struggle, and dreaming. Without these gifts, we cannot sustain the journey of reconciliation. In the following three sections I will briefly explore these gifts as the hallmark of what it means to be a sign of hope and an agent of God's new creation in a broken world.

A Life of Vigilance: The Politics of Naming

> *That is the whirlwind*
> *which does not let us sleep,*
> *The reason why asleep, we keep watch,*
> *and awake, we dream.*

Martyrs keep the church from sleeping. In a number of places in "Threatened with Resurrection," Esquivel speaks of being kept from sleeping. What she is obviously referring to is not the lack of sleep that is usually referred to as insomnia, but a form of watchfulness. That is the reason she notes, "why asleep, we keep watch. . . ." It is through such a vigil that one can keep an eye on "those demented gorillas" — those who sacrifice the innocent.

A Life of Vigilance

Apparently, the early Christians knew something of this watchfulness, for they had no illusion that the world in which they lived was hospitable to the Christian way of life. That is one reason why Christian feast days and holy days were marked by a "vigil" service. This was not simply a way of anticipating the celebration of the feast day with prayer and other liturgical commemoration. It was a reminder of the vigilance that, even in the midst of celebration, Christian life was all about. But this is also the same reason why, as Pope John Paul II has reminded us, in spite of considerable organizational difficulties, the church of the first centuries took care to write down in special martyrologies the witness of the martyrs.[3] The reason, it is now obvious, is that the cultivation of a life of vigil requires and involves memory. Keeping the memory of martyrs was at least one way to remember the journey that the Christian life was all about, as well as naming particular dangers, threats, and temptations on the journey.

In our time, we have mostly lost the sense of the world as a dangerous place. This may sound ironic given the ever-present reality of war, injustice, and conflict. What we have lost is the ability to see these challenges as specifically *Christian* challenges (and not simply as human challenges). Furthermore, we have little sense of the Christian life as a journey according to which we live in the world as "resident aliens."[4] As a result, we have come to be so much "at home" in the world that we readily accept explanations that purport to offer the ultimate account of reality. Thus do sociological accounts lead us to think that "conflict and war" are inevitable; we accept the fact of millions of people going without food as simply an unfortunate consequence of the economic realities of our world. We easily assume "race," "tribe," and "nationality" to be natural identities.

How else does one explain that, in Rwanda in 1994, the majority Hutu Christians tried to wipe out their Tutsi brothers and sisters in a genocide? The fact that they were all Christians and that this happened to be Easter season did not seem to register any significant difference.[5]

In order to pierce through the tragic horror of such tribalism, but also to call back the church to a life of vigil, a life of alertness and resistance, one needs the story of martyrs like Chantal Mujjawamaholo and her friends. On March 18, 1997, three years after the genocide, Interahamwe militia attacked the secondary school at Nyange in Rwanda. The students had finished supper and their evening prayer, and they were in the classrooms doing their daily prep. The rebels attacked Senior 4 and Senior 5 classes and commanded the students to separate Tutsi and Hutu. The students refused; they said they were all Rwandans. The rebels then shot at them indiscriminately and threw grenades into the classroom. Thirteen

3. John Paul II, *Apostolic Letter, Tertio Millennio Adveniente* (Roma, 1994), #37.

4. For a full discussion of Christians as "resident aliens," see Stanley Hauerwas and William H. Willimon, *Resident Aliens: Life in the Christian Colony* (Nashville: Abingdon, 1989).

5. I have argued elsewhere that the depth and type of tribalism revealed in the Rwanda genocide is not an exclusive African phenomenon, but is a widespread and constant and consistent pattern within modern nation-state formation. See my *A Future for Africa: Critical Essays in Christian Social Imagination* (Scranton, PA: University of Scranton Press, 2005), 95-118.

students were killed in all. The victims were all reclaimed by their families and buried near their homes, all except one female student, who was from Changugu (a long distance away). She is buried at the school, and her tombstone bears a simple inscription: "Chantal Mujjawamaholo. B. 24.04.1975. D. 18.03.1997." She was just a month shy of her twenty-second birthday when she was killed.

In a world marked by tribal, racial, and national identities, where we tend to assume that these identities are "natural," we need the story of Chantal and her friends to reveal the idolatrous nature of these so-called natural identities. In this case, the truth that Mujjawamaholo and her martyred friends depict by their refusing to divide between Hutu and Tutsi points to "resistance" as a necessary posture in the face of these identities. But even more important, their story points to the gift for the sake of which "resistance" is possible and necessary. Thus do martyrs name the *telos* of Christian life. Without a clear sense of the gift toward which one's life is directed, resistance can be a form of reckless self-sacrifice or mere expression of radical fundamentalism.[6]

Naming the Gift

That is why martyrs name the gift. The students' refusal to separate Hutu and Tutsi, saying they were all Rwandans, names not only a sense of solidarity but a friendship that cuts across — and whose promise is far richer than — the ideological promises of Hutu or Tutsi. But even more tellingly, Chantal's very name, *Mujjawamaholo,* which in Kinyarwanda means "maiden of peace," points to the gift and goal of Christian living, whose truth and reality can only be grasped to the extent that one is able to resist the many forms of tribalism that characterize our existence in the world.

Thus I am not simply suggesting that the church should name Chantal Mujjawamaholo and her friends as martyrs; I am making the

6. This marks the difference between a life of martyrdom Christianly understood and terrorism that may involve suicide. Martyrs do not want to die; the irony is that, even if they are willing to sacrifice their own lives for the gift, they believe that the gift is not in their own power to realize. Accordingly, they can never sacrifice others in order to bring about the peace for which they are willing to die. In fact, their willingness to die is a confirmation of their belief that such peace has already been given by the one whose death and resurrection we remember. All we are called on to be as Christians is to witness that peace, which might involve surrendering our own lives — a strange kind of peace indeed.

stronger claim that martyrs name the church for what she is: maiden of peace. Without the story of Chantal and her friends, this invitation, call, and gift can very easily be obscured in the assumed inevitability of racial, tribal, or national politics. Martyrs provide a constant reminder of both the Christian gift and the concrete challenges to living out that invitation and journey.

This is why the practice of choosing a child's baptismal name (often the name of a martyr or saint) has deep significance in the Catholic tradition: these names serve as geographies of memory, which keep the church from forgetting — or from "sleeping," to use Esquivel's metaphor. This ancient practice augurs very well with many African traditions, where naming is always a rich cultural event. The naming of a baby is never a private or family matter; it is a social event, and the name is understood not simply as personal tag, chosen because it is "cute," but as the embodiment of social memory and a form of practical wisdom.

Naming Spells

That is what makes the story of the Congolese nun Blessed Annuarite Nengapeta (beatified by Pope John Paul II in 1985) so remarkable. As a young girl, Annaurite joined the convent of the Holy Family Sisters in Isiro-Wamba, where she spent her religious life as a nun and a midwife. In 1964, when the Mulele rebellion broke out, Simba rebels invaded the convent. Annuarite was murdered as she resisted the sexual demands of the rebel leader.

Annuarite's encouragement to her other sisters during the siege, as well as her courage during the ordeal, is exemplary. But what is even more striking is the witness of her names. At birth, she received the name of Nengapeta, which in her native language means "wealth is deceptive." When she started primary school, she was erroneously registered with the name Annuarite. That was the name of her sister. In her language the name means, "I laugh to myself about war."[7]

That is why the church, in naming martyrs, not only names a person's identity as maiden of peace. In the life and name of someone like Annuarite Nengapeta, the church also learns to rightly name the spells that try to convince us that conflict, war, and violence are inevitable, or that the

7. http://nbsc68.tripod.com/id90.htm.

world as we know it is the only world we have to live in.[8] Only if we name the spells for what they are, are we able to cultivate the virtue of alertness through which we resist, "despise," or laugh at the ideologies that would willingly sacrifice lives in the name of "peace," wealth, democracy, development, or security.

A Life of Struggle: Gestures of Peacebleness

> *They have threatened us with resurrection,*
> *Because they are more alive than ever before,*
> *Because they transform our agonies,*
> *And fertilize our struggle. . . .*

There is another sense in which martyrs keep the church from sleeping by calling her into a life of commitment to realize a better world. There are at least two ways martyrs do this. First, martyrs fertilize the church's struggle by drawing the church into a restless posture of lament.

Even though martyrs can be said to be dead, and thus "resting in God," they are never really dead; and they never really rest, since they remain, even in death, restless. According to John's vision in the book of Revelation, the souls of those below the altar remain restless:

> When he [the angel] broke open the fifth seal, I saw underneath the altar the souls of those who had been slaughtered for the word of God and for the testimony they had given. They cried out with a loud voice, "Sovereign Lord, holy and true, how long will it be before you judge and avenge our blood on the inhabitants of the earth?" (Rev. 6:9-10)

If this is the fate of martyrs, then a church that is custodian of their stories finds herself inevitably drawn into the same restless cry of "how long?" Such a cry is at once a posture of lament, which allows Christians to see the extent and depth of brokenness, and a posture of defiance, as it brings the church to the same anger and "breaking point" — a point where "we cannot take it anymore."[9]

8. For the language of "spells" as it applies to modern ideologies, see Katongole, "Violence and Christian Social Reconstruction in Africa": www.theotherjournal.org.

9. Brian K. Blount, "Breaking Point: A Sermon," in *Lament: Reclaiming Practices in Pulpit, Pew, and Public Square,* ed. Sally A. Brown and Patrick D. Miller (Louisville: Westminster John Knox, 2005), 145-53.

The recovery of such anger and passion is a much-needed gift, especially in our time, when most of the church's ministry is carried out as if nothing much is really at stake (save perhaps the church's own institutional security or the *spiritual* security of her members). The restless cry of the martyrs keeps the church from sleeping by reminding her of the promise of new creation for which the martyrs laid down their lives.

That is why the lament of "how long, oh God?" that the martyrs draw the church into is not a forlorn cry of despair, but a form of hope that galvanizes the church into a passionate and relentless struggle for a better society, where human life and dignity is respected, where basic human needs are met, where peace and freedom abound. In other words, the cry of the martyrs calls us to a place where hope becomes concrete in the forgiveness, respect, and tolerance within human interactions.

Second, the martyrs call us back into the everydayness of the struggle for peace. In other words, even though the martyrs are honored for the ultimate sacrifice of their lives, it is not primarily to this, but to the very mundane gestures and practice of peaceableness in their everyday living, that they point.[10] That is why it is not the memory of the martyrs in the abstract that is important, but the telling and retelling of the thick narrative of their particular lives.

When I visited Nyange Secondary School in December 2004 and heard the story of Chantal Mujjawamaholo and her friends, I asked whether there was an explanation for why the students were willing to risk their lives rather than divide between Hutu and Tutsi. Where did such courage come from? A teacher at the school suggested different reasons, including the fact that the students had just finished their evening prayers and could have drawn spiritual strength from that. He also mentioned another teacher — who had since left the school — who would speak to the students every morning before their classes, giving them some insights into unity and nonviolence.

I point to these practices of evening prayers and "some insights" into unity and nonviolence to show that, in a world that is so enamored of grand strategies for how to end poverty and eradicate terrorism, the martyrs remind us that the journey of reconciliation is a journey of tactics and gestures — a story here, a lesson there, and some insights along the way. In this world of gestures, tactics, and ordinary practices, the martyrs show us

10. For more on this point, see Emmanuel M. Katongole, *A Future For Africa: Critical Essays in Christian Social Imagination* (Scranton: Scranton University Press, 2005), 86-88.

the stuff of God's new creation as well as the form and the location of the struggle to realize a different world.

A Life of Dreaming: A Communion of Witnesses

To dream awake,
To keep watch asleep, to live while dying
And to already know oneself,
Resurrected.

If the martyrs fertilize the church's struggle for a better, more peaceful world, what sustains that struggle is the gift of dreaming. While a life of "dreaming" might strike some as a fantasy (as in "daydreaming"), the kind of dreaming the martyrs call the church to is a very concrete discipline. It is a way of living into the future as if the future were already here. Another way to put it is to say that the vision of God's peaceful creation is not a fantastic dream, one that can only be realized in the afterlife, but a concrete possibility in the here and now. That is why to dream — at least in the sense we are using it here — is at the same time to open ourselves to life on the other side of death. It is to live a life of the resurrection, or in the words of Esquivel's poem, it is to "know oneself already resurrected."

The Courage to Dream

There is no doubt that opening oneself to life on the other side of death not only requires courage but also a certain amount of madness — the kind of madness that Thomas Sankara, the slain Burkina Faso revolutionary, had in mind when he said:

> You cannot carry out fundamental change without a certain amount of madness. In this case, it comes from non-conformity; the ability to turn your back on old formulas; the courage to invent the future. . . . We must dare to invent the future.[11]

This is the same kind of madness — of daring to invent the future — with which the martyrs threaten the church. And that is what makes resur-

11. On Thomas Sankara (1985), see: www.littlebluething.com/sankara.

rection both a gift and a threat. In a world built on assumptions of power, self-preservation, and control, the martyrs reveal to us a new future that is built on powerlessness. For, in their being killed, the martyrs are indeed powerless. In their powerlessness, they seem to have nothing to lose. Accordingly, they stand naked in front of their killers and face death.

But if the martyrs seem to have nothing to lose, it is because, as Esquivel says, they know themselves already resurrected. In this way, what they reveal and live into is a vision of the future made present, a radical sense of flourishing that cannot be threatened, not even by death.[12]

A Communion of Witnesses

If the life of resurrection is a threat, it is also as Esquivel says, a "marvelous" adventure:

> Accompany us on this vigil
> And you will know what it is to dream
> And you will know how marvelous it is to live threatened with resurrection.

What makes it marvelous is the fact that a life of dreaming both requires and creates a community. And so, even though martyrs may seem to die alone, what makes it possible for them to willingly accept death is the fact that they are never alone, but that the story and struggle they participate in is bigger than they are. It is a story to which they have been called, but one that will continue after them. Again, in the words of Esquivel:

> Because in this marathon of Hope,
> There are always others to relieve us
> In baring the courage necessary

12. In light of the above considerations, and given the courage and hope that martyrs exemplify, the crucial question for the Christian is not whether to live or die, but how to die better, that is, how to live and die without fear. A recent book that speaks directly to the issue of fear is Scott Bader Saye, *Following Jesus in a Culture of Fear* (Grand Rapids: Brazos, 2007). I also find the story of Robert Sobukwe very inspiring: as one of the early resisters of apartheid in South Africa, he was imprisoned on Robben Island and banished into solitary confinement; nevertheless, he remained hopeful and committed to the struggle. His biography, by Benjamin Pogrund, is appropriately entitled *How Can Man Die Better? Sobukwe and Apartheid* (London: Peter Halban, 1990).

to arrive at the goal
Which lies beyond death.

This observation is significant because, in a world so marked by individualism, the story of martyrs points to and names the church as a body of witnesses. Moreover, in a world marked by the deep divisions of racial, national, and ethnic loyalties, what martyrs name is a communion that cuts across these boundaries. This is what the story of Tonia Locatelli reveals.

Following the invasion of Rwanda in 1990 by the Rwandan Patriotic Front, local militias, together with the police, started a systematic process of killing Tutsis at Nyamata. In 1992, an Italian social worker, Tonia Locatelli, who had lived there for more than twenty years, alerted the international media about the sporadic but systematic killings that were going on around Nyamata. As a result, the international media descended on Nyamata and reported the killings. The police commander was so infuriated by the presence of the international media that he shot Tonia Locatelli. She is buried at the side of the church.

Locatelli's story becomes even more telling in the light of the events of 1994, when, following the United Nations order to airlift foreign nationals from Rwanda, the missionary priests and nuns at Nyamata, who were protecting tens of thousands of Tutsi refugees in the church compound, were evacuated, and immediately after that the Interahamwe militia killed more than two thousand refugees in the church compound.

The fact that Tonia Locatelli lies buried in Nyamata alongside other (Rwandan) victims of genocide not only redefines the concept of "my people" but also announces her resurrection into a new communion beyond black and white. That is why, in a world marked by neat and settled identities of race, gender, nation, and tribe that divide Christians, we need her story. For without a story like hers, we lose the ability to imagine, dream, and live into the reality of the church as a resurrected and "strange" communion of witnesses drawn from all tribes, nations, and languages.

Conclusion: Naming and Remembering Martyrs

Of course, neither Locatelli nor Mujjawamaholo has been officially declared a martyr by the Catholic Church. My referring to them as martyrs is not only an indication that I use the designation "martyr" in a somewhat loose sense; I am also suggesting that a recovery of the gifts of martyrs has to do with the recovery of a vibrant conversation about why and who the church should name as martyrs.[13] If such a conversation becomes dull or uninteresting, then the church is in danger of losing the skills and courage necessary for the Christian journey. But it is also obvious why the church might be unable or even reluctant to engage the conversation about martyrs in a lively, ongoing way. For doing so involves accepting and welcoming the threat martyrs offer. In that case, the church is much "safer" without the stories of the martyrs. And yet, as I have shown, without martyrs the church would not be able to name the gift of God's peace in the world, nor the shape of the journey this gift involves.

I am also suggesting that a recovery of the gifts of martyrs has to do not only with the practice of naming martyrs but also with the rich tradition of remembering martyrs. Such remembering takes many forms: vigils, feast days, storytelling, renaming, and so on. It is through these practices that martyrs are remembered by the church. But it is through such remembering that the church herself is re-membered as community across the divisions of race, tribe, and nation, and constituted as a pilgrim people — a people on a journey toward the peace of God's new creation. A church that does not have the tradition and practice of honoring martyrs not only lives in the ever-present preoccupation of her projects, but it soon loses the skills to name the gifts of God's peace and the habits that sustain the journey.

13. I find Robert Royal, *The Catholic Martyrs of the Twentieth Century* (New York: Crossroads, 2000), very helpful in engaging this conversation, not only because of its attempt to provide a global map for martyrdom in our time, but also for the stories and lives he names as martyrdoms, some of them controversial.

CHAPTER 11

Flashpoints for Future Martyrdom: Beyond the "Clash of Civilizations"

Eric O. Hanson

Introduction

Christian martyrdom remains an important subject in the post–Cold War world, not simply in itself but also because it forces social scientists to give religious traditions their full due in any political explanation. The increased political significance of religious actors and organizations in post–Cold War politics has rendered this balanced approach absolutely essential. Until recently, Western intellectuals, especially social scientists, tended to reduce religious phenomena to political, economic, or psychological causes. Such reductionism remains more difficult in the case of martyrdom since the martyr is willing to sacrifice all other considerations for a religious motive. In global analysis, it is challenging to give all the varying causalities their independent significance, for any such complete analysis calls not only for significant political and economic expertise but also for a deep sensitivity to theological and historical concerns. Martyrdom can thus serve as a touchstone for the social scientist. If the theorist's paradigm does not know what to make of martyrdom, significant basic questions remain.

My chapter in this book belongs to the "Signs of the Times" discernment advocated by the Vatican II Pastoral Constitution on the Church in the Modern World *(Gaudium et Spes)*.[1] What is the current world like, and

1. For Vatican II and its relationship to the Council of Trent, see Raymond F. Bulman and Frederick J. Parrella, eds., *From Trent to Vatican II: Historical and Theological Investigations* (New York: Oxford University Press, 2006).

how does Christian martyrdom fit into that vision? While I hope to be sensitive to the concerns of the theologian and the historian, my assignment begins with an analysis of the post–Cold War world from the perspective of the political scientist. In other words, this analysis should start with the current state of world politics and work its way back to the concerns of other authors. Most fortunately for me, Emmanuel Katongole has contributed a very fine piece on Africa. I readily confess my inadequate knowledge of that continent, so his article has liberated me from the temptation to discuss Africa in detail, just because of the crucial significance of that continent for the future of Christianity.[2] Historians and theologians, of course, would also point to Africa's Christian heritage from Roman times and to the contemporary political significance of Christian-Muslim relations on that continent.

My political education began on another continent, with five years in East Asia during the 1960s (Mao and the Cultural Revolution) and the 1970s (the coming of Deng Xiaoping), so I will naturally focus on that region more than others. Since I have also written on global Catholic politics, however, Latin America and Europe have become natural secondary interests.[3] And finally, my recent book *Religion and Politics in the International System* focused on the global political roles of seven religions: Christianity, Judaism, Islam, Hinduism, Buddhism, Confucianism, and Maoist Marxism.[4] Therefore, I hope that this chapter will benefit from an interfaith context while it covers the following three questions:

1. What are the most salient characteristics of the contemporary post–Cold War world?
2. What might be the specific Christian political vocation in such a world?
3. How does Christian martyrdom fit into this vocation?

2. See, for example, Lamin Sanneh, *Whose Religion is Christianity? The Gospel beyond the West* (Grand Rapids: Eerdmans, 2003), and Lamin Sannah and Joel A. Carpenter, eds., *The Changing Face of Christianity: Africa, the West, and the World* (New York: Oxford University Press, 2005). See also two books by Philip Jenkins: *The Next Christendom: The Coming of Global Christianity* (New York: Oxford University Press, 2002), and *The New Faces of Christianity: Believing the Bible in the Global South* (New York: Oxford University Press, 2006).

3. Eric O. Hanson, *The Catholic Church in World Politics* (Princeton, NJ: Princeton University Press, 1987).

4. Eric O. Hanson, *Religion and Politics in the International System Today* (New York: Cambridge University Press, 2006).

The great danger in beginning with international affairs, of course, is that it can subordinate religious belief and practice to political impact. It is because of this danger that some theologians suspect even traditional Catholic social thought of being too close to "the powers that be" in its evaluation of the church in the world. I note the danger, and hope to avoid it by paying close attention to the principles of Catholic spirituality, especially as found in the thought of the twentieth-century Trappist monk Thomas Merton.[5] In a piece on Christian martyrdom, it is good to remember that Merton emphasized "the word of the Cross" as giving "the Christian a radically new consciousness of the meaning of his life and of his relationship with other men and with the world around him."[6] Merton locates martyrdom in its religious context by pointing out that, for the Christian, "martyrdom is the perfect response to the baptismal vocation." He explains: "By baptism, a man becomes another Christ and his life must be that of another Christ. . . . The saint, or *hagios,* is one who is sanctified in the sense of sacrifice."[7] So this subject is not just about politics and economics.

The Contemporary Post–Cold War World

If we start with a case study such as Iraq in the twenty-first century, the first thing that strikes even the casual observer is the pervasiveness of chaos. No one national actor, including the sole superpower (the United States), the premier international organization (the United Nations), or the religious leader of the majority Shiites (Grand Ayatollah Sayyid Ali al-Sistani), is capable of bringing order to the country, even if — contrary to fact — they were to develop a close alliance. Many individuals and organizations, from the local Sunni insurgency, to the governments of Iran and Syria, to the United States Defense Department, hold a black ball that enables each group or nation individually to block social order. Second, in contrast to the Cold War period, when military and economic power

5. For this discussion, see Kristin E. Heyer, *Prophetic and Public: The Social Witness of U.S. Catholicism* (Washington, DC: Georgetown University Press, 2006). Heyer contrasts the opposing views of J. Bryan Hehir and Michael Baxter, and then offers a synthetic position. For Merton, see Lawrence S. Cunningham, ed., *Thomas Merton: Spiritual Master; The Essential Writings* (New York: Paulist Press, 1992).

6. Cunningham, *Merton,* 414.

7. Cunningham, *Merton,* 202.

largely determined the global political structure, symbolic and communication "soft power" exercised by actors as disparate as Moktada al-Sadr, following his martyred father, and the television network Al-Jazeera, have grown in salience, especially in terms of creating political chaos.

My image for contemporary challenges such as Iraq or Israeli-Palestinian relations is that of a ten-tumbler slot machine on which every tumbler must show the same sign simultaneously to produce a political solution. In the Oslo Process, for example, the summer of 2000 brought about the agreement of nine tumblers, but not that of Yasir Arafat, who pulled his lever again. Then Ariel Sharon pulled his by visiting the Temple Mount in September. As Mao learned in the Cultural Revolution, it is much easier to destroy order than to create it.

For an African example, one could study the progressive deterioration of politics since the 1960s in Zaire/Congo. Even the most expensive election in history seems not to have made much difference.[8] Of course, the tragedy of Darfur remains the world's largest humanitarian disaster. Sri Lanka constitutes an example in South Asia, with fighting escalating again after relative calm following the Norway-brokered cease-fire of 2002. Increased global fragmentation also results partially from recent scientific and technological progress. Think, for example, of the global political impact of the hidden cell phone video coverage of the guards' verbal abuse at Saddam Hussein's execution when that coverage appeared on the Internet. None of the above crises, however, threatens a global conflagration in the way that conflicts over the Korean peninsula, the Taiwan Strait, or Kashmir would. The latter tensions all represent issues that remain nonnegotiable to major military powers, thus threatening at least a regional war.

What paradigm, then, could we use to describe the new realities of the post–Cold War period? My book starts with the intersection of four independent global systems: economic, military, communication, and political.[9] The global economic system calls our attention to the great world disparities of income and the continued damage to the human and physical environment from phenomena like SARS, AIDS, and climate change.[10] In-

8. See *The New York Times*, March 28, 2007. The front-page headline is: "After Congo Vote, Neglect and Scandal Still Reign."

9. Hanson, *Religion and Politics*. The paradigm can be found in chap. 1: "A New Paradigm for World Politics?" (17-46).

10. The starting point for a general overview of the economic system should be the yearly *United Nations Human Development Report*.

deed, while the developed countries have added most of the greenhouse gases to the atmosphere, it will be the poor developing countries' deltas and river valleys that will suffer most as sea levels rise.

The global military system differs from its Cold War counterpart in the recent emphasis on nuclear proliferation and long-running chaotic civil wars fought with varying levels of conventional weapons. The global communication system of the nearly instantaneous Internet and satellite television fosters the formation of communities that are not geographically based — as well as new types of self-identity. And the global political system combines a weak internationalism centered in the United Nations with an expanded role for transnational organizations like multinationals, churches, NGOs, and nonprofits. It also features a weakening sole national superpower, the United States, and rising regional powers such as China, India, and Brazil. Human rights issues belong to this political system.

Each of these economic, military, communication, and political systems exists as an independent and autonomous regime with its own rules and methods of interaction, but what distinguishes this half of the global paradigm is the constant interaction among the four systems. That means that ethical considerations about one system need to relate to all other systems. For example, Williams and Caldwell tie just-war theory more tightly to the contemporary human rights regime and the global economic system by adding a "jus post bellum" to the traditional categories of *ius ad bellum* and *ius in bello.*[11] As in Iraq, what happens in civilian reconstruction at the end of the military phase really matters ethically. This constant interaction among the four separate systems produces fifteen separate types of issues, from solely political ones to situations like the Iraq War, which combine all four concerns.

The second half of the paradigm focuses on the political actors at various levels: individual, local, national, regional, and global. It is at these levels that religious decisions influence the paradigm. There is no global religious system, however, that is composed of, for example, Judaism, Hinduism, and Confucianism any more than there is a global linguistic system composed of Arabic, Basque, and Cantonese. Because of the great differences among religious beliefs and structures, the noun "religion" denotes a category of ultimate meaning, not a system. My book gives both an obser-

11. Robert E. Williams, Jr., and Dan Caldwell, "*Jus Post Bellum:* Just War Theory and the Principles of Just Peace," *International Studies Perspectives* (November 2006): 309-20.

vational and a judgmental definition of religion. The former is "that pattern of beliefs and activities that expresses ultimate meaning in a person's life and death"; the latter is "that pattern of beliefs and activities which predispose and accompany the person's contact with the Other in which one accepts one's inmost self."[12] In the judgmental case, one can distinguish between true and false religion. But even if religion is nonsystemic, religious inspiration remains terribly important in today's world. Think of the twentieth-century political influence of, for example, Mohandas K. Gandhi, Desmond Tutu, the Dalai Lama, and John Paul II. Each religious tradition has produced men and women generally recognized as combining great sanctity with heroic service to others.

The fall of the Berlin Wall constituted a great shock to those political analysts, national populations, and movie screenwriters grown comfortable with the Cold War paradigm based on nuclear deterrence and competition between the Kremlin and the White House. The most popular post–Cold War explanation of the 1990s, "the clash of civilizations," came from Harvard University Professor Samuel P. Huntington. It seems to me that most paradigms begin with the theorist's attempt to explain a particular large event that does not fit the previous dominant paradigm. For the West, the most significant crisis of the 1990s was the war in the former Yugoslavia. When the Cold War lynchpin of the Tito government was removed, the preexisting regional, ethnic, and religious interests reasserted themselves. This conflict engaged first the European Union and then the United States in trying to sort out the conflict among Catholic Croatians, Orthodox Serbs, and Bosnian Muslims. Suddenly, the Catholic-Orthodox split of 1054, and the sixteenth- and seventeenth-century expansion of the Ottomans into the Balkans, even to the gates of Vienna in 1529 and 1683, when Polish King John Sobieski saved the city, were influencing today's headlines.

Huntington duly noted that the Yugoslavian opponents seemed to be engaged in a "clash of civilizations," and that the civilizations seemed to be based on religious differences. The theory also proved useful if one thought that the greatest threats to the West came from Islam and China, or — even more terrible — from an alliance between the two, which would greatly surprise the Muslims of China's Xinjiang Province. Huntington even supported concern about Hispanic immigration into the United States. Such immigration could change the United States from a Western

12. Hanson, *Religion and Politics,* 76.

civilization into a Latin American one, at least in states such as Arizona, California, New Mexico, and Texas. In the end, Huntington posited nine civilizations: Western, Latin American, African, Islamic, Sinic (Chinese), Hindu, Orthodox, Buddhist, and Japanese, all with varying links to the other eight.

There are significant theoretical problems associated with the different meanings of "civilization" in the above designations, and quantitative studies did not support the paradigm. Scholars Bruce Russett and John Oneal, for example, found that for global conflicts between states, traditional realist and liberal theories better explain the data.[13] In another study, Errol Henderson found that, while a common religion reduces the frequency of such wars, common ethnicity and language increase it.[14] Most critics, however, focused on the significant similarities *among* some civilizations and the even more significant differences *within* other civilizations. For example, the Iran-Iraq War between Saddam Hussein and Ayatollah Khomeini constituted a terrible bloodbath within Islam.[15] Or think of the different civilization orientations — from Arab nationalism to universal Islamism to Shiite regionalism — of the current Muslim political actors in the Iraqi conflict. An extremely thoughtful Muslim critique of the theory came from Roy Mottahedeh, chairman of Harvard's Committee on Islamic Studies. Mottahedeh welcomed Huntington's reemphasis on culture and "identity politics," but savaged his description of Islamic civilization and its theoretical links to actual political events.[16] Indeed, Huntington's theory cannot explain the current system. At the most abstract theoretical level, a global explanation at least demands additions from the political economy of Wallerstein's world-system theory and the consideration of *Realpolitik* "national interest" alliances like that between the United States and Saudi Arabia.

While Huntington rightly takes into account the significance of political identities and of religion in the formation of those identities, he focuses on an essentialist understanding of the more general term, his "civilization," while the most relevant marker is often the most local, for

13. Bruce Russett and John R. Oneal, *Triangulating Peace: Democracy, Interdependence, and International Organization* (New York: Norton, 2001), 239-69.

14. Russett and Oneal, *Triangulating Peace*, 247.

15. For Sunni-Shia relations, see Vali Nasr, *The Shia Revival: How Conflicts Within Islam Will Shape the Future* (New York: Norton, 2006).

16. Roy P. Mottahedeh, "The Clash of Civilizations: An Islamicist's Critique," *Harvard Middle Eastern and Islamic Review* 2 (1995): 1-26.

example, very disparate Sunni political actors in Baghdad in 2007. In addition, religious traditions change significantly over time, as illustrated by the Second Vatican Council in world Catholicism[17] and the global rise of Engaged Buddhism during the last fifty years.[18] Indeed, religious traditions are reacting to the various currents of modernity and to the adaptations of other religious traditions to these currents at the same time. Yet religious traditions are not multinational corporations; they must maintain their traditional links to have any reason for existence. It is not an easy time to be a religious leader.

So Huntington remains correct in emphasizing the crucial significance of religion, using it as his principal civilization marker; but he fails to appreciate its relevance at all political levels, from the individual to the global. He also never discusses the multiple ways in which it makes a difference. One could focus, for example, on the separate political impacts of spirituality, ritual, Scripture and prophecy, cultural worldview, doctrine, ecclesiastical organization, and morality and law. For example, rituals like the funeral of Steve Biko played a major role in South African antiapartheid politics. Pilgrimages tie groups together, for example, Iraqi Shiites going to Karbala. For the last category, all political analysts, especially those from an American culture that tends to identify religion and ethics, should note that the importance of the latter varies greatly across religions.

Ethics tends to be more important in the religions of the book — Christianity, Islam, and Judaism. But not all ethical systems come from a religious base, nor do all religions give the same emphasis to ethics. Even in the case of religious-based ethics, these systems do not serve as basic religious touchstones. Merton warns that "[t]o imprison ethics in the realm of division, of good and evil, right and wrong, is to condemn it to sterility, and rob it of its real reason for existing, which is *love*."[19] Humanity had fallen into the knowledge of good and evil, according to Merton, so that the genius of the Protestant Reformation consisted in that "it focused from

17. The classic short history is Giuseppe Alberigo, *A Brief History of Vatican II* (Maryknoll, NY: Orbis, 2006). Orbis also published the definitive 5-volume history by the scholarly team put together by Alberigo, which has been translated into many other languages.

18. See, e.g., Christopher S. Queen and Sallie B. King, eds., *Engaged Buddhism: Buddhist Liberation Movements in Asia* (Albany: State University of New York Press, 1996); Peter Harvey, *An Introduction to Buddhist Ethics* (Cambridge: Cambridge University Press, 2000); and Christopher Queen, Charles Prebish, and Damien Keown, eds., *Action Dharma: New Studies in Engaged Buddhism* (London: Routledge Curzon, 2003).

19. Cunningham, *Merton*, 153 (italics in original).

the beginning on the ambiguities contained in 'being good' and 'being saved' or 'belonging to Christ.'"[20]

The Christian Political Vocation in the Contemporary World

I judge Huntington's paradigm to be severely limited, but the concept of the Christian political vocation in this post–Cold War world does not depend on that judgment. It depends on the common spiritual experience of religious traditions that union with the Other and union with all of one's fellow humans deepens as a single experience. Even if Huntington's paradigm were the best available, religious spirituality, for example, as articulated by Merton, should inspire us to question Huntington's acceptance of a regionalized, culturally balkanized vision that divides all humanity into "us" and eight varieties of "them." Reconciliation among all peoples and all religions remains a Christian vocation, whether the Christian is Catholic, Orthodox, or Protestant; it also remains a specifically religious vocation, whether the believer is Buddhist, Confucian, Hindu, Jewish, or Muslim.[21]

However, regardless of what specific religions do individually, political salvation in the current fragmented post–Cold War world will come only through cooperative action nurtured by interfaith dialogues. What do I mean by political salvation? I mean development and equity in the global economic system, peace and reconciliation in the global military system, strengthened personal and communal values in the global communication system, and human rights in the global political system.[22] Thus the contemporary religious vocation remains tied to the economic, military, communication, and political systems, even though it cannot be reduced to any or all of these systems. Let's take the Catholic political vocation as an example of the application of this approach.

Religion can affect politics at the individual, local, national, regional, and international levels. At the individual level, the person is inspired to

20. Cunningham, *Merton,* 155.

21. For a comparative religious perspective of ethics, see the body of work by ecumenical theologian Hans Küng, for example, *Global Responsibility: In Search of a New World Ethic* (New York: Crossroads Publishing, 1991). The statement *A Global Ethic* was adopted by the Parliament of the World's Religions. It can be found in Hans Küng and Karl-Josef Kuschel, eds., *A Global Ethic* (New York: Continuum, 1993).

22. For a fine treatment of the global communication system, see Michael Budde, *The (Magic) Kingdom of God: Christianity and the Global Culture Industries* (Boulder, CO: Westview Press, 1997).

the conversion of his or her life to serve God and God's people in a special way. Both Oscar Romero of El Salvador and Samuel Ruiz of Chiapas were selected as bishops precisely because their respective political establishments thought that they would never disturb what was — at least for the powerful — the comfortable status quo. However, both bishops experienced *metanoia* (conversion) as they interacted with the people of their dioceses. Romero was changed by the murder of one of his priest friends, Rutillo Grande, and the murders of countless other Salvadorans. Ruiz rode a burro through the mountains to visit his Mayan parishioners in their small villages. We need to keep the individual level in view, because the basis of any true religious political vocation is the continual process of self-conversion. For the social analyst, such religious conversions should be one of the significant sources of change within the whole system.

The local level most often provides the context for that personal conversion. For example, to grow up Catholic in Northern Ireland over the last one hundred years constituted, by that very fact, a vocation to reconciliation with Protestants — for example, in John Hume, winner of the Nobel Peace Prize. The joining of a unified government by Gerry Adams of Sinn Fein and radical Protestant minister Ian Paisley gave the people of Northern Ireland hope for a better future.[23] Note that neither Hume nor his fellow Nobel Prize winner David Trimble headed the government. In the March 2007 elections, Paisley's Democratic Unionists garnered first place with 30 percent of the vote, and Sinn Fein won 26 percent. Paisley became first minister, and Martin McGuinness, negotiator for Sinn Fein, served as his deputy. Often the politicians who most strongly supported reconciliation, in this case the above Nobel laureates, do not succeed to power.

Indeed, sometimes the very fact of the renunciation of power can lower political hostility. In 2004, India's Italian-born leader of the just-victorious Congress Party, Sonia Gandhi, stepped aside for the current prime minister, Sikh economist Manmohan Singh. She served her country exceedingly well by that personal sacrifice in the face of opposition from her closest allies. Such a renunciation was not easy, but it was necessary for the good of India. Otherwise, the country would have been engulfed in strife over the accession of Sonia, who was born an Italian Catholic (she then joined the Nehru dynasty as wife of the former prime minister, Rajiv Gandhi). There was also an economic consideration: Singh was widely re-

23. *The New York Times*, March 27, 2007.

spected by the business community as the architect of the open market under Prime Minister Narasimha Rao.

At the national level, the Catholic Church has played many roles, some positive, some not so positive. For example, the Brazilian, Chilean, Philippine, and South Korean churches of the 1960s through 1980s can generally be very proud of their role in protecting human rights within authoritarian and brutal military regimes. The current Brazilian president, Luiz Inácio Lula da Silva, comes from the worker-church alliance that resisted the military National Security State in the 1960s and 1970s. Cardinals Aloísio Lorscheider and Paolo Arns (Brazil), Raúl Silva Henríquez (Chile), Jaime Sin (Philippines), and Stephen Kim Sou Hwan (South Korea) all led the ethical opposition in their countries to dictators backed by the United States.

Not so ideal was the response of the Argentine Catholic Church.[24] When the Democratic Party could not unify around an alternative to the Reagan military buildup of the 1980s, the United States Bishops Conference did.[25] For regional examples, the Latin American Bishops Conference (CELAM) was instrumental in defending human rights during the military period, and European Catholic and Protestant organizations have supported the formation of the European Union. At the global level, the Vatican has been especially supportive of the role of the United Nations and transnational organizations. It is on this point of strong support for international organizations that papal foreign policy, no matter who the pope is, most differs from that of the United States.

That's the good news. But organizational structure can also be a negative, for example, the close identification of the papal nuncio, Archbishop Bruno Torpigliani, with the Marcos administration in the Philippines.[26] The central Catholic political temptation since Constantine has always been the worship of the institutional arrangements. Merton terms this "the Carolingian suggestion," whose false argument he sketches as follows: "We are living in the last age of salvation history. A world radically evil and doomed to hell has been ransomed . . . and is now simply marking time until the message of salvation can be preached to everyone. Then will

24. Emilio F. Mignone, *Witness to the Truth* (Maryknoll, NY: Orbis Books, 1988). For the difficult history of the Catholic Church in Argentina, see Austen Ivereigh, *Catholicism and Politics in Argentina, 1810-1960* (Oxford: St. Martin's Press, 1995).

25. Eric O. Hanson, *The Catholic Church in World Politics* (Princeton, NJ: Princeton University Press, 1987), 285-301.

26. Hanson, *World Politics*, 331.

come the judgment. Meanwhile men . . . must be prevented by authority from following their base instincts and getting lost."[27] So the Christian emperor maintains the order that prevents evil. In addition, there are holdovers from the Cold War period. For example, the justly praised role of Pope John Paul II — in the United Nations, in Eastern Europe, in Israeli-Palestinian relations (remember his March 2000 visit to the Holy Land) — could support that temptation on future issues if one tries to generalize postwar Polish politics. Karol Wojtyla was an excellent Cold War pope. But we are no longer in the Cold War period, and the current fragmentation of power calls for a different, if complementary, approach.

At the global level, the current state of world affairs remains much more chaotic than the Cold War system. We have nation-states of various strengths and generally weak transnational and international organizations. The military system's regime of nonproliferation is breaking down. In the economic system, however, the WTO, the IMF, and the World Bank exercise considerable clout, but not always in an intelligent way. The global communication system has introduced and heightened tension in various "culture wars." To build a viable international system, we need to pursue reconciliation initiatives in all four systems and at all five levels of interaction. Each of us has a special vocation that impacts all. Indeed, in the post–Cold War world, everything influences everything else.

The nation-states must come up with a new way to aggregate their alliance structures in ways that will replace the Washington-Moscow axis as a source of global stability. Transnationals such as NGOs and multinationals must find their proper role in the formation of the new "international civil society." Then international organizations, especially the United Nations, must become effective peacemakers and development agents of last resort. Individual international leadership will be most legitimate globally when it comes from small and medium states such as Ghana (Kofi Annan), Ireland (Mary Robinson), and South Korea (Ban Ki-moon). The global challenges at all levels and in all systems have never been greater, nor have the forces of chaos. Technological advancement works for both good and evil.

Just advocating the international solution of problems won't work without confidence-building measures among the nation-states. Nation-states retain their major causality in global affairs. In addition, the most powerful (the United States) and the rising regional powers like China, In-

27. Cunningham, *Merton,* 378-79.

dia, and Brazil show no signs of giving up their nationalist sentiments in the near future. The world needs a new national architecture in international affairs, but it must be based on the relationships of current nation-states.

My proposal and the relationship of religion and politics in that proposal are the following: to replace the Cold War paradigm and to structure the global architecture on the relationship between two poles — the Western alliance of North America and the European Union as one pole, and an Asian alliance of East Asia and South Asia as the other pole. The Western alliance points to the crucial significance of restoring comity to the Atlantic Pact, and of the extension of the European Union to include Turkey, Russia, and the Ukraine. The Asian alliance would be formed of two poles itself, an East Asian cluster led by China and mediated by the Republic of Korea, and a South Asian cluster led by India. The ASEAN nations would mediate between Seoul/Beijing/Tokyo and New Delhi/Islamabad. The final step would be a cooperative relationship between the Atlantic and Asian groupings that would structure cooperative arrangements for Central Asia, the Middle East, Africa, and Latin America. Regional powers such as Nigeria, South Africa, and Brazil would continue to play significant regional and international roles in integrating Central Asia, the Middle East, Africa, and Latin America into the above global structure.

The point of this proposal is that, although international arrangements for the economy and nuclear proliferation remain absolutely essential, they will not succeed without confidence-building networks among the principal nation-states and regions. Otherwise, the world ends up with the 190 plus nations of the UN General Assembly and global chaos. Some theorists may want to start by just centralizing power globally, but they must also build ever more secure linkages among the national actors that will give national capitals the confidence to trust shared sovereignty on the increasing number of issues that demand such action, for example, global environmental issues. What the final world structural arrangements might be has to wait for the coming of the right *kairos.*

What role would religious traditions play in such a proposal? Interfaith dialogue would be absolutely essential in the confidence-building. Let me illustrate by looking at the three principal parts of the Asian pole.

East Asia: China constitutes the principal rising power, and the China-Korea-Japan triangle offers significant opportunities joined to tremendous challenges. Christian-Buddhist relations on the Korean peninsula remain crucial, with the East Asian dialogue in general focused on discussions between Confucian-Marxist state ideologies and the local practices of Buddhists, Taoists, and Christians. After a rocky stretch in Beijing-Vatican relations, on January 23, 2007, the Chinese government stated that it appreciated the Vatican's willingness to have "constructive dialogue."[28]

South Asia: The principal challenge, of course, is Hindu-Muslim relations across the subcontinent. As in Japan, Christianity has been active in opposing extreme cultural nationalism and working for social equality.[29]

ASEAN unites ten countries, but six remain especially suitable for interfaith dialogue: Malaysia, Indonesia, the Philippines, Singapore, Thailand, and Vietnam. Singapore is a high-development country according to the United Nations Human Development Index, and the other five are medium-development nations. Medium development and the presence of multiple religions both facilitate religious dialogue. The ASEAN nations include significant representation from Buddhism, both Theravada and Mahayana; Christianity, both Catholic and Protestant; Confucianism; Hinduism; Islam — Sunni, Shia, and Sufi; and Marxism. Very populous countries, such as Indonesia (majority Muslim, minority Christian) and the Philippines (majority Christian, minority Muslim), make fine dialogue partners, and the interfaith interchange between Manila and Jakarta is already promising. Christian-Muslim dialogue is much easier in Southeast Asia than it is in the Arab context. Cardinal Julius Darmaatmadja of Jakarta, for example, has praised the anticorruption work of the two major Muslim organizations, Nahdlatul Ulama and Muhammnadiyah. The Vietnamese government has entered into a dialogue to normalize relations with the Holy See. The effort began with a visit of Prime Minister Nguyenh Tan Dung to Pope Benedict XVI on January 25, 2007, and continued with a government white paper on religious toleration and a six-day March visit to Vietnam by a delegation from the Holy See.[30]

28. *Asia Focus,* February 2, 2007. For the historical background of Vatican-Chinese relations, see Eric O. Hanson, *Catholic Politics in China and Korea* (Maryknoll, NY: Orbis Books, 1980).

29. See chaps. 6 and 7 in Hanson, *Religion and Politics.*

30. *Asia Focus,* February 2 and 9; March 16, 2007. At the end of the preceding year, considerable tension was created by the government ordination of bishops without Vatican

Readers will find it much easier to sketch in the necessary interfaith dialogues for the Atlantic pole, but the Catholic-Orthodox and Catholic-Muslim interactions emphasized in Pope Benedict XVI's trip to Turkey remain crucial. Europe faces the twin challenges of re-Christianization and of the linking of traditionally secular (laïcité), Catholic, Protestant, Orthodox, and Muslim religious traditions. These dialogues are made all the more necessary because of the presence of many immigrants from North Africa, the Middle East, and the Balkans within the European Union. For example, Turks who immigrated to Germany when they were young and thought that they would soon return home now have reached retirement age in Germany.[31] The relationship of national identity and immigration became the major issue in the 2007 presidential election in France. Perhaps the most famous case in this adjustment was the controversy surrounding the murder of Theo van Gogh after he produced the movie *Submission* with Ayaan Hirsi Ali, a Dutch member of parliament who had emigrated from Somalia.[32]

These issues all focus on questions of identity at various levels. First, can the West maintain its unity and cooperation? Andrei S. Markovits's *Uncouth Nation: Why Europe Dislikes America* focuses on the tradition of anti-Americanism that reached a high point in the February 15, 2003, pan-European demonstrations just prior to the U.S. invasion of Iraq.[33] Markovits overstates the case in a Fox News-like manner, but there are tensions, especially between American religious conservatives and secular Franco-German élite intellectual positions. The book's major lacuna is its lack of coverage of Eastern Europe. The EU's admission of ten new nations in 2004 greatly changed the European dynamic and made religious dialogue more significant.[34]

Second, the future of the European Union and the nature of a European identity remain unclear. The French and Dutch electoral defeats of the proposed European Constitution on May 29 and June 1, 2005, signaled

---

consent. See, e.g., the ordination of twenty-seven-year-old coadjutor, Bishop Wang Renlei, in Xuzhou. *Asia Focus*, December 8, 2006.

31. *The New York Times*, March 25, 2007.

32. Ian Buruma, *Murder in Amsterdam: The Death of Theo van Gogh and the Limits of Tolerance* (New York: Penguin, 2006).

33. Andrei S. Markovits, *Uncouth Nation: Why Europe Dislikes America* (Princeton, NJ: Princeton University Press, 2007).

34. See Timothy A. Byrnes and Peter J. Katzenstein, eds., *Religion in an Expanding Europe* (New York: Cambridge University Press, 2006).

mass popular distrust of the élite position of support. Much work needs to be done at the grassroots level to democratize pan-European institutions. Part of that conversation must be a dialogue on the role of religion in Europe, a source of tension in the drafting of that constitution.

Third, an increased emphasis on national identity within the uncertainties and challenges of globalization also poses some risks. France is having a particularly hard time formulating a self-identity. For example, *The New York Times* describes the spring 2007 presidential campaign as "seized by a subject long monopolized by the extreme right: how best to be French."[35] Conservative Nicolas Sarkozy proposed a "ministry of immigration and national identity," and Socialist Ségolène Royal advocated memorizing "La Marseillaise" and displaying the French flag on Bastille Day. The longtime far-right candidate, Jean-Marie Le Pen, declared that both had stolen the message of his National Front Party, "France for the French." Thomas Merton, of course, would pose the dangers of an exclusive focus on any "external" identity, dividing humanity into "us" and "them," at any level. He warns that "if we think our mask is our true face, we will protect it with fabrications even at the cost of violating our own truth."[36] This "collective endeavor of society" ends up in "the enormous, obsessive, uncontrollable dynamic of fabrications designed to protect our fictitious identities."[37] Our true identity, says Merton, is an event, not an external label, and that event joins us with all humanity.

Interfaith dialogues can bring us to a realization of the unity of humanity. In pursuing this course, the Catholic Church would be following in the footsteps of John Paul II. During his long papacy, John Paul II distinguished himself in interfaith dialogue, especially with Protestants, Orthodox, Jews, and Muslims. In the year 2000, for example, the pope orchestrated a trip to the Holy Land during March and a millennial confession of church faults in July. During the former he visited both the Holocaust museum and the Palestinian refugee camp, and in the latter he confessed Catholic Church sins during the Crusades, the Inquisition, and Western imperial expansion, including those against Jews, other Christians, and women. John Paul II also supported the Catholic lay organization Sant'Egidio, which became very active in Christian-Muslim dialogue and in peaceful reconciliation in nations like Algeria and Mozambique. Inter-

35. *The New York Times*, March 30, 2007.
36. Cunningham, *Merton*, 392-93.
37. Cunningham, *Merton*, 393.

faith dialogue requires four different kinds of exchanges: the dialogue of life among ordinary people; the dialogue of action among activists; the dialogue of religious experience among spiritual adepts; and the dialogue of theological/philosophical exchange among religious scholars.[38]

The chapters by Brad Gregory and William Cavanaugh have shown that the Catholic Church did not lack the faults to confess, but also that these faults remained entwined in national and social dynamics that make it difficult to impute specific percentages of religious causality to each atrocity. What we do know is that all religions can point to examples of the good and the bad in the partial and confused political effects of their beliefs and actions. Merton emphasizes that "[i]t is important at all times to keep clear the distinction between true and false religion, true and false interiority, holiness and possession, love and frenzy, contemplation and magic. In every case, there is an aspiration toward inner awakening, and same means, good or indifferent in themselves, may be used for good or evil, health or sickness, freedom or obsession."[39] In the first chapter of this volume, Lawrence Cunningham rightly takes pains to dissociate true martyrdom from the contemporary phenomenon of suicide bombing. My book offers nine rules for religion's contribution to a better world. The most important is the first: "A refusal to advocate religious violence in any situation remains the first political hallmark of religious depth! Gandhi was right! Political leaders must sometimes make difficult judgments about the legitimacy of coercion in protecting the human rights of the weak, but religious leaders should sacrifice their own lives before advocating violence."[40] It is at this cardinal point that the willingness to die, but not to kill, becomes the hallmark of truly religious participation in political affairs. Such an orientation is the great witness *(martyr)* of Christian belief in national and world affairs.

Christian Martyrdom in the Contemporary Christian Political Vocation

In the global economic system, blessed are those who labor for sustainable development and just distribution. In the global military system, blessed are

38. "Our Mission and Interreligious Dialogue," Decree Five of the 34th General Congregation of the Society of Jesus: www.jesuit.org/sections.

39. Cunningham, *Merton,* 318.

40. Hanson, *Religion and Politics,* 320.

the peacemakers. In the global communication system, blessed are those journalists who speak truth to power. In the global political system, blessed are those who institutionalize justice, promote social order, and defend the rights of the poor. All four of the above vocations have become extraordinarily risky in the post–Cold War system, when extreme political movements on many sides of national, regional, and global conflicts use killing to promote chaos. Let's take a particular political vocation as an example.

UN analyst James Traub called the Brazilian Sergio Vieira de Mello the "most experienced crisis manager in the U.N. and perhaps its single most gifted official."[41] In 2003, Vieira de Mello had just finished overseeing East Timor's transition to independence and had become the UN's High Commissioner for Human Rights. He had no desire to lead the UN's re-entry into Iraq. However, UN Secretary-General Kofi Annan had become desperate to improve life for the Iraqis and to restore relations with Washington, so he convinced his Brazilian friend to go to Baghdad as UN special representative. Vieira de Mello then met with Ayatollah al-Sistani and others to work on national stability, but he refused tight security measures like those in the U.S. "Green Zone," viewing them as incompatible with the UN mission of reconciliation.

On August 7, 2003, insurgents bombed the Jordanian embassy, but Vieira de Mello continued his work under the same porous UN security arrangements. Twelve days later, a flatbed truck pulled up directly under de Mello's office, the corner window of the Canal Hotel. When a ton of high explosives was detonated, the floor of the special representative's office vaporized, and de Mello was crushed to death before medical help could reach him. Altogether, twenty-two UN officials were killed in the blast, the worst debacle ever to befall UN civilian officials. The rules of engagement have changed in the post–Cold War world. Peacekeeping has become a terribly dangerous occupation, even if — maybe especially if — one is wearing a blue hat. And this is also true for obvious humanitarian efforts such as aid to Darfur,[42] or patrolling the streets of Haiti.[43] Yet there are some things that only a lightly defended international civil servant can do, such as meeting with al-Sistani and arranging legitimate elections in the Iraqi case.

41. Traub, *The Best Intentions,* 195.

42. *The New York Times,* August 9, 2006, reported the previous July as the most deadly for aid workers since the beginning of the latest conflict in 2003. The top UN official, Manuel Arnada da Silva, said, "The level of violence being faced by humanitarian workers in Darfur is unprecedented."

43. *The New York Times,* January 10, 2007.

I am focusing here on Vieira de Mello's willingness to risk death not because of his high position, but because of his willingness to risk death. The Iraq conflict includes many other examples of dying for others by persons holding far less exalted positions. For example, the young American activist Marla Ruzicka founded CIVIC (Campaign for Innocent Victims in Conflict) to help Iraqi and Afghan families and orphans harmed by the war. She even began a door-to-door survey in Baghdad the day after the toppling of Saddam Hussein's statue. On April 16, 2005, Marla was killed by an Iraqi car bomb blast. Marla may have received Santa Clara University's Architects of Peace award posthumously, but her story is not widely known.[44] Another example of pairing the more famous and the less famous martyrs for human rights would be in El Salvador. The more famous is the late Archbishop Oscar Romero, who has become a global icon for resistance to authoritarian brutality. He was shot while celebrating Mass on March 24, 1980. The less famous is the laywoman Jean Donovan, who died for the same cause. She and three companions were raped and killed on December 2 of the same year by a Salvadoran death squad.

The above four martyrs — famous and less so — died attempting to protect the human rights of innocent people suffering in the midst of civil war. They died, according to Lawrence Cunningham, *in odium caritatis*, like the Jewish theologian Edith Stein, who died because she was a Jew, or the Polish priest Maximilian Kolbe, who died because he took the place of a married man in a Nazi starvation bunker.[45] The Iraqi and Salvadoran political dynamic of the above four martyrs is well understood. As the political and military situation polarizes, the more violent parties of both the right and the left continue to grow in strength. The moderates, who are in the middle and who often refuse special protection so that they can continue their work of reconciliation, get assassinated by both the right (85 percent in El Salvador, according to the UN report) and the left (the other 15 percent).[46] Should we call these nonviolent reconcilers Christian martyrs, or maybe "just" peacemakers who embrace high-risk civil war situations to do their work? Does it make any difference what we call them? Does the contemporary global situation add any special considerations?

44. For the story and teaching materials, see: scu.edu/ethics/architects-of-peace/Ruzicka/homepage.html.

45. See Lawrence S. Cunningham, "On the Contemporary Martyrs," in *More than a Memory: The Discourse of Martyrdom and the Construction of Christian Identity in the History of Christianity*, ed. Johan Leemans (Leuven: Peeters, 2005), 451-64.

46. United Nations, *United Nations Report on El Salvador*, April 1, 1993.

There are, of course, "purer" cases where we would have no problem extending the exact terminology of the first three centuries. For example, in the wake of the controversy over the Danish cartoons, a Turkish teenager killed a priest at the altar in the port city of Trabazon. There is no question that that priest died *in odium fidei* in imitation of the martyrs of the Roman Empire.[47] And we can think of other examples throughout Christian history, for example, the monks, nuns, and laity at the heights of the Wars of Religion, documented by Brad Gregory in *Salvation at Stake,*[48] and the French Revolution, its fundamentalist secular counterpart.[49]

As the period of Roman persecution came to a close, however, Christians meditated on "the next step" in demonstrating their witness to Christ. Merton points out that many of those who left for the solitary life in the deserts of Egypt and other Middle Eastern lands saw their lives as a continuity of the martyrs' witness.[50] They would save their lives and witness Christ by focusing on "the one thing necessary," living in the radical simplicity of God's love. This call to leave a corrupt society, says Merton, became even more urgent when that society converted to official Christianity under Constantine. And today's situation, says Merton, has become "far more desperate."[51] Such a religious movement emphasizes the relationship between interior spirituality and the experience of Christian martyrdom. Irish monks, while they "failed" in the Green Martyrdom of the hermit, took the next step and embraced the White Martyrdom of leaving their own isle to sail into the white sky of morning to convert the new tribes of Europe.[52] This stage emphasized the evangelizing call to leave one's home and preach Christ to all the nations. Now — in the current post–Cold War period — what would be a concept of Christian martyrdom that especially fits this era?

Post–Cold War martyrdom would be a life of high physical risk, liv-

47. See the discussion by Lawrence S. Cunningham, "Christian Martyrdom: A Theological Perspective," chap. 1 above.

48. Brad S. Gregory, *Salvation at Stake: Christian Martyrdom in Early Modern Europe* (Cambridge, MA: Harvard University Press, 1999).

49. See Michael Burleigh, *Earthly Powers: The Clash of Religion and Politics in Europe, From the French Revolution to the Great War* (New York: HarperCollins, 2005).

50. Cunningham, *Merton,* 265-77.

51. Cunningham, *Merton,* 277.

52. Thomas Cahill, *How the Irish Saved Civilization* (New York: Doubleday, 1995), 183-84. "[T]hey sailed into the white sky of morning, into the unknown, never to return." Cahill says that the Irish failed at the Green Martyrdom of the hermit life because they were just too sociable (171).

ing as a stranger with the poorest of the poor, embraced as a witness to God's love for the world in Christ, focused on reconciliation and human development. To differentiate it from harmful phenomena like suicide bombing, it would be nonviolent, interfaith-oriented, and indifferent to actual physical martyrdom and political power. The first characteristic ("nonviolence") links it to the rules for religious political activity above. The second characteristic ("interfaith orientation") divides it from the "Holy War mentality" that views one's coreligionists as allies and others as enemies. Such a crusade viewpoint has produced most of the damage done by religious groups through the centuries. Third, one must be indifferent to both the actual martyrdom and the political impact of one's life. The person must strive to accept the risk of death without any desire to actually die or not die. An analogy can be seen in Merton's treatment of solitude: "It is not talking that breaks solitude, but the desire to be heard."[53] The crucial point is the willingness to risk death, not the actual attainment of martyrdom. That is in God's hands, and any focus on that fact focuses on the person, not God's will. The indifference to political position and political impact gives the person freedom in the most crucial way. For the seeking of political power in order to make moral changes is the root of most of the evil that otherwise good people do.[54] Finally, such a life would normally be led in the rural areas of the developing world: the lower the country's Human Development Index rating, the more fitting. One characteristic of even "successful" developing countries, such as China and India, is the great gap between the urban and the rural areas. And to reach the poorest of the poor, this life would engage the development of rural women in a special way.

Such an extraordinary life would require heroic sanctity and a deep life of prayer. In that sense, it would go directly against the American desire for the quick technological fix. Such a project would call for constant religious conversion, no matter what the religion. Such an orientation would remain radically countercultural, no matter what the culture. And such a position cannot be associated with a particular political party or a particular political movement. Merton often took radical stands, but he also declares that "the contemplative mind today will not normally be associated too firmly or too definitely with any 'movement' whether political, reli-

53. Cunningham, *Merton*, 246.

54. For a book-length series of illustrations of the above point, see David Kuo, *Tempting Faith: An Inside Story of Political Seduction* (New York: Free Press, 2006).

gious, liturgical, artistic, philosophical or what have you. . . . He does not need them and can go farther by himself than he can in their formalized and often fanatical ranks."[55] Elsewhere he observes: "Even those strange ones who still see fit to dissent, tend to think now that massive protest is more valid. Yet the more massive a movement is, the more it is doctored and manipulated."[56]

Such a willingness to risk death for the global service of humanity would certainly constitute a major inspiring challenge, no matter how talented the person. In addition to religious depth, think of the extraordinary "secular" skills required: deep cultural and linguistic understanding of multiple cultures, disciplines, and political ideologies and organizations. These twenty-first-century martyrs would also focus on human development, communication, and/or on conflict-resolution skills. And since the challenges are so multicultural and multidisciplinary, the ability to work in multinational groups would be essential. This new vocation of the global religious-based international servant of humanity could inspire a new generation of young people to live out their faith in situations that would be more, rather than less, demanding than that of facing the lions in the Roman Coliseum. The generosity is there: witness the number of young domestic and international volunteers for groups like the Peace Corps, Doctors Without Borders, and various religious volunteers. In our contemporary world, whether or not we get religion right — whether or not we get martyrdom right — will go a long way toward determining the nature of the twenty-second century.

For the Christian, then, the ultimate goal is not martyrdom but the love of Christ and of all other persons for whom Christ died, whether by one's life or one's death. Paul corresponds to the Philippians: "My eager expectation and hope is that I shall not be put to shame in any way, but that with all boldness, now as always, Christ will be magnified in my body, whether by life or death. For to me life is Christ, and death is gain. If I go on living in the flesh, that means fruitful labor for me. . . . And this I know with confidence, that I shall remain and continue in the service of all of you for your progress and joy in the faith" (Phil. 1:20-23, 25). If we situate this passage for a post–Cold War reading, we note that since the fall of the Berlin War, the odds of being killed in the midst of political chaos has risen significantly for international civil servants, journalists, relief workers, and

55. Cunningham, *Merton,* 344-45.
56. Cunningham, *Merton,* 149.

those of religious vocation. True peacemakers will not have to look for martyrdom. In today's world, martyrdom — and the concomitant depth of the love of Christ and of their fellow human beings — will easily find them.

Contributors

LAWRENCE CUNNINGHAM is the John A. O'Brien Professor of Theology, University of Notre Dame.

TRIPP YORK is Instructor of Religious Studies at Western Kentucky University.

STEPHEN FOWL is Professor of Theology at Loyola College of Maryland.

JOYCE E. SALISBURY is the Frankenthal Professor Emerita of History at the University of Wisconsin–Green Bay.

ANN ASTELL is Professor of Theology at the University of Notre Dame.

BRAD GREGORY is the Dorothy G. Griffin Associate Professor of Early Modern European History at the University of Notre Dame.

WILLIAM CAVANAUGH is Professor of Catholic Studies and Senior Research Scholar in the Center for World Catholicism and Intercultural Theology at DePaul University.

MICHAEL L. BUDDE is Professor of Catholic Studies and Political Science and Senior Research Scholar in the Center for World Catholicism and Intercultural Theology at DePaul University.

D. STEPHEN LONG is Professor of Theology at Marquette University.

EMMANUEL KATONGOLE is Associate Professor of Theology and World Christianity and Co-Director of the Center for Reconciliation at Duke Divinity School.

ERIC O. HANSON is the Patrick A. Donohue, S.J., Professor of Political Science at Santa Clara University.